Suk Yu Chan

Heavenly Providence

A Historical Exploration of the Development of
Calvin's Biblical Doctrine of Divine Providence

Vandenhoeck & Ruprecht

Bibliographic information published by the Deutsche Nationalbibliothek:
The Deutsche Nationalbibliothek lists this publication in the Deutsche Nationalbibliografie;
detailed bibliographic data available online: https://dnb.de.

Typesetting: le-tex publishing services, Leipzig
Cover design: SchwabScantechnik, Göttingen
Printed and bound: Hubert & Co. BuchPartner, Göttingen
Printed in the EU

Vandenhoeck & Ruprecht Verlage | www.vandenhoeck-ruprecht-verlage.com

ISSN 2198–8226
ISBN 978–3–525–56071–6

Preface

Heavenly Providence is a revised version of my doctoral thesis supervised by Professor Mark W. Elliott at the University of St Andrews, Scotland. I am especially grateful to Professor Elliott, Dr William Hyland, Dr Jon Balserak, and to the editors of Vandenhoeck & Ruprecht for their comprehensive reviews and helpful feedback to enhance this version. I am also indebted to the E-library of Hong Kong Evangel Seminary, which made its resources accessible during the Covid-19 pandemic. I am grateful to the donors, my home church, and Hong Kong Alliance Bible Seminary, who supported me continuously. I wish to thank the management team of my seminary for recommending me to apply for the Ming Yee Scholarship from North Point Baptist Church. I am extremely grateful for this scholarship which was the major financial source for my doctoral study. I am also very grateful for the Student Research Fellowship granted to me by the H. Henry Meeter Center for Calvin Studies in Grand Rapids, which enabled me to work on my research at this center from April-May 2019. In addition, I would like to thank my family in Hong Kong for their love, humour, and blessings, regardless of the difficult times they were experiencing. From all these people's selfless support, I have experienced divine providence.

This study is a revisit of John Calvin's interpretation of the doctrine of divine providence and it builds upon a vast repository of quality research conducted by previous Reformation scholars. It adopts an historical approach to explore Calvin's works from 1534–1559, and it argues that from 1534–1541, Calvin uses the image of the fountain to portray God as the source of everything, who has power to preserve and give life to all creatures on earth. Between the Latin edition of the *Institutes* in 1539 and the French translation of that work in 1541, Calvin is indecisive about the definition of special providence, articulating a fitful relationship between providence and soteriology in these two texts. In 1552, Calvin gradually ceased using the image of the fountain to portray God as the source of everything, and he also delivered three definitions of divine providence: general providence, special providence, and the very presence of God. Based on the theological understanding of divine providence which he developed from 1534–1552, Calvin presented his exegesis on the Book of Job and the Book of Psalms through his sermons and commentaries. He contrasts two biblical figures, Job and David, to support his exegesis and to present a more detailed elaboration of providence through the doctrine of heavenly providence. Furthermore, Calvin also discusses the importance of the human role in God's providence. While Calvin's theological understanding of God's providence was inherited by his successor, Theodore Beza, Beza applied it differently in his exegesis on the Book of Job.

This research argues that through an historical analysis, a full picture of the spectrum of Calvin's development of the doctrine God's providence from 1534–1559 can be appreciated. While God's providence is gradually less associated with soteriological matters for the ungodly, salvation in heavenly providence for the godly is increasingly assured. Calvin conveys the message that divine providence is truly heavenly providence from the point of view of the faithful. There is a genuine existence of human agency as secondary cause in heavenly providence.

Contents

Iob respondant au Seigneur, dit,
Ie say que tu peux tout, et que nulle pensee ne sera empeschee de toy.
Qui est celuy qui obscurcist le conseil sans science? i'ay parlé, et n'entendoye point:
ces choses sont merveilleuses sur moy: ie ne les ay point cognues.
Escoute donc, ie parleray: ie t'interrogueray, afin que tu m'enseignes.
l'avoye ouy de toy de mon aureille: maintenant mon œil t'a veu.
Livre de Iob 42:1–5

1. Introduction

Research related to John Calvin's interpretation of *providentia Dei*[1] has adopted various methodologies, including philosophical and historical approaches. Researchers

---

1   William J. Abraham, "Divine Action in Predestination in John Calvin" in *Divine Agency and Divine Action, Volume II* (Oxford: Oxford University Press Scholarship Online, 2017), 1–24; Josef Bohatec, "Calvin's Vorsehungslehre", in *Calvinstudien: Festschrift Zum 400. Geburtstage Johann Calvins* (Leipzig: Rudolph Haupt, 1909), 339–441; I. Bohatec "Gott Und Die Geschichte Nach Calvin", *Philosophia Reformata*, vol. 1, no. 3, (1936): 129–161; Oliver D. Crisp, "Calvin on Creation and Providence", in *John Calvin and Evangelical Theology: Legacy and Prospect*, edited by Sung Wook Chung (Louisville, KY: Westminster John Knox Press, 2009), 43–65; Edward A. Dowey, *The Knowledge of God in Calvin's Theology* (Grand Rapids, MI: W.B. Eerdmans Publishing Company, 1994), 239–240; Mark W. Elliott, *Providence Perceived: Divine Action from a Human Point of View* (Berlin/Boston: De Gruyter, 2015), 141–148; Mary Potter Engel, *Perspectival Structure of Calvin's Anthropology* (Eugene, OR: Wipf and Stock Publishers, 2002), 123–149; David Fergusson, *The Providence of God: A Polyphonic Approach* (Cambridge: Cambridge University Press, 2018), 84–109; Bruce Gordon, *John Calvin's Institutes of the Christian Religion: a Biography* (Princeton: Princeton University Press, 2016); Paul Helm, "Calvin, the 'Two Issues' and the Structure of the Institutes", *Calvin Theological Journal* 42, no. 2 (2007): 341–48; Paul Helm, "Providence and Predestination", in *Calvin at the Centre* (Oxford: Oxford University Press, 2010), 132–162; Paul Helm, *John Calvin's Ideas* (Oxford: Oxford University Press, 2004), 93–128; Paul Helm, *Calvin and the Calvinists* (Edinburgh: The Banner of Truth Trust, 1982), 16–17; Stephen Leigh Hunt, "Predestination in the Institutes of the Christian Religion, 1536–1559", in *An Elaboration of the Theology of Calvin*, edited by Richard C. Gamble (New York: Garland, 1992), 185–192; Sung-Sup Kim, *Deus Providebit-Calvin, Schleiermacher, and Barth on the Providence of God* (Minneapolis, MN: Fortress Press, 2014); W. J. Torrance Kirby, "Stoic and Epicurean? Calvin's Dialectical Account of Providence in the Institutes", *International Journal of Systematic Theology* 5, no. 3 (2003): 309–322; Christian Link, "Wie handelt Gott in der Welt?-Calvins Vorsehungslehre", in *Calvin entdecken: Wirkungsgeschichte-Theologie-Sozialethik*, edited by Traugott Jähnichen, Thomas K. Kuhn, and Arno Lohmann (Berlin: Lit, 2010), 65–79; Peter Miln, "Hommes D'une Bonne Cause: Calvin's Sermons on the Book of Job" (PhD diss., University of Nottingham, 1989); Richard A. Muller, "Reception and Response Referencing and Understanding Calvin in Seventeenth-Century Calvinism", in *Calvin and His Influence, 1509–2009* (Oxford Scholarship Online: 2011), 182–196; Richard A. Muller, "The Placement of Predestination in Reformed Theology: Issue or Non-Issue?", *Calvin Theological Journal*, 40, (2005): 184–210; Joseph P. Murphy, *The Fountain of Life in John Calvin and the Devotio Moderna: Metaphorical Theology of the Trinity in Word and Sacrament* (Palo Alto, CA: Academica Press, 2011), 59–60; Wilhelm Niesel, *The Theology of Calvin*, translated by Harold Knight (London: Lutterworth Press, 1956), 61–79; Meng-Chai Ong, "John Calvin on Providence: The *Locus Classicus* in Context" (PhD diss., King's College, London, 2003); Charles Partee, *Calvin and Classical Philosophy* (Leiden: E. J. Brill, 1977); Joseph A., Jr Pipa, "Creation and Providence: Institutes 1.14, 16–18", in *A Theological Guide to Calvin's Institutes: Essays and Analysis*, edited by

such as Paul Helm[2] who follow the philosophical approach, only focus on *De occulta providentia Dei* 1558 and the 1559 *Institutes*, so they miss many critical links between *providentia Dei* and other theological elements in different genres of Calvin's writings. Researchers who follow the historical approach, such as Stephen Leigh Hunt, explore the development of the doctrine of predestination from the 1536 to 1559 *Institutes*, which simply provides an historical outline of various editions of that work, while other works in different genres, such as commentaries, sermons, and treatises are ignored. The recent discussion by William J. Abraham adopts both approaches in a work that considers topics concerning divine agency and divine action, and that amounts to three volumes of systematic theology.[3] Abraham offers a diachronic analysis of the interpretation of divine agency by theologians, such as the Apostle Paul, Athanasius, various Cappadocians, Augustine, Aquinas, and Calvin. Abraham reminds readers that the chapter, 'Divine action in predestination in John Calvin' is for theologians and philosophers to appreciate.[4] Using mainly the

---

David W. Hall and Peter A. Lillback (Phillipsburg: P & R Publishing, 2008), 123–150; Michelle Chaplin Sanchez, "Providence: from pronoia to immanent affirmation in John Calvin's Institutes of 1559" (PhD diss., Massachusetts: Harvard University, 2014); Susan Schreiner, "Exegesis and Double Justice in Calvin's Sermons on Job", *Church History*, vol. 58, 03 (September 1989): 322–338; Susan Schreiner, "Why do the wicked live? Job and David in Calvin's sermons on Job", in *The Voice from the Whirlwind*, edited by Leo G. Perdue and W. Clark Gilpin (Nashville, TN: Abingdon Press, 1992), 129–143; Susan Schreiner, *Where Shall Wisdom Be Found? Calvin's Exegesis of Job from Medieval and Modern Perspectives* (Chicago: The University of Chicago Press, 1994); Susan Schreiner, *The Theater of His Glory* (Grand Rapids, MI: Baker, 1995); Susan Schreiner, "Calvin as an Interpreter of Job", in *Calvin and the Bible*, edited by Donald K. McKim (Cambridge: Cambridge University Press, 2006), 53–84; Susan Schreiner, "Creation and Providence", in *The Calvin Handbook*, edited by Herman J. Selderhuis (Grand Rapids, MI: William B. Eerdmans Publishing Company, 2009), 267–275; Herman J. Selderhuis, *Calvin's theology of the Psalms* (Grand Rapids, MI: Baker Academic, 2007); Herman J. Selderhuis, "God, the Caring One: The Providence of God According to Calvin's Psalms Commentary", *La Revue Farel* 1 (2006): 17–32; Richard Stauffer, *Dieu, la Création et la Providence dans la Prédication de Calvin* (Bern: P. Lang, 1978); George Stroup, *Calvin* (Nashville: Abingdon Press, 2009): 30–33; George H. Tavard, "The Mystery of Divine Providence", *Theological Studies* 64, no. 4 (2003): 707–718; Derek Thomas, *Proclaiming the Incomprehensible God: Calvin's Teaching on Job* (Fearn: Mentor, 2004); Francois Wendel, *Calvin: Origins and Development of His Religious Thought* (New York: Harper & Row, 1963), 177–184.

2 Helm, *Calvin at the Centre*, 132–162

3 William J. Abraham, *Divine Agency and Divine Action, Volume I: Exploring and Evaluation the Debate* (Oxford: Oxford University Press, 2017); Abraham, *Divine Agency and Divine Action, Volume II: Soundings in the Christian Tradition*; William J. Abraham, *Divine Agency and Divine Action, Volume III: Systematic Theology* (Oxford: Oxford University Press, 2018).

4 Abraham, *Divine Agency and Divine Action, Volume II*, 176.

1559 *Institutes* to support his arguments, Abraham asserts that Calvin's doctrine of predestination does not allow any influence of secondary causes in predestination. It appears that most studies concerning Calvin's doctrine of *providentia Dei* only refer to the 1559 *Institutes*,[5] just as David Fergusson asserts in his recent monograph, *The Providence of God: A Polyphonic Approach*, '...the most influential Reformed approach to providence is set out in John Calvin's *Institutes*'.[6]

My research addresses the questions of how and why Calvin interpreted God's providence at different stages of his life. To answer these questions, it is necessary to adopt an historical analysis to obtain a detailed investigation into the development of Calvin's doctrine of *providentia Dei* from 1534 to 1559, and to grasp how this development affects the message Calvin delivered to believers. This historical analysis involves exploring Calvin's formulation of the doctrine of *providentia Dei* in his treaties, commentaries, sermons, and polemical works published during this period to revisit all the related issues. This kind of analysis has not been comprehensively done by any previous scholars, and therefore my study aims to fill this research gap to discover a more complete picture of Calvin's development of the doctrine of *providentia Dei*.

I argue that Calvin's development of *providentia Dei* can be divided into two stages, but also that his interpretation is consistently related to soteriological matters. How does Calvin support this argument? This work will show that he uses the doctrine of heavenly providence to link providence to predestination. Furthermore, does Calvin agree that human beings participate in *providentia Dei*? If yes, how does this work? Calvin's successor, Theodore Beza appreciates Calvin's interpretation of the doctrines of *providentia Dei* and predestination, but he also uses other methods to explain many aspects of these doctrines. Does the use of these methods cause any differences in Beza's application? Hence this work also looks at the differences between Beza and Calvin in their exegesis of the Book of Job, their application of the doctrines to analyse Job's case, and their understanding of the issues concerning causality. Before offering an outline of this work, the most recent research, and some representative findings on Calvin's doctrine of *providentia Dei* need to be analysed.

---

5 "Book 1, Chapters 16–18 of the 1559 *Institutes*, according to Calvin himself, is definitive and can, therefore, be safely considered the *locus classicus* of his thought on providence." Ong, "John Calvin on Providence: The *Locus Classicus* in Context", 31; Sanchez, "Providence: from Pronoia to Immanent Affirmation in John Calvin's Institutes of 1559", 4; Tavard, "The Mystery of Divine Providence", 710; Kirby, "Stoic and Epicurean? Calvin's Dialectical Account of Providence in the Institutes", 309–322; Pipa, "Creation and Providence: Institutes 1.14, 16–18", 123–150.

6 Fergusson, *The Providence of God*, 84. See also Bruce Gordon's analysis of a worldly reception of the 1559 *Institutes* from the end of the sixteenth century to the twenty first century. Gordon, *John Calvin's Institutes of the Christian Religion*.

There is some discussion about the placement of the doctrines of providence and predestination in Calvin's works over the years.[7] In *Calvin at the Centre*, Helm suggests that the change in the placement of the doctrines of providence and predestination is because of pedagogic reasons only, and not because there is a doctrinal separation between the two topics.[8] This work agrees with Helm's argument that 'the two doctrines are nevertheless closely interrelated in Calvin's thought',[9] however, it also suggests that there is another doctrine, which is developed later in Calvin's life, to link these two doctrines together.

Abraham has recently contributed a total of three volumes of theological work concerning the topic of divine agency and divine action, and in volume II, he introduces a chapter concerning divine action in Calvin's understanding of predestination.[10] Writing within the Arminian tradition, he alleges that 'Calvin cannot allow for genuine human action and thus Calvin eliminates human agency as a crucial category in Christian theology'.[11] Abraham's argument is based on his belief that Calvin's doctrine of predestination to salvation is to be found in his doctrine of justification, and that people are not saved by works.[12] He also argues that Calvin's description of the fall of Adam in the 1559 *Institutes* implies that God is the author of sin, as He decides Adam's fall.[13] Furthermore, Abraham also asserts that Calvin's reasoning of the hiddenness of God as an explanation of Him condemning some people is too vague and unconvincing.[14] Based on only one of Calvin's works, Abraham concludes: Calvin's radical theocentric doctrine suggests that there is no human freedom in predestination but just a matter of necessity.[15] Abraham's arguments lack validity as they only rely on one source-the 1559 *Institutes*, and hence he misses significant features of Calvin's doctrines. Abraham is not alone in this failing, but he is representative of a fairly widespread view of Calvin as a monist or determinist. Importantly, Calvin's doctrine of predestination is not to be understood through the lens of the doctrine of justification, but through the doctrine of heavenly providence.

---

7 Wendel, *Calvin: Origins and Development of His Religious Thought*, 178; Muller, "The Placement of Predestination in Reformed Theology: Issue or Non-Issue?"; Helm, "Calvin, the 'Two Issues' and the Structure of the Institutes".

8 Helm, *Calvin at the Centre*, 135, 143.

9 Ibid.,143.

10 Abraham, *Divine Agency and Divine Action, Volume II: Soundings in the Christian Tradition*, 176–197.

11 Ibid., 196.

12 Ibid., 179–180.

13 Ibid., 185.

14 Ibid., 186.

15 Ibid., 196.

Calvin's doctrine of predestination is always related to the doctrine of providence, and it also reveals the interaction between divine and human actions. Calvin suggests that there is a seamless relationship between the doctrine of *providentia Dei* and predestination. For example, the involvement of secondary cause in the reprobation aspect of predestination, is explained in the area of *providentia Dei*, which is in the area of secret providence precisely, but not in the area of predestination. The people who can benefit from predestination are those being cared for by very special providence. However, it is impossible to spot this relationship in just one of Calvin's works because his theology is 'in process' throughout his life. Therefore, one needs to read a more comprehensive selection of Calvin's works in order to appreciate this link.

In *Providence Perceived: divine action from a human point of view*, Mark W. Elliott gives an historical account of the doctrine of providence from the era of the early Christian church up to recent times.[16] Elliott's monograph includes a section on the current discussion of Calvin's doctrine of providence, and he asserts that the central tenet of God's providence is that He endows believers with special providence to enable them to live on earth. Thus, God's providence should be understood as special providence. Elliott agrees with Charles Partee that God's providence is not universal, implying that certain aspects in *providentia Dei* are related to predestination.[17] '*Providentia specialissima*' is a term used by theologians after Calvin, including Gulielmus Bucanus,[18] J. F. König,[19] Partee, and Werner Krusche,[20] to describe this non-universal providence for believers. The working of the Holy Spirit is in this aspect of providence,[21] and the question must be asked: does Calvin have a similar thought or a specific term to describe the relationship between the doctrines of

---

16 Elliott, *Providence Perceived: Divine Action from a Human Point of View*.

17 Ibid., 142. Cf. Partee, *Calvin and Classical Philosophy*, 135.

18 Gulielmus Bucanus could be the first Reformed theologian who used '*specialissima*' to describe this non-universal providence. Gulielmus Bucanus, *Institio theologica* (Lausanne, 1605), 151. Also quoted in Elliott, *Providence Perceived: Divine Action from a Human Point of View*, 154.

19 The influence spread to Lutheran theology in the seventeenth century. J. F. König, a Lutheran theologian, discussed *providentia* as having the most particular objects *(specialissime objectum)* of each believer briefly in 1664. He was one of the early Lutheran theologians who used this term, and to include *concursus* in it: "Specialissime autem objectum ejus sunt homines pii & fideles, Deut 32:9. seqq. Ps(s) 4:4; 33:18; 37:19,25; 73:24; 77:20; 91:11; Heb 1:14; Matt 10:31." J. F. König, *Theologia Positiva Acroamatica* (Rostock 1664), edited and translated by Andreas Stegmann (Tübingen: Mohr Siebeck, 2016), §260, §277. Cf. Christopher R. J. Holmes, *Revisiting the Doctrine of the Divine Attributes–in dialogue with Karl Barth, Eberhard Jüngel and Wolf Krötke* (New York: Peter Lang, 2007), 215.

20 Werner Krusche, *Das Wirken des Heiligen Geistes nach Calvin* (Göttingen: Vandenhoech & Ruprecht, 1957), 14. Also in Partee, *Calvin and Classical Philosophy*, 135.

21 Partee, *Calvin and Classical Philosophy*, 135.

providentia Dei and predestination? Furthermore, how does Calvin's thinking on this very special kind of providence develop? These questions are left unanswered by Elliott's work, which admittedly is not a work devoted to Calvin.

Sung Sup Kim's doctoral thesis considers a comparison between Calvin, Schleiermacher, and Barth on the providence of God.[22] In particular, Kim uses Calvin's doctrine of predestination and the theology of prayer to defend Calvin's doctrine of God's providence against Barth's criticism of a lack of Christology in this doctrine. Kim stresses that there are three kinds of providence in Calvin's doctrine of providence. *Providentia universalis/generalis* is God's creation, guidance, and preservation in the order of nature. *Providentia singularis* is God's guidance for individual creation, which involves '*concursus*' and '*gubernatio*'.[23] Kim uses the terms from seventeenth-century Reformed theology to explain Calvin's meaning of special providence in the sixteenth-century context,[24] and although divine concurrence is not a theological term which Calvin adopts, it does explain the working of secondary causes in Calvin's doctrine of *providentia Dei*. However, the question arises: what precisely does human participation mean when divine concurrence is involved?

The third kind of providence is one especially for the Church and it is also the point Kim uses to argue that Calvin's doctrine of providence is Christocentric and inseparable from his doctrine of predestination.[25] Kim believes that Barth has missed this point, since Barth only focused on Calvin's later work such as the 1559 *Institutes*, but Calvin's doctrine of providence and its relationship with predestination should be understood in the various editions of the *Institutes* together with commentaries.[26] Calvin uses a special term to define this kind of providence for the Church in *De aeterna Dei praedestinatione* 1552. It was probably the first work in which Calvin used this term to describe God's providence for the Church. There is no mentioning of this significant work of Calvin in Kim's thesis even though he highlights the importance of reading different works of Calvin. While there is a development of God's providence for the Church in Calvin's formulation of the doctrine of *providentia Die*, Kim misses this. Furthermore, Kim asserts that prayer is necessary as it is a response to God's faithful providence,[27] but how does human prayer influence *providentia Dei* according to Calvin?

---

22 Kim, *Deus Providebit: Calvin, Schleiermacher, and Barth on the Providence of God.*

23 Ibid., 26.

24 Cf. Crisp, "Calvin on Creation and Providence", 52. Crisp also refers Calvin's doctrine of God's providence to divine concurrence. In addition, Crisp uses the term 'meticulous providence' but Calvin does not use this term.

25 Kim, *Deus Providebit: Calvin, Schleiermacher, and Barth on the Providence of God*, 46.

26 Ibid., 43.

27 Ibid., 76.

Calvin was already emphasising the relevance of prayer in providence when he preached his sermons on Job early in 1554, and he also used a biblical illustration to both encourage the public congregation, and to testify to his own personal conviction. Calvin's argument about the significance of prayer offered in his sermons on Job provides an indispensable support to his claim in the 1559 *Institutes*. However, Calvin's sermons are absent in Kim's discussion, and instead Kim's view of prayer focuses rather too much on the 1559 *Institutes*.[28] Kim's discussions of the three kinds of providence and of the gradual relationship between providence and predestination are helpful to understanding Calvin's doctrine of providence. However, some questions stemming from his arguments raised above need further exploration. If one reads Calvin's works across their different genres, one can locate a deeper relationship between different kinds of providence and then, a stronger bond between the doctrines of providence and predestination can also be found. The indivisible relationship between these two doctrines allows human participation and it can confirm that there is a genuine existence of secondary causes in God's providence.

Richard Stauffer studies Calvin's sermons in a chronological order and subsequently discusses them according to the topics of general revelation, special revelation, the attributes of God, the Trinity, creation, and providence.[29] Under the topic of providence, Stauffer's focus is on general providence and special providence, and '*le probléme de théodicée qu'elle ne manque pas de poser*'.[30] In the discussions on the two kinds of providence, Stauffer consults many sermons on different Biblical books of Calvin including his *Sermons sur le livre de Job*. He demonstrates that things do not happen by coincidence, and that God's general providence governs in the order of nature.[31] Also, God governs human history with His power and justice in His special providence.[32] In both kinds of providence, God uses human beings as the intermediaries to accomplish His purpose and he describes this process as '*concursus*'.[33]

Stauffer considers God's actions in His special providence is particularly for the Church,[34] and his study commences the interest in the exploration of Calvin's

---

28 Ibid., 53.

29 Stauffer, *Dieu, la création et la Providence dans la prédication de Calvin*.

30 Ibid., 261.

31 Ibid., 262, 267.

32 Ibid., 272.

33 "Manifestation de la puissance et de la justice de Dieu, la Providence spéciale agit dans l'histoire avec le concours des hommes *(concursus)*. De même que Dieu se sert des créatures pour œuvrer dans l'ordre de nature, de même il a recours à des 'moyens inférieurs.'" Ibid., 273.

34 "Si, comme nous venons dele voir, la Providence spéciale exerce une activité de 'maintenance' et de 'pourvoyance' en faveur de l'humanité, elle joue aussi pour celle-ci un rôle de 'direction' et de 'gouvernement'. A la *manutenentia* et à la *conservatio* effectuées par la Providence spéciale s'ajoutent

sermons. However, there are many critical questions stemming from Stauffer's research which need further investigation. For instance, Stauffer observes that God governs human history with His actions of power and justice, but are these actions also related to the doctrine of predestination? Furthermore, what is the relationship between the doctrines of providence and predestination according to Calvin's sermons on Job. Undoubtedly, the special providence of God is related to providence for the Church, but how precisely is this link developed? Additionally, what is the process of '*concursus*' being explained by Calvin in the sermons on Job? Job has shown his humility,[35] but is this a norm or is it the result of the trial for the goodness of his nature? These questions are not elaborated in Stauffer's monograph.

Edward Dowey's work on *The Knowledge of God in Calvin's Theology* endeavours to explain Calvin's meaning of the knowledge of God. Dowey argues that people are unable to know God directly through His creative activity, but only through His revelation in Scripture and redemption. Therefore, only the faithful can attain to the knowledge of God.[36] This assertion is insightful but how does Calvin describe the links between God's activity, His revelation, and the knowledge of God?

Although this work only reviews the studies of scholars on Calvin's interpretation of *providentia Dei* spanning the last 50 years, two significant works of Josef Bohatec published in the early 1900s need to be examined.[37] In the chapter of '*Calvins Vorsehungslehre*', Bohatec aims to refute Alexander Schweizer's arguments for the doctrine of predestination as being Calvin's central doctrine. Bohatec examines the interpretation of *providentia Dei* by Calvin's predecessors, and he discovers that Zwingli used the term '*summum bonum*' at the beginning of his sermons on God's providence. Bohatec finds this term connotes ethical issues because it includes the meaning of goodness, wisdom, and justice, and also has the metaphorical concept

---

la *rectio* et la *gubernatio*. Dieu conduit et gouverne en effet les sociétés humaines, et, *a fortiori,* cette société particulière qu'est l'Eglise." Ibid., 270.

35 Ibid., 278.

36 Dowey, *The Knowledge of God in Calvin's Theology*, 239–240.

37 Bohatec, "Calvins Vorsehungslehre", 340–441; Bohatec, 'Gott und die Geschichte nach Calvin', 129–161.

of Plato.[38] This is insightful, but Bohatec does not attend to Calvin's reception. Does Calvin's interpretation of *providentia Dei* relate to 'goodness, justice, and wisdom'?

Bohatec quotes some of Ritschl's arguments on the individual treatment of the doctrines of God's providence and predestination, but he opposes Ritschl's conclusion. For Ritschl argues that God's actions in the world have objective and subjective purposes, and that God acts upon everything by means of secondary causes for the '*gloria Dei*' through salvation and damnation.[39] In God's glory, He shows His mercy and righteousness, which are the objective deeds of God.[40] Other than the objective purpose, God also shows His subjective purpose, which is the assurance of salvation for humankind.[41] Bohatec does not seem to disagree with Ritschl on this objective and subjective understanding of God's purposes in His actions,[42] but he refutes Ritschl's assertions on the denial of the connection between the teachings in

---

38 "Zwar beginnt er sein Sermonis de Providentia Dei anamnema mit dem Begriff summum bonum, der scheinbar ethisch klingt ; aber die folgende spekulativ-aprioristische Begriffsentwicklung beweist, daß der Begriff summum bonum der platonisch gefärbte metaphysische Seinsbegriff ist, wonach auch die ethischen Eigenschaften (Güte, Weisheit, Gerechtigkeit) bemessen sind." Bohatec, "Calvins Vorsehungslehre", 392–393. Cf. "…Zwingli argues that all things have their being from God…The chapter draws heavily on non-biblical sources: Aristotle, Plato…" W. P. Stephens, *The Theology of Huldrych Zwingli* (Oxford: Oxford University Press, 1986), 94. See also "The mercy and righteousness of God are held together in the goodness of God…Zwingli has engaged in a defence of God's goodness and wisdom in relation to man. 'When we see him created and redeemed, we contemplate the fact with reverence and cannot praise enough the wisdom, goodness, power, and providence of the creator in all things.'" Stephens, *The Theology of Huldrych Zwingli*, 95–96. Cf. Huldrych Zwingli, *Huldreich Zwinglis Sämtliche Werke* (Berlin, Leipzig, Zurich, 1905–), VI iii 149.14–17; *Works* II 179–180, 223.24–225.14. See also Ulrich Zwingli, "Reproduction from memory of a sermon on the providence of God, dedicated to his highness, Philip Hesse August 20, 1530", *On providence and other essays*, chapter V (Eugene, OR: Wipf and Stock Publishers, 1999), 128–234. Calvin could have inherited the terms goodness, power, wisdom, and justice to describe God's actions from Zwingli. This topic will be explored in chapter 3.

39 "Im Willen Gottes ist beides auf gleiche Weise enthalten, sowohl die Seligkeit als auch die Verdammnis; und wenn man auch darum nicht die Kategorie der Notwendigkeit, sondern nur die der Möglichkeit anwenden kann, so gleicht sich in der Wirklichkeit beides dadurch aus, daß es keine Verdammten geben könnte, wenn nicht auch sie dazu dienten, den höchsten Zweck, die gloria dei, zu verherrlichen." Bohatec, "Calvins Vorsehungslehre", 395.

40 "Auch in der Bestimmung des Zweckes stimmt die Prädestinationslehre mit der Vorsehungslehre überein: a) Calvin will in erster Reihe die objektiven Taten Gottes (Gnade und Gerechtigkeit) beschreiben." Ibid., 394–395.

41 "Neben diesem objektiven Zweck Gottes steht, wie in der Vorsehungslehre, der subjektive, die salus hominum (Inst. III, 21.7; 24.3.5). Neben dem warmen Bestreben, den majestätischen Gott in seiner Allwirksamkeit aufzuzeigen, geht der große echt reformatorische Zug. die certitudo salutis, durch die Sätze Calvins hindurch: der majestätsvolle Objektivismus wird durch den zuversichtlichen Subjektivismus ergänzt." Ibid., 395.

42 "Kurz: Handelt es sich um das (subjektive) Sehgkeitsinteresse so sucht Calvin die Heilsgewißheit in dem Erlösungswerk Christi; handelt es sich ihm um die Wahrung der göttlichen Allwirksamkeit, um

the doctrines of predestination and of providence.[43] Bohatec argues that salvation is the ultimate end of God's providence.[44]

Thus, it brings us back to Bohatec's argument against Schweizer's assertion: while the doctrine of predestination is Calvin's core doctrine, Bohatec also stresses that for Calvin, it is the doctrine of providence and not predestination that is a dogmatic principle.[45] Bohatec argues that in divine providence, God's actions operate in His righteousness and goodness[46] and hence, the doctrine of providence is the fundamental in Calvin's theology. Also, Calvin's doctrines of providence and predestination are interwoven, but they work differently. God acts through created causes in God's providence, but He assures that the godly with salvation in a non-causative way, and that they are justified by faith.

Bohatec observes that prayer is a special action undertaken by humankind to attain an intimate relationship with God, and through this action, they are strengthened in peace and tranquility.[47] All the wonderful states for humankind that result from prayer are a foretaste of eternal life enjoyed in God's providence.[48] This segment on prayer about Calvin's doctrine of providence is often not noticed by Calvin

---

die objektive Begründung dieses Heilsbewußtseins, so geht er zurück auf den göttlichen Ratschluß als die logisch und zeitlich höchste causa." Ibid., 413.

43 "In der der Institutio von 1559 angehörenden Lehre von der Providenz wird, so meint Ritschl, keine vorschauende Rücksicht auf die doppelte Prädestination genommen. In dieser Lehre (von der Prädestination) fehle jede Unterordnung unter die Lehre von der Providenz. Beide verhalten sich gleichgültig gegeneinander..." Ibid., 394.

44 "So müssen wir fragen, wenn wir die volle Koncinnität der Prädestinationslehre mit den Erörterungen über den Zweck der Vorsehung bewahren wollen. In der letzteren ordnet, wie wir sahen, Gott alles so, daß schließlich dabei die salus der Seinigen herauskommt. Ritschl, der den Zusammenhang beider Lehren in dieser Hinsicht leugnet, muß selber zugeben..." Ibid., 402.

45 "Die Providenzlehre, in der die allgemeine göttliche Allwirksamkeit beschrieben wird, bildet für die dogmatische Betrachtung die Grundlage der Prädestinationslehre." Ibid., 413; cf. Niesel argues that Calvin's theology is Christo-centric, but this does not mean that redemption is the central thought of this scheme. He considers that the knowledge of God is the fundamental. Niesel, *The Theology of Calvin*, 61–79.

46 "In der Geschichte kommt die göttliche Majestät zu ihrer Auswirkung; sie ist das Handeln der göttlichen Vorsehung, die Betätigung der Gerechtigkeit und Güte Gottes (ut providentiam Domini, erga suos iustitiam ac bonitatem, erga reprobos iudicia demonstraret)." Bohatec, "Gott und die Geschichte nach Calvin", 133.

47 "Die Gewißheit der Nähe und Gegenwart der göttlichen Providenz holt sich der Mensch von Gott im Gebet...Dadurch wird der Friede und die Ruhe begründet und bekräftigt." Bohatec, "Calvins Vorsehungslehre", 433.

48 "Ein männlicher Friede, welchen die göttliche Vorsehung ins Herz gießt und mitten in Kampf und Not erhält, die Demut, welche sich in aller Verworrenheit der irdischen Dinge von den göttlichen Ratschlüssen geduldig und zu Ehren des unbedingten Herrschers leiten läßt, das Gebet, welches den erhabenen, ewigen Gott als den gegenwärtigen mit heiligen Banden umschlingt – und alles das ein Vorgeschmack des ewigen Lebens, welches der Mensch hienieden bereits wesentlich, ob auch

scholars. This observation of Bohatec is perceptive because he connects the objective side of displaying glory for God in His providence through created means with the subjective side of assurance of salvation for the faithful in predestination through justification by faith. This foretaste of eternal life is gained after a believer is justified by faith. Bohatec concludes that Calvin is a witness of providence,[49] but how does Calvin apply the doctrine of divine providence in his exegesis? To answer this question, an historical analysis of how Calvin becomes the witness of providence serves the purpose.

In *The Theater of His Glory: Nature and the Natural Order in the Thought of John Calvin*, Susan Schreiner argues that God's providence is the proscenium arch forming the theatre of God's glory, suggesting providence is God's power and that this power governs the world and everything in it.[50] Furthermore, God's providence is an assurance for the believers to affirm God's special care for His people.[51] This argument is insightful and it is elaborated in her another monograph, *Are You Alone Wise?: The Search for Certainty in the Early Modern Era* in 2012.[52] Randall Zachman, in his review of Schreiner's *The Theater of His Glory*, reinforces that Calvin speaks of the universe as a theatre of God's glory because God portrays Himself to humanity as 'the fountain of every good by representing his powers, for example life, wisdom, power, mercy, and goodness', for the assurance of faith.[53] He argues that Schreiner misses this central theme in her discussion on the providence of God. Zachman's recognition of the importance of the image of the fountain in Calvin's doctrine of God's providence is insightful, however, did Calvin continue using this image? Calvin does use God's action in His goodness and justice to address the assurance of salvation, but he also adopts another doctrine to explain this issue. Zachman's contribution does not extend very far into these issues. Schreiner recognises the inseparability of God's power, goodness, justice, and wisdom as a central theme in Calvin's interpretation of divine providence in his sermons on Job.[54] Chapter 3 of this book extends her discussion on this topic.

A central text for this book is that of the *Sermons sur le livre de Job* 1554–1555 in which Calvin offers a detailed description of *providentia Dei*. Schreiner contributes

---

verborgen und im Keime in sich trägt und auf dessen herrliche Offenbarung im Jenseits er sehnend hofft – das ist der Grundzug der Frömmigkeit Calvins nach seiner Vorsehungslehre." Ibid., 434.
49 "Calvin ist Theologe der Vorsehung geworden, da er Werkzeug der Vorsehung sein durfte." Ibid., 441.
50 Schreiner, *The Theater of His Glory: Nature and the Natural Order in the Thought of John Calvin*, 34.
51 Ibid., 33–35, 37.
52 Susan Schreiner, *Are You Alone Wise? The Search for Certainty in the Early Modern Era* (Oxford Studies in Historical Theology. New: Oxford University Press, 2012), 38–77.
53 Randall C. Zachman, Review of *The Theater of His Glory: Nature and the Natural Order in the Thought of John Calvin*, by Susan Schreiner, *Journal of Religion*, vol. 73, Issue 3 (Jul 1993), 413–414.
54 Schreiner, *The Theater of His Glory: Nature and the Natural Order in the Thought of John Calvin*, 34.

a crucial analysis of Calvin's sermons on Job by first discussing the exegesis of this book offered by medieval scholars.[55] Schreiner observes that various medieval thoughts influence Calvin's interpretation of the Book of Job. To summarize, Calvin refrains from using the allegorical explanation suggested by Gregory the Great but adopts the literal interpretation proposed by Thomas Aquinas. Calvin uses 'double justice' as a hermeneutical key to explain Job's case and argues that human justice can never attain divine justice because it is high and hidden in God.[56] Therefore, the problem of God as a tyrant making people suffer by using His absolute power arises. To avoid this problem, Schreiner asserts that for Calvin, the inseparability of divine 'essence', for instance, God is powerful, good, and just, can ease the tension of God's capriciousness while still declaring His omnipotence.[57]

Instead of 'essence', Calvin describes God's goodness, power, wisdom, and justice as His 'choses' (a French term, meaning 'things'), and they show God's glory. This description is in the 1541 *Institutes*, which is a French translation of the second edition of the *Institutes* he wrote in 1539. The French term 'choses',[58] is used by Calvin in his 1541 *Institutes* and one would expect the term to be translated from 'res' in the Latin edition of the 1539 *Institutes*. However, there is no mentioning of 'res' in the sentence, which is supposed to contain the term, but instead 'quibus' is

---

55 Schreiner, *Where shall wisdom be found? Calvin's exegesis of Job from medieval and modern perspectives*; Schreiner, "Creation and Providence", 267–275; Schreiner, "Calvin as an Interpreter of Job", 53–84.

56 Schreiner, *Where shall wisdom be found? Calvin's exegesis of Job from medieval and modern perspectives*, 105–120.

57 Schreiner, "Exegesis and Double Justice in Calvin's Sermons on Job", 338.

58 "Certes ces trois choses nous sont principallement necessaires à congnoistre: sa misericorde, en laquelle consiste le salut de nous tous; son judgement, lequel journellement il exerce sur les iniques, et lequel il leur reserve plus rigoreux à confusion eternelle: sa justice, par laquelle ses fideles sont benignement entretenuz. Ces choses comprinses, le Prophete tesmoigne que nous avons abondamment de quoy nous glorifier en Dieu." Jean Calvin, *Institution de la Religion Chrétienne* 1541 Tome I, edited and translated by Olivier Millet (Genève: Librairie Droz S.A., 2008), 234–235.

used.[59] Elsie McKee translates 'ces choses' as "these things" in the English version of the 1541 *Institutes*.[60]

Regarding the definition of essence or attributes in Calvin's works, Forrest Buckner and Richard Muller contribute a significant discussion.[61] Buckner distinguishes between the relative attributes and absolute attributes of God, and he asserts that human beings can obtain positive knowledge of God's powers through His acts. Muller argues that power is God's intrinsic essence, which belongs to Him only, and therefore cannot be simply referred to words of God *ad extra*.[62] Muller argues that Buckner has a wrong translation of *virtutes* which leads him into a false interpretation. This book agrees with Muller but Calvin's sermons on Job also emphasises that God allows the faithful to participate in His providence through His acts in His goodness, power, wisdom, and justice. However, this participation is not the positive knowledge of God's power as suggested by Buckner. Instead, it is a taste of God's goodness in His providence that only the faithful can enjoy.

In Calvin's sermons on Job, he has a lot more to say about God's glory to demonstrate these 'things' in *providentia Dei*. God's glory, in His power, goodness, justice, and wisdom together, displays God's providence in the order of nature, in all of His creation, and in His Elect, while human participation is contained in *providentia Dei*. Calvin demonstrates this participation using Job's situation. Schreiner has not explored God's 'choses' in *providentia Dei* thoroughly, and the issue of human participation according to Calvin in his sermons on Job is not discussed.

---

59 "Virtutes porro easdem hic enumerari audimus, quas notabamus in coelo et terra relucere: clementiam, bonitatem, misericordiam, iustitiam, iudicium, veritatem. Nam virtus et potentia, sub titulo Elohim continetur...Tria certe haec apprime nobis cognitu sunt necessaria. Misericordia, qua sola consistit nostra omnium salus; iudicium, quod in flagitiosos quotidie exercetur et gravius etiam eos manet in aeternum exitium; iustitia, qua conservantur fideles et benignissime foventur. Quibus comprehensis, te abunde habere vaticinium testatur, quo possis in Deo gloriari. Neque tamen ita omittuntur aut veritas eius, aut potentia, aut sanctitas, aut bonitas. Quomodo enim constaret, quae hic requiritur, iustitiae, misericordiae, iudicii eius scientia, nisi veritate eius inflexibili niteretur? Et quomodo crederetur terram iudicio et iustitia moderari, nisi intellecta eius virtute?" CO1:304.

60 John Calvin, *Institutes of the Christian Religion 1541*, translated by Elsie Anne McKee (Grand Rapids, MI: William B. Eerdmans Publishing Company, 2009), 46.

61 Forrest Buckner, "Calvin's Non-Speculative Methodology: A Corrective to Billings and Muller on Calvin's Divine Attributes", in *Calvinus Pastor Ecclesiae*, ed. Herman J. Selderhuis (Göttingen: Vandenhoeck & Ruprecht, 2016), 233–243; Richard A. Muller, "Calvin on Divine Attributes: A Question of Terminology and Method", *Westminster Theological Journal* 80, no.2 (2018): 199–218. See also Alden C. McCray, "'God, We Know, Is Subject to No Passions.' The Impassibility of God in Calvin's Commentaries as a Test-Case for the Divine Attributes", *Calvinus frater in Domino*, Papers of the Twelfth International Congress on Calvin Research, edited by Arnold Huijgen and Karin Maag (Gottingen: Vandenhoeck & Ruprecht, 2020), 295–308.

62 Muller, "Calvin on Divine Attributes: A Question of Terminology and Method," 211.

John Rziha's monograph, *Perfecting Human Actions: St Thomas Aquinas on Human Participation Eternal Law*, explores Aquinas' interpretation of the relationship between eternal law and providence. While eternal law is 'God's command to order well the subjects of creation, divine providence is God's foresight to order well all things to their final ends'.[63] Rziha argues that *providentia* is a broader concept than eternal law because *providentia* includes the act of counsel, judgement, and command.[64] Also, eternal law is God's providential wisdom directing all creatures to the end. The creatures, as beings, participate in providence because their actions are caused by the eternal law. Rziha asserts that because all effects are like their cause, therefore, one can understand more the way the creatures participate in God, who is the efficient cause.[65] Humans depend on God, but they also participate rationally in divine direction.[66] Thus, human actions are both passive and active in God's providence. Participation is a sharing in a perfection of God's providence from the finite to the infinite.[67]

For Paul Helm, Aquinas's interpretation of predestination is 'not on account of any foreseen merits, but they are the cause of it only in the sense that they are part of the ordained divine sequence which begins in the calling of men and women and ends in their glorification'.[68] Helm then asserts that Calvin and Aquinas both treat predestination as *pars providentiae*:[69] God's general providence and His special care for the Church are interconnected.[70] Helm believes that Calvin adopts the medieval tradition of explaining primary and secondary causes, and that Calvin finds it difficult to give a satisfactory explanation that God is not the author of sin, because God as the primary cause of creation and human action also signifies that He is responsible for the sin that human beings participate in it. Regardless of this difficulty, Calvin's main purpose is not to explain until people nod their heads but to foster the correct practical religious responses to the doctrine of providence and to deliver what Scripture teaches.[71] Calvin's understanding of the causality in providence does show that he adopts the medieval tradition. However, when Calvin preaches his sermons on Job, Calvin's understanding of human participation is not so much related to eternal law as defined by Aquinas, but to having a taste of

---

63 John Rziha, *Perfecting Human Actions: St Thomas Aquinas on Human Participation In Eternal Law* (Washington, DC: Catholic University of America, 2009), 42.

64 Ibid.

65 Ibid., 43.

66 Ibid., 185.

67 Ibid., 255–6.

68 Paul Helm, *Calvin at the Centre* (Oxford University Press, 2011), 143.

69 Ibid.

70 Ibid.

71 Ibid., 248–249.

eternal life on earth. Perhaps this is what Helm described that Calvin is ultimately concerned to foster the correct practical religious responses to *providence de Dieu*. Chapter 3 will deliver a detailed explanation.

Schreiner also argues that Calvin uses an additional Biblical figure to illustrate that suffering can happen to God's loved ones. Calvin suggests that Job and David lead parallel lives in the way that God raises and afflicts them.[72] The similarities between the lives of Job and David are important, but Calvin praises David for his virtues, as he believes that David is blessed in God's three kinds of providence, and that David's prayer leads to God's revelation in His providence. Furthermore, Calvin in his sermons on Job promotes David so often, sometimes even over Job, because Calvin sees himself in David. However, Schreiner leaves the above underdeveloped and so what follows will provide an in-depth exploration of David's situation in relation to *providentia Dei*.

Joseph Murphy observes that in the 1559 *Institutes*, Calvin adopts the fountain metaphor to describe God in many aspects, such as His character, location, indefinite quantity, nourishment, and benefits including God's providence, wisdom, righteousness, and truth.[73] No doubt Murphy asserts that Calvin uses this metaphorical image of a fountain because it is a biblical (even if deuterocanonical) metaphor, a classical metaphor, an ancient patristic metaphor, a humanist metaphor, a Reformation metaphor, a common metaphor, and a traditional metaphor.[74] He also ascribes spiritual meaning to this term and argues that this metaphor reminds people to go back to God for the source of all goodness. Therefore, the true meaning of the imitation of Christ in the movement of the *devotio moderna* is the understanding of Scripture for the revelation of God, the source of all good things.[75] That is, the importance of the imitation of Christ is to seek God who provides all goodness.

Murphy suggests that the fountain is a literary image which Calvin uses to describe God as the source of all goodness. The image of the fountain serves an adjectival function in Calvin's writing, and in fact, when Calvin wrote his first theological work, *Psychopannychia*, he did not adopt the image of the fountain from the Hebrew Bible or canonical Old Testament but from the deuterocanonical Book of Baruch.[76] One can locate many places in the Bible where the term fountain is

---

72 Schreiner, *Where shall wisdom be found? Calvin's exegesis of Job from medieval and modern perspectives*, 96.

73 Murphy, *The Fountain of Life in John Calvin and the Devotio Moderna: Metaphorical Theology of the Trinity in Word and Sacrament*, 59–60.

74 Ibid., 63–64, 83.

75 Ibid., 85–87.

76 By 1547 in his Antidote to the Council of Trent, Calvin does not include Baruch among the 'ecclesiastical' (deuterocanonical – good for piety but not doctrine) books. Georges Bavaud, "La position

used to describe God, especially in Psalms, but Calvin, in his early works, rarely referred to these sources when he explained *providentia Dei*. Instead, he followed the common medieval usage of this term and also adopted this term in light of the Book of Baruch. If one adopts an historical approach to analyse Calvin's usage of the image of the fountain, one will identify an historical development of Calvin's interpretation of the image of the fountain in relation to *providentia Dei*.

The main theme, 'incomprehensibility' of Derek Thomas's Doctoral thesis, *Proclaiming the Incomprehensible God: Calvin's teaching on Job*, is a theme Thomas takes up from Peter Miln's unpublished thesis.[77] Thomas notices 'the doctrine of incomprehensibility' was not addressed sufficiently by Miln. Thomas appreciates Schreiner's work, *Where Shall Wisdom be Found? Calvin's Exegesis of Job from Medieval and Modern Perspectives*, with an analysis of the interpretation of the Book of Job by Calvin's three predecessors, but he does not agree with her implication about Calvin coming close to nominalism in his rhetoric of God's absolute power.[78] Thomas argues that Schreiner's misjudgement about this aspect of Calvin's theology is because she has not discussed the 'doctrine of incomprehensibility' adequately.[79] While Schreiner's Calvin argues that the 'hermeneutical key' to understand the Book of Job is double justice,[80] Thomas believes that the 'interpretative key' in the understanding of Calvin's sermons on Job is the 'doctrine of God's incomprehensibility'.[81] Thomas argues that 'Calvin's doctrine of the incomprehensibility of God informs his understanding of divine providence, and that Calvin uses this insight as a pastoral tool to teach the lesson on suffering'.[82] Thomas makes a valuable contribution to the pastoral dimension of Calvin's sermons on Job as this aspect is not explored by previous research. However, regarding the argument of incomprehensibility, is the 'doctrine of the incomprehensibility of God', as considered by Thomas, a doctrine in Calvin's theology? Or is it a descriptive word used in conjunction with the 'doctrine of secret providence'? These questions deserve more exploration.

Some theologians have special interest in Calvin's interpretation of the Book of Psalms. Nevada Levi DeLapp argues that rather than using Scripture as the vertical vehicle to mystical communion with the divine, Calvin finds in the Bible

---

du Réformateur Pierre Viret à face aux Deutérocanoniques", in *Le canon de l'Ancien Testament: sa formation et son histoire* , edited by Jean-Daniel Kaestli and Otto Wermelinger (Geneva : Labor et Fides, 1984), 245–252.

77 Miln, "Hommes D'une Bonne Cause: Calvin's Sermons on the Book of Job"; cf. Thomas, *Proclaiming the Incomprehensible God*, 13–15.

78 Thomas, *Proclaiming the Incomprehensible God*, 13, 35.

79 Ibid., 13, 17, 35.

80 Schreiner, "Exegesis and Double Justice in Calvin's Sermons on Job," 322.

81 Thomas, *Proclaiming the Incomprehensible God*, 16.

82 Ibid., 13, 93.

linear historical typologies, and therefore biblical figures and events can pre-figure modern persons and events.[83] Following this methodology of historical typology, DeLapp further argues that Calvin reads the biblical figure of King David in two ways: an example of a good king and a model of political non-resistance and patient suffering.[84] He observes that for Calvin, David is a righteous king who 'looks out for the common good of his people through mercy and judgement'.[85] Also, Calvin feels that the Church is a remnant in a hostile world in the sixteenth century but he finds comfort in David's example as it provides a model of political non-resistance and patient suffering under persecution.[86] DeLapp's analysis is helpful to an understanding of Calvin's David but the issue of God's providence is not discussed enough, provided providence is the main theme of Calvin's *Commentarius in librum Psalmorum*. However, Herman J. Selderhuis recognises this theme.

Selderhuis admits the theological importance of *providentia Dei* in Calvin's commentary on Psalms, and he further argues that *providentia Dei* is the most significant motif in this commentary.[87] He explains that God's activities in His general, special, and hidden providence govern the world and all affairs related to his creations. Selderhuis suggests that Calvin intends to provide some pastoral encouragement through the commentary on Psalms by suggesting to the faithful that their suffering will come to an end through God's intervention.[88] Yet, how will this happen? Will the faithful influence God's intervention? Selderhuis asserts, "David is a God–given mirror in whom we can see what must incite us to prayer and what must move us to praise him when he answers our prayer."[89] Although Selderhuis offers insightful discussions about *providentia Dei* and prayer, he treats these two topics independently. The link between *providentia Dei* and prayer receives little attention, and presumably other works of Calvin are not consulted.

Barbara Pitkin is another theologian who recognises the importance of the doctrine of providence in Calvin's commentary on Psalms and she further argues that faith is not only necessary for the godly to understand God's redemptive activity, but also to appreciate God's creative and providential activity.[90] Pitkin describes Calvin as distinguishing God's providential word from God's providential

---

83 Neveda Levi DeLapp, *The reformed David(s) and the question of resistance to tyranny: reading the Bible in the 16th and 17th centuries* (London: T&T Clark, 2016), 26.

84 Ibid., 29, 41.

85 Ibid., 43.

86 Ibid., 44–45.

87 Selderhuis, *Calvin's theology of the Psalms*, 118.

88 Ibid., 114, 118.

89 Ibid., 23.

90 Barbara Pitkin, *What Pure Eyes Could See: Calvin's Doctrine of Faith in its Exegetical Context* (New York: Oxford University Press, 1999), 4, 99.

work: while God's providential word is His eternal counsel, God's providential work is the execution of His counsel.[91] Pitkin also argues that for Calvin, God's providential word is linked to God's power and that the godly should not only admire God's power but also have faith in its magnitude.[92] She stresses that 'it is only the godly, who through the eyes of faith contemplate God's counsel, who benefit: they alone perceive and rest on a providential ordering that is invisible to those without faith.'[93] Therefore, she suggests that faith in God's providential promise can be distinguished from saving faith while providential faith, however, arises out of saving faith. Both kinds of faith are 'Christocentric' as while providential faith looks to the Son as Logos, saving faith looks to the Son as the incarnate Christ.[94] Some of the findings in this research concerning Calvin's doctrine of divine providence in relation to soteriological matters echo Pitkin's arguments. However, while Pitkin makes reference to God desiring prayer from the godly when discussing Calvin's commentary on Psalm 9,[95] she does not sufficiently discuss the link between faith and prayer. This work explores this link in chapter 4.

Christian Link, in a study based on Calvin's *De occulta Dei providentia*, suggests that prayer both draws the presence of God and establishes His will. While God's will is ordained well in advance of events in which believers must cooperate, all these proceedings are not simply fixed in place but are part of God's purpose for believers as pilgrims to be able to witness the coming reign of Christ.[96] It should be noted that the discussion about prayer and God's will that Link refers to is not initiated by Calvin. Instead, it arises as part of Sebastian Castellio's refutation of Calvin's doctrine of predestination because Castellio thinks that this doctrine implies that God's will is contradicting in Article 7.[97] However, Calvin did not respond to Castellio's refutation, therefore other works of Calvin should be consulted to locate Calvin's opinion on prayer. Link seems to agree with Castellio's charges on Calvin's doctrine of predestination, as Link suggests that while God is active in history, not all the events are fixed in advance.[98] This research does not aim to debate this topic, but it argues that if one wants to explore the relationship between Calvin's understanding of providence, predestination, and prayer, an historical study of Calvin's doctrine of divine providence certainly helps to reveal this relationship.

---

91 Ibid., 105. CO31:325.
92 Pitkin, *What Pure Eyes Could See: Calvin's Doctrine of Faith in its Exegetical Context*, 105–106.
93 Ibid., 107.
94 Ibid., 108.
95 Ibid., 123.
96 Link, "Wie handelt Gott in der Welt?-Calvins Vorsehungslehre", 75–77.
97 Iohannis Calvini, *De occulta Dei providentia*, CO9:279.
98 Link, "Wie handelt Gott in der Welt?-Calvins Vorsehungslehre", 78–79.

In *John Calvin's Perspectival Anthropology*, Mary Potter Engel argues that Calvin's anthropology can be viewed from two perspectives: 'the relative perspective of humankind' and 'the absolute perspective of God'.[99] She uses these two perspectives to explain many aspects of Calvin's theology including the doctrine of God's providence. Engel argues that Calvin distinguishes two kinds of providence: 'creative providence' and 'redemptive providence'. She asserts that in Calvin's doctrine of creative providence, God's power does not operate separately but together with His goodness, wisdom, and justice, and therefore she concludes that God does not act with His power but with His righteousness.[100] In redemptive providence, God acts from the absolute perspective and therefore it appears that all human freedom is lost and free choice obliterated.[101] However, it is from the relative perspective of humankind that human beings appear to retain the faculty of the will and freedom from coercion.[102] It could be that the recasting of Calvin's terminology into anthropologically related concepts might distort what Calvin aims to do, that is, maintain a primary focus on God. Calvin does not use the terms 'relative perspective of humankind' or 'creative providence', for example, to explain the doctrine of divine providence. Hence, we could ask after reading Engel, does Calvin's theology constitute a separate division called anthropology? Engel perceptively acknowledges the relationship between goodness, wisdom, power, and justice, but she concludes that 'creative providence' is only God's righteousness. Chapters 3 and 4 in this book will address the role of humankind and God's action in His goodness, power, wisdom, and justice in relation to *providentia Dei*. The following discusses the methodology adopted in this study.

Richard Muller published *The Unaccommodated Calvin* in 2000 and proposed that a methodology to examine Calvin must embrace his *Institutes*, treatises, commentaries, and sermons.[103] Muller stresses that Calvin has to be examined through sixteenth-century eyes of Calvin's predecessors and successors, and Muller demonstrates this importance in his 1986 publication *Christ and the Decree: Christology and Predestination in Reformed Theology from Calvin to Perkins*.[104] The synchronic and diachronic methods have subsequently been adopted in many studies of Calvin scholars, however these methods have also been the subject of criticism.

---

99 Engel, *Perspectival Structure of Calvin's Anthropology*, 3.

100 Ibid., 131–132.

101 Ibid., 143.

102 Ibid., 144.

103 Richard A. Muller, *The Unaccommodated Calvin: Studies in the Foundation of a Theological Tradition* (Oxford: Oxford University Press, 2000).

104 Richard A. Muller, *Christ and the Decree: Christology and Predestination in Reformed Theology from Calvin to Perkins* (Durham, NC: Labyrinth Press, 1986).

Carl Trueman asserts that the reception of Calvin's ideas in later Reformed theology is a complex matter and one factor contributing to this complexity is that none of Calvin's theology originated from Calvin.[105] Therefore, Trueman suggests that one can interpret the 'continuity thesis', proposed by Muller, from three perspectives. Firstly, it is about the direct continuity of doctrine between Calvin and his successors. Trueman calls this a confessional continuity as this continuity adopts a confessional and catechetical style.[106] Secondly, the adoption of the philosophical framework over the period prior to the sixteenth century in the wider medieval context is considered a continuity.[107] Thirdly, the fact that the same questions and problems raised by the different Reformers on the same doctrine in the Reformed tradition demonstrates continuity.[108] Therefore, Trueman argues that the efforts made by Calvin's successors are called 'historical actions', rather than 'continuity or discontinuity'.[109] Discontinuity shown in Calvin's successors' interpretation of certain doctrines is also a development of the formulation of the doctrines in the Reformed tradition. Trueman appears to position Calvin as the centre of all issues related to continuity and discontinuity in the Reformed tradition regardless of his recognition of the lack of originality in Calvin's thoughts.

Muller also argues that Calvin's theology is 'seldom highly original', and therefore the questions of continuity, discontinuity, development, and diversity cannot 'merely' be discussed in terms of Calvin's relationship to the later Reformers. Instead, Muller asserts that Calvin's thoughts must be related to his predecessors and contemporaries in the Reformed tradition.[110] Thus, Muller objects to Trueman's argument of considering the 'continuity thesis' simply as advocacy of 'Calvin for the Calvinists' or 'Calvin against Calvinists'.

This study adopts the historical method of seeking the continuities and discontinuities, between the theology of Calvin and 'his predecessors and successors' proposed by Muller. It shows that Calvin's interpretation of the doctrine of divine providence is adopted from his predecessor, Zwingli, and Calvin also influences his successor, Beza, in his understanding of the same doctrine.[111]

---

105 Carl R. Trueman, "The Reception of Calvin: Historical Considerations", *Church History and Religious Culture* 91, no. 1–2 (2011): 19.

106 Ibid., 21–22.

107 Ibid., 22.

108 Ibid., 23.

109 Ibid., 21.

110 Richard A. Muller, "'The Reception of Calvin' in Later Reformed Theology: Concluding Thoughts", *Church History and Religious Culture* 91, no. 1–2 (2011): 257.

111 See also chapters three and six.

Around the time of his response to Trueman, Muller also examined the reception of Calvin's thought in the works of the seventeenth-century Calvinist theologians.[112] Muller has done an historical analysis on the reception of Calvin's thoughts by these Calvinist theologians, but he has not undertaken an historical analysis of Calvin's thoughts on God's providence or Beza's reception of this doctrine. This research project aims to fill this scholarship gap.

This book adopts a synchronic and diachronic approach to track the answers to the above questions, and also to investigate other issues related to Calvin's doctrine of *providentia Dei*. Synchronically, it explores the historical development of Calvin's interpretation of *providentia Dei* in light of his treatises, commentaries, sermons, and polemic works. The research concerning the reception of the Church Fathers and the medieval predecessors in Calvin's thoughts of *providentia Dei* is accomplished by Schreiner in her monographs, *The Theater of His Glory*[113] and *Where shall wisdom be found?*.[114] The reception of Calvin's teaching of *providentia Dei* in the seventeenth century Calvinism is explored by Muller. Bruce Gordon contributes a study on the reception of the 1559 *Institutes* from the sixteenth century to the twenty first century.[115] In regard to the diachronic analysis, this work will only explore the historical continuity of Calvin's thoughts in several works from Calvin's successor, Theodore Beza. Beza thus functions as a longstop for Calvin's immediate influence, an influence also witnessed to by Arthur Golding's 1574 translation into English of *Sermons sur le livre de Job* 1554–1555.

This study is divided into seven chapters, including this Introduction. Chapter 2 provides a comprehensive research of Calvin's thoughts on *providentia Dei* in all major related works that he composed from 1534 to 1552: *Psychopannychia* 1534,[116] the 1536, 1539, 1543 and 1550 *Institutes, Commentarius in epistolam Pauli ad Romanos* 1540, and *De aeterna Dei pradestionatione* 1552. In this period, Calvin uses the image of the fountain to portray that God's providence is the source of eternal life. This chapter traces Calvin's use of the image of the fountain throughout his earlier works. General providence and special providence are the two major topics concerning *providentia Dei* that are usually discussed by Calvin scholars. Chapter 2 also discusses when these two kinds of providence start to take shape in Calvin's

---

112 For the reception of Calvin from the 18th century to the 21st century, see Gordon, *John Calvin's Institutes of the Christian Religion: a Biography*.

113 Schreiner, *The Theater of His Glory: Nature and the Natural Order in the Thought of John Calvin*, 7–15.

114 Schreiner, *Where shall wisdom be found? Calvin's exegesis of Job from medieval and modern perspectives*, 22–90.

115 Gordon, *John Calvin's Institutes of the Christian Religion: a Biography*.

116 *Psychopannychia* was written in 1534 but was not published until 1542. Refer to footnote 14 in chapter 2.

theology. Chapter 3 focuses on Calvin's *Sermons sur le livre de Job* 1554–1555. Calvin argues that God's actions in power, goodness, wisdom, and justice are *providentia Dei* and that human participation in God's providence genuinely exists. Calvin does not regard Job as a good example for the godly to follow and this chapter considers Job's change and his role in *providentia Dei*. Chapter 4 includes a discussion about David with reference to *Commentarius in librum Psalmorum* 1557, and it is an extension of chapter 3 because Calvin suggests to his congregation in his sermons on Job that the example of David is the right example to follow. This chapter investigates the reason David is an example of a virtuous sufferer in different kinds of *providentia Dei*. Chapter 5 offers a detailed exploration of three works: *Sermons sur le livre de Job* 1554–1555, *De occulta providentia Dei* 1558 and the 1559 *Institutes*. By reading these three works together, one can conclude that Calvin gradually formulates a doctrine to link the doctrines of providence and predestination together. Chapter 6 discusses Beza's formulation of the doctrine of predestination in *Tabula Praedestinationis*, and his interpretation of God's providence from 1555–1589. Special attention is given to his *Jobus Theodori Bezae partim commentariis partim paraphrasi illustratus* 1589 to locate if there is a line of continuity with Calvin's interpretation of Job reference to the doctrine of *providentia Dei*. This chapter discusses Beza's agreements with Calvin's arguments of *providentia Dei*, and Beza's exegesis of Job's suffering according to the Book of Job and his own theological conviction. Last chapter is a discussion of the findings and the conclusion of this work.

2. Calvin's interpretation of the doctrine of *providentia Dei* from 1534 to 1552

John Calvin (1509–1564) was born in the era when King Francis I ruled France (1515–1547). During his reign, Francis I encouraged the cultivation of art and literature. He promoted Renaissance humanism and hired many Italian artists and scholars to work on architectural and cultural aspects in the kingdom of France. Learning the scholastics or following the footsteps of a priest was anachronistic to the learned people in France but instead, they were aspired to study humanism.[1] This was a pattern familiar to Calvin who had been raised in a reforming epoch like this, before he was involved in reforming religion.

In 1523, the young Calvin, under aristocratic patronage, left his birthplace of Noyon for Paris, where he learned Latin from a renowned teacher to prepare himself for his humanist studies. In Paris, he also studied subjects including rhetoric, logic, and geometry to pave the way to more advanced theological studies.[2] Calvin's father originally planned this programme of study in order for Calvin to be ordained as a priest, but he later decided that a legal career would lead to a more profitable future for his son. Calvin received his legal education in Orleans and Bourges, in 1528 and 1529 respectively. In 1532, the ambitious Calvin published *L. Annei Senecae, Romani senatoris ac philosophi clarissimi, libri duo de Clementia, ad Neronem caesarem: Ioannis Calvini Noviodunaei commentariis illustrati* (short form: *Commentary on Seneca's De Clementia*) in Paris, just after the completion of his law degree in 1531.

In the 1970s, Robert M. Kingdon asserted that Calvin's *Commentary on Seneca's De Clementia* is seemingly not the work of a theologian as it contains "practically no references to formal theology or to the Scriptures, and that its references to the Church Fathers are sparse and mainly copied from the *Corpus Juris Canonici*".[3] In 2018, Wim A. Dreyer published an article with a very different conclusion. Based on a definition of public theology, Dreyer suggests that Calvin's *Commentary on Seneca's De Clementia* is a reflection on faith and has significant implications for society.[4] He, therefore, considers that Calvin was a public theologian at this

---

1 Quirinus Breen, *John Calvin: a Study in French Humanism* (Hamden, CT: Archon Books, 1968), 4–7, 10.

2 Bruce Gordon, *Calvin* (New Haven: Yale University Press, 2009), 4–8.

3 Robert M. Kingdon, "Reviewed Work: *Calvin's Commentary on Seneca's De Clementia*", by John Calvin, *Renaissance Quarterly*, 25, no. 4 (Winter, 1972): 467–469.

4 Wim A. Dreyer, "John Calvin as 'public theologian' in view of his '*Commentary on Seneca's De Clementia*'", *HTS Teologies Studies/Theological Studies*, 74, no. 4, (June 2018), a4928. https://doi.org/10.4102/hts.v74i4.4928

time because in his theological writing, Calvin engaged socio-political issues.[5] Bruce Gordon, however, stresses that Calvin truly knew that he was a novice in the sixteenth–century intellectual world, so, he considers that the commentary was intended to 'demonstrate to a learned French audience Calvin's legal, philological, and philosophical skills'.[6] Gordon also believes that this work shows the development of Calvin's knowledge gained from his previous education, both from his language and legal studies.[7] However, this is no 'public theology' as his thoughts found in *Commentary on Seneca's De Clementia* are neither political nor theological.

Contrary to Kingdon's assertion, Calvin does include Scripture when he comments on Seneca's *De Clementia*. For example, in chapter one, Calvin quotes Romans 13:1 to support his agreement with Seneca's Stoic teaching that gods are superintendents of human affairs, and that they do not leave events to chance but protect humans in their providence.[8] Hence, Kingdon's argument that no Scriptures are found in this commentary is not justifiable. However, whether Calvin uses the Scriptures according to his own faith (which was Catholicism at the time when he wrote his *Commentary on Seneca's De Clementia*) is questionable as he was hardly a Christian theologian at this stage.

Dreyer uses a twenty-first century term, 'public theologian' to describe Calvin's role when he was writing *Commentary on Seneca's De Clementia* in the sixteenth century. This use of the term seems somewhat anachronistic. Calvin was not yet a theologian in 1532 when he published the commentary and thus, this publication is apparently intended to mark the commencement of a long intellectual journey by a humanist lawyer.[9] Breen argues that if "Calvin had not been converted to radical Protestantism, he would have increasingly become a humanist as demonstrated in his *Commentary on Seneca's De Clementia*".[10]

Most probably, Calvin did not write the *Commentary on Seneca's De Clementia* based on his faith or as a theological treatise, but two points need to be highlighted before leaving this topic. Firstly, in 1531, Calvin was struggling with the question of whether to continue his path as a jurist or a scholar.[11] His work *Commentary on*

---

5 "Calvin's fundamental understanding of law and justice, as well as his theological engagement with socio-political issues, made him a public theologian par excellence." Ibid., 1.

6 Gordon, *Calvin*, 24.

7 Ibid.; see also Breen, *John Calvin: a study in French humanism*, 67.

8 "Haec autem oratio ex opinione Stoicorum pendet, qui diis rerum humanarum procurationem tribuunt; providentiam asserunt, nihil fortunae temeritati relinquunt…Est etiam illa confessio religionis nostrae, non esse potestatem nisi a Deo, et quae sunt, a Deo ordinatas esse, ad Rom XIII." *L. Annei Senecae, Romani senatoris ac philosophi clarissimi, libri duo de clementia, ad Neronem Caesarem: Ioannis Calvini Noviodunaei commentariis illustrati, CO5:18.*

9 Gordon, *Calvin*, 24.

10 Breen, *John Calvin: A Study in French Humanism*, 8.

11 Gordon, *Calvin*, 21.

Seneca's De Clementia shows that he is drawn to both. Secondly, the Stoic philosopher, Seneca endeavours to encourage King Nero to hold just trials when judging civilians, free from any personal emotions or the taking of revenge. Ruling with justice is essential and yet clemency is also needed to make people love the ruler. Calvin seems to be influenced by this aspect of Seneca's thoughts, especially his philosophy of Stoicism. Breen suggests that the revival of Stoicism is a contributing factor in the commencement of the Reformation.[12]

Calvin's first book shows his rhetoric and legal knowledge,[13] and it also conveys a message that he attends to Stoic teachings on the ruler's responsibility in governing with justice and clemency. It is found that Calvin's development of the doctrine of *providentia Dei* reflects an extension of these Stoic teachings after 1532, when he converted from his old faith to the evangelical movement, and began to write works that were motivated and informed by his religious perspective.

This chapter contributes four arguments. Firstly, in 1534, Calvin started to use some theological ideas with reference to the Apocrypha or the Deuterocanonical books to help him to understand *providentia Dei*. These are not theological ideas drawn from the Apocrypha but rather 'already existing theological ideas supported by texts from the Apocrypha'. He argues that there is a resemblance between the concept of the *fons* and *providentia Dei* because *providentia Dei* as a source of everything, functions like a fountain. Secondly, he dropped this reference when he composed his second edition of the *Institutes* and thereafter also gradually reduced the use of the term, *fons* as a heuristic key to explain *providentia Dei*. Thirdly, in the second edition of the *Institutes*, he formally started to discuss soteriological matters in relation to *providentia Dei*. Fourthly, in 1552, he defined three kinds of providence: '*generalis mundi gubernatio*', '*speciali providentia*', and '*praesentissima Dei*'.

The following discussion explains how Calvin develops his interpretation of *providentia Dei* in his theological works written between 1534 and 1552. The works include: *Psychopannychia*, the 1536, 1539, 1541, 1543, and 1550 *Institutes*, *Commentarius in epistolam Pauli ad Romanos*, and *De aeterna Dei praedestinatione*.

---

12 Breen, *John Calvin: A Study in French Humanism*, 69. Cf. "Calvin had become Seneca and Francis was his Nero." Gordon, *Calvin*, 58.

13 Quirinus Breen, *Christianity and Humanism: Studies in the History of Ideas*, edited by Nelson Peter Ross (Grand Rapids, MI: W.B. Eerdmans Publishing Company, 1968), 107–129.

Psychopannychia 1534[14] – *vivere apud Christum non dormire animis sanctos qui in fide Christi decedunt, assertio Ioannis Calvini*

Did Calvin convert from his old faith to the evangelical movement when he wrote *Psychopannychia* in 1534? In 1557, he asserted that he had a sudden conversion and that God called him to be a minister of the Church. Calvin seldom talked about his conversion but in 1557, he admitted that it was by God's secret providence that he had begun a different life when he stopped following his father's will.[15] It was only until later in his life in 1557, that Calvin personally testified of God's revelation of His secret providence concerning his special mission as an evangelist, which he had received from God when he was young. Yet, what did God's providence mean to him when he wrote his first theological work?

Scholars of studies on Calvin rarely examine *Psychopannychia* to study Calvin's interpretation of *providentia Dei*, but instead investigate the link between Calvin's life and his theology in this work.[16] However, Calvin contributes a short but significant description of his understanding of *providentia Dei* in *Psychopannychia* and he continues to develop this doctrine throughout his early works.

According to a verse from 4 Esdras 7:32, which specifies that "The earth will render up those things which sleep in it, and dwell in silence; and the storehouses will render up the souls which were committed to them", the Anabaptists argue that the soul sleeps or dies after life.[17] They believe that the storehouse is God's providence, and so when a person dies, his soul dies as well but the souls of the faithful are

---

14 *Psychopannychia* was written in 1534 but was not published until 1542. It is noted that Calvin's referencing in *Psychopannychia* relied extensively on the Apocryphal or Deuterocanonical books, and the literary style he adopted was apparently entirely different from his works written from 1536 onwards. Although it is difficult to predict the exact time Calvin wrote *Psychopannychia*, this work should be regarded as his early formation of his ideas.

15 "Verum, sicuti ille a caulis ovium ad summam imperii dignitatem evectus est, ita me Deus ab obscuris tenuibusque principiis extractum, hoc tam honorifico munere dignatus est, ut evangelii praeco essem ac minister…Ita factum est, ut revocatus a philosophiae studio, ad leges discendas traherer, quibus tametsi ut patris voluntati obsequerer fidelem operam impendere conatus sum, Deus tamen arcano providentiae suae fraeno cursum meum alio tandem reflexit." Ioannis Calvini, *Commentarius in librum Psalmorum*, Author's Preface CO31:21.

16 Besides learning about Calvin's arguments against "soul sleep", historians try to find out the kind of books Calvin read, the timing of Calvin's conversion to an evangelical movement, the places Calvin stayed, and the relationships between Calvin and his friends, based on the content of *Psychopannychia*. Alexandre Ganoczy and Joseph Lortz, *Le Jeune Calvin* (Wiesbaden: Franz Steiner Verlag GMBH, 1966), 74–83. Cf. Gordon, *Calvin*, 46, 57 and see also T.H.L. Parker, *John Calvin: A Biography* (London: J.M. Dent & Sons Ltd., 1975), 31–32.

17 John Calvin, *Soul Sleep: Psychopannychia*, translated by Henry Beveridge (Legacy Publications: 2011), 24. Cf. "Audiant igitur sum Esdram: Terra reddet quae in ea dormiunt, et in silentio habitant: et promptuaria reddent quae illis commendatae sunt animae (4 Esd 7:32)." Ioannis Calvini, *Psy-*

kept in the storehouse, which is known as God's providence. Furthermore, they allege that souls are thoughts and that the Book of Life displays these thoughts in storehouses.[18] Calvin does not agree with these interpretations of the soul and reminds his readers to take note of 4 Esdras 4:35 as it says, "Did not the souls of these petition in their abodes, saying, how long do we hope this, O Lord? When will the harvest of our reward come?"[19] Therefore, the soul does not die but instead it hopes for the reward of resurrection. Calvin argues that God's providence is not a storehouse but is God's power, and that souls are not thoughts but life,[20] and that the soul never loses its life.[21] This chapter explores no further details concerning Calvin and the Anabaptists' discussion on the soul, but it focuses on the aspect of providence.

Providentia Dei is not a storehouse but God's power:[22] '*virtus*'.[23] In '*virtute Dei*', which is *providentia Dei*, human beings are cared for by God's remembrance and are promised resurrection after death. So, what is God's power? Calvin argues that God's power is the fountain of life. He claims that people do not need to ask "*si abscissi sunt a virtute Dei*" because their names are written in the book of life, and

---

chopannychia 1534, vivere apud Christum non dormire animis sanctos qui in fide Christi decedunt, assertio Ioannis Calvini, CO5:186.

18 "Audiant igitur suum Esdram: Terra reddet quae in ea dormiunt, et in silentio habitant: et promptuaria reddent quae illis commendatae sunt animae (4 Esd 7:32). Nugantur, promptuaria esse providentiam Dei: animas vero, cogitationes: ut liber vitae offerat cogitationes in conspectu Dei." CO5:186. Calvin, *Soul Sleep*, 24.

19 "Nonne de his interrogaverunt animae istorum in promptuariis suis dicentes: Usque quo Domine speramus sic? quando veniet fructus areae mercedis nostrae? etc. (4 Esd 4:35). Quae sunt istae animae, quae interrogant et sperant? Hic cuniculum alium effodere eos oportet, si subterfugere volunt." CO5:186–187. Calvin, *Soul Sleep*, 24.

20 "Et si fidelis animae vita, Deus est, perinde atque ipsa, vita est corporis: quid est quod anima..." CO5:195.

21 "Caeterum, anima vitam suam nunquam perdidit, quae patri commendata non poterat non salva esse." CO5:192.

22 The debate over God's power as His absolute attribute vs God's power as His revealed attribute is discussed in chapter one of this work. See also Forrest Buckner, "Calvin's Non-Speculative Methodology: A Corrective to Billings and Muller on Calvin's Divine Attributes," in *Calvinus Pastor Ecclesia*, ed. Herman J. Selderhuis (Göttingen: Vandenhoeck & Ruprecht, 2016), 233–243; Richard A. Muller, "Calvin on Divine Attributes: A Question of Terminology and Method," *Westminster Theological Journal* 80, no.2 (2018): 199–218.

23 "Nos docemus, Dei benignitate ac virtute sustineri: quoniam ipse solus habet, immortalitatem (1 Tim 6:16): et quidquid est vitae, ab eo est." CO5:222. Cf. "Quid, inquiunt, si abscissi sunt a virtute Dei, si providentia eius et memoria exciderunt, nonne esse desierunt? Quasi vero non liceat mihi retorquere: Quid? si abscissi sunt a virtute Dei, si memoria exciderunt, quomodo rursum erunt?" CO5:222. Calvin, *Soul Sleep*, 82.

God's immortal power supports the mortal humans and guarantees resurrection.[24] Certainly, people will not be cut off from God's power because God's power is the fountain of life. Calvin supports his argument using a verse from the Book of Baruch,[25] where he contends, "For thus speaks the Prophet, when he would show that the fountain of life is with God, learn where there is prudence, where there is virtue, where there is understanding, where there is length of life and food, where there is light to the eyes and peace (Baruch 3:14)".[26] Calvin shows that God's power functions like a fountain to give blessings for humans. What kind of blessings does this fountain spring?

Calvin clarifies that God's power functions as a fountain,

> from which all drink, and from which streams flow and are derived, is said to have water in itself; yet it has it not of itself but of the source, which constantly supplies what may suffice both for the running streams and the men who drink of it. Accordingly, Christ has life in himself, i. e., fullness of life, by which he both himself lives and quickens others; yet he has it not of himself, as he elsewhere declares that he lives by the Father.[27]

---

24 "Ille ait hominem, si ab eo auferat suam misericordiam Dominus, ruere ac perire (Psal 104:29). Nos docemus, Dei benignitate ac virtute sustineri: quoniam ipse solus habet, immortalitatem (1 Tim 6:16): et quidquid est vitae, ab eo est…Quid? si abscissi sunt a virtute Dei, si memoria exciderunt, quomodo rursum erunt? Et ubi erit resurrectio? Rursum qui convenient isthaec? Iustorum animae in manu Dei sunt (Sapient 3:1). Aut, ut certis Dei oraculis agamus: In memoria aeterna erit iustus (Psal 112:6). Non igitur exciderunt a manu Domini, nec memoriam eius fugerunt. Quin potius hoc loquendi genere percipiamus gravem sensum hominis afflicti, qui apud Deum conqueritur, se paene desertum cum impiis in perditionem: quos Deus non nosse, et oblitus esse dicitur, quia nomina eorum in libro vitae scripta non sunt: et de manu sua abiecisse, quia eos non regit spiritu suo." *CO*5:222–223.

25 Disce ubi sit prudentia; ubi sit virtus; ubi sit intellectus; ut scias simul ubi sit longiturnitas; vitae et victus; ubi sit lumen oculorum et pax. *Biblia Sacra Vulgata*, editio quinta (Deutsche Bibelgesell- schaft, 2007), Baruch 3:14. Cf. Learn where there is wisdom, where there is strength, where there is understanding, that you may at the same time discern where there is length of days, and life, where there is light for the eyes, and peace. (Bar 3:14 RSV)

26 "Nullo denique vitae officio fungitur. Sic enim loquitur propheta (Bar 3:14), quum vult ostendere fontem vitae esse apud Deum: Disce ubi sit prudentia, ubi sit virtus, ubi sit intellectus, ubi sit diuturnitas vitae et victus, ubi sit lumen oculorum et pax." *CO*5:205. Cf. Calvin, *Soul Sleep*, 53–54.

27 "Quod familiari similitudine planum fieri potest. Fons, ex quo omnes hauriunt, ex quo rivuli defluunt et derivantur, aquam in semetipso habere dicitur: nec tamen ex semetipso, sed ex scaturigine, quae illi assidue subministrat quod et rivis labentibus, et haurientibus hominibus sufficere possit. Ergo Christus habet vitam in semetipso, hoc est, vitae plenitudinem, qua et ipse vivat, et suos vivificet: non tamen habet ex semetipso, quemadmodum ipse alibi testatur, quod vivit propter patrem (Ioann 6:57)." *CO*5:192; Calvin, *Soul Sleep*, 32–33.

Two crucial points need to be highlighted. Firstly, God's power benefits all people in the world, including the godly and ungodly. Secondly, God's providence is God's power, which is a source, providing fullness of eternal life through Christ. Hence, relationships between God's power, God as the fountain of life and *providentia Dei* are identified: *providentia Dei* is God's power and God's power functions like a fountain.

Calvin goes through three steps to identify the above relationships between God's power, providence, and fountain. Firstly, Calvin stresses that God cares for people after death by refuting the teaching of the Anabaptists about storehouse. Secondly, he emphasises that people's lives will not be cut off from God's power as their names are written in the book of life as a guarantee. Thirdly, the fountain of life is in God and this fountain is the source of the fullness of life. However, it must be asked how Calvin's young mind formulated these thoughts? The answer can be observed in Calvin's adopting of the medieval practice of using the Apocryphal or Deuterocanonical books to support his interpretation of God's power.

George Tavard argues that Calvin's explanation of the image of the fountain is related to the union with God in His kingdom, and that "to be one with God is to be in God, to be filled with God, to adhere to God, to possess God".[28] This explanation constitutes the tradition of medieval mysticism and Tavard asserts that Calvin follows Bonaventure's theology '*fontalis plenitudo*', and that the fountain of all fullness is in God the Father's kingdom, and that the believers will receive a plenitude of all riches.[29] Tavard stresses that Calvin's first Christian work is humanistic yet that at the same time he is influenced by medieval mysticism.[30]

Admittedly, Calvin adopts the term '*virtus*' from the Book of Baruch to show God's power through the giving of life and he interprets the term using the image of the fountain, which is Bonaventure's idea to show God's fullness, giving all the riches that humans need. Calvin might not have access to Bonaventure,[31] but Bonaventure does deliver the best explanation of '*fontalis plenitudo*'. Although it is not known from where Calvin adopted the image of the *fons*, it seems to act as a heuristic key to unlock the meaning of '*virtute Dei*' in Baruch 3:14.

In *Psychopannychia*, Calvin briefly expresses his preliminary thoughts on *providentia Dei*, but the core teaching is clear: God's providence is His power, and people

---

28 George H. Tavard, *The Starting Point of Calvin's Theology* (Cambridge: William B. Eerdmans Publishing Company, 2000), 91.

29 Ibid., 91.

30 Ibid., 72.

31 "Parmi Les anciens, l'école augustinienne ne reçoit pas non plus les égards qu'on attendrait de calviniens. Elle est représentée par un seul volume de Grégoire de Rimini. Ni Bonaventure, ni Gilles de Rome..." Alexandre Ganoczy, *La Bibliothèque de l'Académie de Calvin. Le Catalogue de 1572 et ses Enseignments* (Genèva: Librairie Droz, 1969), 107.

will not be cut off from lives because God has power over life and His riches spring like an image of a fountain. Calvin affirms that God's power is acted upon all human beings when they are alive, and the same power continues in the afterlife for them,[32] implying that this power continues in the afterlife for all, including the Reprobate.

The 1536 *Institutes*

The 1536 *Institutes* is a more structured theological work compared to *Psychopannychia*. While *Psychopannychia* is a short treatise Calvin composed to refute the teaching of a specific group of people, the *Institutes* address the ruler of the country, hoping that he would administer in a godly way. Some specific incidents that happened in Calvin's younger life might have influenced the way he composed the first edition of the *Institutes*. One of these could have been the poor sales of his first humanistic work, *Commentary on Seneca's De Clementia*. Calvin had wanted to use this commentary to gain a reputation as a humanist scholar but was not successful in doing so. However, after some chaos in his younger life, Calvin fled Paris to live in the Swiss city of Basel, from where he published the first edition of the *Institutes*, which gained for him enormous fame, far beyond his expectations.

Calvin published his first edition of the *Institutes* at the age of 27, and this work achieved what *Commentary on Seneca's De Clementia* failed to achieve, as the publication was an immediate success and was highly regarded by Reformers. In the 1536 *Institutes*, Calvin gave the faithful an instruction to become learned interpreters of the Word.[33] The contents of the 1536 *Institutes* resemble the form of a catechism and show significant divergence from Calvin's early works in the use of Scripture.

The 1536 *Institutes* does not give a major discussion on the topic of *providentia Dei*. Calvin mentions the term *providentia* in three chapters (chapters two, three, and six) under four topics: faith, prayers, church governance, and country administration. Calvin also uses this term to describe how God appoints rulers in His *providentia*.[34] The ruler has special divine responsibilities to fulfil and they should show "some image of divine providence, protection, goodness, benevolence, and

---

32 "Iam ut virtutem ipsam ad se quoque pertinere fideles intelligerent, subiungit Christum hanc virtutem erga alios exseruisse: neque erga vivos modo, sed etiam mortuos: deinde non tantum erga servos suos, sed incredulos quoque ac gratiae suae contemptores." CO5:185.

33 Gordon, *Calvin*, 62.

34 Four times in chapter two, four times in chapter three, and seven times in chapter six of the 1536 *Institutes*.

justice".[35] However, the discussion of *providentia* in the 1536 *Institutes* is primarily directed to the relationship between God and people from different classes, including the godly, the ungodly, and country leaders. Chapter two is '*de fide, ubi et symbolum, quod apostolicum vocant, explicatur*'. He argues that in God's providence, His power is over everything, including salvation for the faithful and the affliction of humankind.[36] Chapter three is '*de oratione, ubi et oratio dominica enarratur*', and its mention of providence appears in the exposition of the Lord's prayer. In this section, God's providence is parental which Calvin portrays as a true and deep love from the heavenly father,[37] where through God's providential care, He nourishes and preserves humankind.[38] In divine providence, both God and human beings have a role: God shows His presence and the faithful persevere to pray.[39]

Chapter six is '*de libertate christiana, potestate ecclesiastica, et politica administratione*'. In this section concerning Christian freedom, Calvin asserts that in God's providence, He appoints humanity to manage the resources He created.[40] In addition, Calvin suggests both ecclesiastical power and political administration are in God's providence. In a church situation, prophets, priests, apostles, and disciples have not been endowed with any power to command unless they are appointed by God.[41] Prophets in the past gained this power from the fountain of God's knowledge

---

35 "In summa, si se Dei vicarios esse meminerint, omni cura, sedulitate, industria invigilent oportet, qui hominibus quandam divinae providentiae, custodiae, bonitatis, benevolentiae, iustitiae, imaginem in se repraesentent." Ioannis Calvini, *Institutio Religionis Christianae* 1536, CO1:231.

36 "Talem patrem grata pietate ardentique amore sic colamus, ut nos totos eius obsequio devoveamus, illum in omnibus honoremus; omnia, adversa quoque, aequis placidisque animis, quasi ex eius manu suscipiamus, cogitantes eius providentiam sic quoque nobis ac saluti nostrae prospicere, dum affligit et tribulat." CO1:63.

37 "Iam si ita, ut par est, vicissim manum porrigere atque opem ferre cupimus, non est in quo magis commodare fratribus possimus, quam si optimi patris curae ac providentiae commendemus: quo propitio ac favente nihil omnino desiderari potest. Et sane hoc ipsum patri etiam nostro debemus. Ut enim qui patrem aliquem familias vere et ex animo diligit, totam simul eius domum amore ac benevolentia complectitur; ad hunc modum, quo simus in hunc coelestem patrem studio atque affectu, erga eius populum, eius familiam, eius denique haereditatem ostendere convenit, quam tantopere honoravit, ut plenitudinem unigeniti filii sui vocaverit (Eph 1)." CO1:91.

38 "Qua breviter nos in eius curam tradimus ac providentiae committimus, ut nos pascat, foveat, servet." CO1:95.

39 "Si animis in hanc obedientiam compositis, providentiae divinae legibus nos regi patimur, facile discemus in oratione perseverare, ac suspensis desideriis patienter expectare Dominum; certi, etiam si minime apparet, nobis tamen semper adesse, suoque tempore declaraturum, quam non habuerit surdas aures precibus, quae in hominum oculis neglectae videbantur." CO1:100–101.

40 "Certe et ebur et aurum et divitiae bonae Dei creaturae sunt, hominum usibus permissae, imo Dei providentia destinatae." CO1:200.

41 "Quidquid autoritatis ac dignitatis scriptura, sive prophetis, sive sacerdotibus, sive apostolis, sive apostolorum successoribus defert, id totum non hominibus ipsis dari, sed ministerio, cui praefecti sunt; vel, ut expeditius loquamur, verbo Dei, in cuius ministerium vocati sunt." CO1:205–206.

and wisdom,[42] as God reveals himself in the fountain: "From the same fountain Adam, Noah, Abraham, Isaac, Jacob, and others, whoever God deigned from the beginning to give a knowledge of Himself, have also drunk all they have taught of heavenly teaching".[43]

In this description, Calvin links the image of the fountain to God's wisdom and he further suggests that in this fountain of God, believers will see some revelation of Him through His word. Regarding the appointment of bishops, Calvin does not deny that their appointment is in divine providence, but he has a negative impression of their administration especially the claim that bishops represent the church and cannot err.[44] Calvin specifically despises the fact that bishops ignore the truth of God's words while promulgating the truth of their own words. Regarding civil government, Calvin emphasises that rulers and kings administer the earth in '*divina providentia*' and '*sancta ordinatione*'.[45] Furthermore, the people who serve as the magistrates are God's representatives.[46] Calvin's tone and the use of words to describe the function of the emperor are more positive compared to his description of the role of bishop, following his predecessors, for instance Marsilius of Padua.[47] In particular, Calvin stresses that the rulers are vicars of God and that they

---

42 "Ipse enim aeternus ac unicus patris consiliarius, qui in eius sinu semper fuit, sic a patre accepit, ut simul omnes scientiae et sapientiae thesauros habuerit in se reconditos (Col 2). Ex hoc fonte hauserunt omnes prophetae, quidquid unquam coelestium oraculorum ediderunt." CO1:207.

43 John Calvin, *Institutes of the Christian Religion* 1536, translated and annotated by Ford Lewis Battles (London: Collins, 1975), 187. Cf. "Ex hoc fonte hauserunt omnes prophetae, quidquid unquam coelestium oraculorum ediderunt. Ex eodem Adam, Noah, Abraham, Isaac, Iacob et alii, quoscunque ab initio Deus sui cognitione dignatus est, hauserunt et ipsi quoque quidquid coelestis doctrinae didicerunt." CO1:207.

44 "Eandem ergo certitudinem veritatis, quae apud ecclesiam est, habere etiam ecclesiae concilia quibus ipsa vere repraesentatur et ne errare possint, immediate regi a spiritu sancto." CO1:210. Cf. "Quod ultimo inferunt, errare non posse ecclesiam in iis quae sunt ad salutem necessaria, minime reclamamus. Sed hic etiam plurimum sensu variamus. Errare non posse ideo sentimus, quod abdicata omni sua sapientia, a spiritu sancto doceri se per verbum Domini patitur." CO1:215.

45 "Perinde enim istud valet, ac si dictum esset, non humana perversitate fieri ut penes reges et praefectos alios sit in terris rerum omnium arbitrium, sed divina providentia et sancta ordinatione, cui sic visum est res hominum moderari." CO1:231.

46 Later in the 1539 *Institutes*, Calvin describes the function of a church minister and implies that a pastor is a representative of God on earth. The discussion is both of the 1539 & 1541 *Institutes*.

47 "Audio, quid ipsi pro se respondeant: suas traditiones non a se, sed a Deo esse; non enim se propria commenta effutire, sed quod a spiritu sancto acceperint veluti per manus tradere christiano populo, cui regendo divina providentia praefecti sunt." CO1:210. Cf. CO1:231–233. Marsilius of Padua has the same comments on the king and bishop. Regarding the king: "…in te quoque respiciens singulariter, tamquam Dei ministrum huic operi finem daturum, quem extrinsecus optat inesse, inclitissime Ludovice Romanorum imperator…" Marsiglio da podova, *Defensor Pacis*, Monumenta Germaniae Historica (Turnhout: Brepols Publishers, 2010), 1.1.6, and regarding bishop: "Hiis consequenter ostendere convenit, nihil per hominem aliquem singularem, cuiuscumque dignitatis

should show "some image of divine providence, protection, goodness, benevolence, and justice".[48] These descriptions of divine providence are first mentioned at the beginning of the 1536 *Institutes*, and they will be discussed later in this section.

Calvin might have written the 1536 *Institutes* as a textbook, a handbook for understanding the Holy Scripture correctly, or a catechism for believers to study, but he also intends to create a political purpose through this work. In the letter to the king, Calvin states that the content was originally formulated as a catechism, but he also intended to explain to the ruler that the persecutions of the believers happening at that time were a mistake. The writing style and the ostensible purpose of the 1536 *Institutes* seems to follow that of Calvin's first scholarly work, his *Commentary on Seneca's De Clementia*, in which Seneca admonishes King Nero to have mercy on other religious groups.[49] Regardless of the many purposes of the main theme of the *Institutes*, Calvin reminds the rulers to reign according to God's rules as they are His vicars.

In the early work of Philip Melanchthon—the 1521 *Loci Communes*, Melanchthon considers two kinds of magistrates: civil and ecclesiastical who are both in God's providence. A civil magistrate piously administers the sword to establish public stability,[50] while an ecclesiastical magistrate is responsible for the correct Scriptural teaching.[51] Although both magistrates are appointed by God, anything they proclaim that proves to be contrary to God is "not to be obeyed

---

aut condicionis existat, statui posse circa ecclesiasticum ritum, quod homines ad observacionem obliget sub aliqua pena pro statu presentis seculi vel venturi, nisi per generale concilium immediate aut inde sumpta prius auctoritate... Amplius, quoniam nullus episcopus in alium auctoritatem habet aliquam a Christo immediate...Ex quibus eciam deduci potest et convenit, ad solius iam dicti concilii, non autem ad solius episcopi aut presbyteri vel alicuius ipsorum particularis collegii auctoritatem pertinere...magnum inde scandalum paci et quieti fidelium omnium evenire contingit." Marsiglio da podova, *Defensor Pacis* 2.21.8–9.

48 "In summa, si se Dei vicarios esse meminerint, omni cura, sedulitate, industria invigilent oportet, qui hominibus quandam divinae providentiae, custodiae, bonitatis, benevolentiae, iustitiae, imaginem in se repraesentent." *CO*1:231.

49 "Seneca requests Emperor Nero urgently that he should show clemency to the heretics in Rome. Similarly, Calvin dedicates the 1536 *Institutes* to King Francis I hoping to remind him that his kingship is appointed in God's providence and that the king, and every king, actually should show mercy towards Christians." Wulfert de Greef, *The Writings of John Calvin - an Introductory Guide*, translated by Lyle D. Bierma (Grand Rapids, MI: Baker Books, 1993), 85.

50 "Magistratus alios censent ciuiles esse, alios ecclesiasticos. Ciuilis magistratus est qui gladium gerit, & ciuilem pacem tuetur. Hunc probat Paulus Roma.xiii...Adeo pie administrat gladium magistratus." Philipp Melanchthon, *Loci communes rerum theologicarum seu hypotyposes theologicae* (Vvittembergae: Zentralbibliothek Zürich, 1521), 136.

51 "Primum ergo si doceant Scripturam, sic audiendi sunt Christus." Ibid., 137.

and heard".[52] Regarding the divine appointment of church ministers and public rulers, the early interpretation of Calvin shows some continuity with Melanchthon's understanding of *providentia Dei* although Calvin uses a more encouraging tone to the civil rulers than to the bishops.

Calvin stresses that kings are God's vicars and they should model themselves on the image of divine providence, protection, goodness, benevolence, and justice.[53] This description of God's actions is an echo of Calvin's description of the list of God's activities in the first paragraph of the first chapter of the 1536 *Institutes*. Calvin argues that God is infinite wisdom, righteousness, goodness, mercy, truth, power, and life, and adopts this idea from the Book of Baruch 3:14,[54] the same quotation he used when he described God's power in *Psychopannychia* in 1534. However, in the 1536 *Institutes*, God is not just power, as Calvin described in *Psychopannychia*. Although the term *fons* is not mentioned by Calvin in the first paragraph of the first chapter, the reference to Baruch 3:14 is quoted in the text. Also, the description about the function of the fountain appears twice in the second chapter, which is a discussion about faith, where Calvin argues that one can find the fountain of living water in Christ.[55] This living water comes from the source of God, and it nourishes human beings.

From *Psychopannychia*, it is found that Calvin gets the idea of the fountain of life from the Book of Baruch. In the 1536 *Institutes*, Calvin continues to use this idea and portrays God as not only powerful, but he also as wise, righteous, good, merciful, faithful, and life giving. In the 1539 & 1541 *Institutes*, Calvin's use of the term *fons* displays some nuanced differences, but the meaning is enormous. He adds the term, fountain, to both the Latin and French editions without reference to the Book of Baruch.

---

52 About a civil magistrate: "…Primum si quid contra deum imperarint principes, non esse obtemperandum." Ibid., 136. Cf. About an ecclesiastical magistrate: "Deinde si quid contra Scripturam decuerint, non sunt audiendi…Tertio si quid praeter Scripturam statuerint, in hoc, ut conscientias obstringant, non sunt audiendi." Ibid., 137.

53 CO1:231.

54 "Primum, ut certa fide constitutum habeamus, ipsum infinitam esse sapientiam, iustitiam, bonitatem, misericordiam, veritatem, virtutem ac vitam: ut nulla sit prorsus alia sapientia, iustitia, bonitas, misericordia, veritas, virtus et vita (Bar 3; Iac 1)." CO1:27.

55 "Cum, enim fides Christum amplectatur ut nobis offertur a patre, ille vero non modo sit remissio, iustitia, pax, et reconciliatio apud patrem, sed etiam sanctificatio et fons aquae vivae, indubie in eo caritatem reperit quae donum est et fructus spiritus sancti opusque eius sanctificationis (Gal 5)." CO1:80. Cf. "Credimus postremo vitam aeternam, hoc est: futurum, ut tum suos Dominus corpore et anima glorificatos in beatitudinem accipiat, sine fine perstaturam, extra omnem mutationis aut corruptionis sortem; quae vera erit solidaque in vitam, lucem, iustitiam perfectio, cum inseparabiliter Domino adhaerebimus, qui earum, velut fons inexhaustus, plenitudinem in se continet (1 Cor 15)." CO1:79.

The 1539 Latin edition of the *Institutes* and its 1541 French translation

Following the invitation of Guillaume Farel and his own confirmation of the calling, Calvin arrived in Geneva in August 1536 to become pastor of the Genevan Church. However, in May 1538, the city of Geneva deported both Calvin and Farel. Calvin found exile in Strasbourg, from where he published the second edition of the *Institutes*. Calvin wrote the 1539 *Institutes* in Latin as he had also done for the 1536 edition, and when he returned to Geneva in 1541, Calvin published the first French edition, entitled *Institution de la religion chrétienne*. This was a translation of the 1539 edition for the Genevans and for the Reformed Christians in France, most of whom did not read Latin.

Significantly, the first paragraph in the opening chapter 'Of the Knowledge of God' in the 1539 *Institutes* has three changes from the first paragraph of the 1536 *Institutes*. It is likely that Calvin wanted to immediately bring the reader's attention to these important changes at the very beginning of this section. The first change was in the wording 'sacred doctrine' in the first sentence of the 1536 *Institutes* which was changed to 'our wisdom' in the 1539 *Institutes*, or to put it in Latin and French terms, for '*sacra doctrina*', he substituted '*sapienta nostra*' and '*nostre sagesse*'.[56] Furthermore, Calvin argues that our wisdom consists of two parts, specifically, the knowledge of God and the knowledge of ourselves. In the first edition of the *Institutes*, Calvin explores this twofold knowledge based on the doctrine of the Apostolic Creed, however, for the second edition, the focus is toward the wisdom of humanity. Although the focus seems to change from creator to creature, the emphasis is that for human beings, to gain wisdom they must acknowledge God, and thus, Calvin employs the entire *Institutes* to elaborate this idea.

The second change concerns the use of the image of the *fons*. In the second edition of the *Institutes*: the 1539 *Institutes* as well as in the 1541 edition, Calvin argues that God is the *fons* or the *fonteine* of all truth, wisdom, goodness, righteousness, judgment, mercy, power, and holiness but he does not include a reference to the Book of Baruch.[57] He used the term and the concept of the *fons* to describe God's

---

56 "Tota fere sapientiae nostrae summa, quae vera demum ac solida sapientia censeri debeat, duabus partibus constat: cognitione Dei, et nostri." *CO*1:279. Cf. "Toute la somme de nostre saigesse laquelle merite d'estre appellée vraie et certaine saigesse, est quasi comprinse en deux parties, à sçavoir la congnoissance de Dieu, et de nousmesmes." Jean Calvin, *Institution de la Religion Chrétienne* 1541 Tome I, edited and translated by Olivier Millet (Genève: Librairie Droz S.A., 2008), 187.

57 In the 1539 *Institutes*: "Illa scilicet, quae non modo unum esse Deum ostendat, quem ab omnibus oporteat coli et adorari, sed simul etiam doceat, illum unum omnis veritatis, sapientiae, bonitatis, iustitiae, iudicii, misericordiae, potentiae, sanctitatis fontem esse, ut ab ipso et exspectare et petere universa ista discamus, praeterea cum laude et gratiarum actione accepta illi referre." *CO*1:279. Cf. In the 1541 *Institutes*: "Dont la premiere doibt monstrer non seulement qu'il est un seul Dieu, lequel il fault que tous adorent et honorent, mais aussi qu'iceluy est la fonteine de toute verité, sapience, bonté,

'*virtus*' and God as the source of life in both *Psychopannychia* and the 1536 *Institutes* with reference to the Book of Baruch but he dropped this reference in the second edition of the *Institutes*. This indicates that he was moving away from including this Apocryphal or Deuterocanonical book in his bible when it is a matter of Christian truth, and probably toward a more narrowly defined biblical way in his quest to understand God.

The third change is that in the 1536 *Institutes*, Calvin introduces God's '*choses*'[58] as truth, wisdom, goodness, righteousness, mercy, power, and life.[59] This list is included in both the 1539 and the 1541 *Institutes* except that Calvin added '*iudicii*' and '*sanctitatis*', but dropped '*vitam*'. Judgement and righteousness are similar, so they do not present a significant difference. However, Calvin replaces life with holiness indicating that his concern is shifted to the sanctification of the Elect and the salvation of the Church. He specifies that the life given is one of holiness befitting the Elect.

These three aspects show that as Calvin tries to formulate his theological understanding about God and His creation, he confirms that God's '*choses*' (things) are salvific. This omission of the Baruch quote signifies something critical: in the second edition of the *Institutes*, Calvin started to disassociate his explanation of God's '*choses*' with the Apocrypha or the Deuterocanonical books. Furthermore, in this edition, Calvin clearly shows that God endows human beings with both salvation and benefits. Besides the discussion of a long list of the 'things' of God in the first paragraph of chapter one, Calvin repeats the discussion of this long list at the end of the first chapter of 'Of the Knowledge of God'. Calvin reminds readers to gain the knowledge of God in His truth, wisdom, goodness, righteousness, judgement, mercy, and power in a wholesome manner, then His holiness will shine in them, and they can glorify God.[60] Admittedly, this list is very important and thus, Calvin

---

justice, jugement, misericorde, puissance, et saincteté, afin que de luy nous aprenions d'attendre et demander toutes ces choses." Calvin, *Institution de la Religion Chrétienne* 1541, 187–188.

58 "...est la fonteine de toute verité, sapience, bonté, justice, jugement, misericorde, puissance, et saincteté, afin que de luy nous aprenions d'attendre et demander toutes ces choses." Calvin, *Institution de la Religion Chrétienne* 1541, 188.

59 CO1:27.

60 "...Quiconque se glorifie, dit-il, qu'il se glorifie en cela, c'est de me congnoistre le Dieu qui faictz misericorde, justice et jugement en la terre. Certes ces trois choses nous sont principallement necessaires à congnoistre: sa misericorde, en laquelle consiste le salut de nous tous; son judgement, lequel journellement il exerce sur les iniques, et lequel il leur reserve plus rigoreux à confusion eternelle: sa justice, par laquelle ses fideles sont benignement entretenuz. Ces choses comprinses, le Prophete tesmoigne que nous avons abondamment de quoy nous glorifier en Dieu. Neantmoins en cela faisant, n'est pas obmise ne sa puissance, ne sa verité, ne sa saincteté, ne sa bonté. Car comment consisteroit l'intelligence de sa justice, misericorde, et jugement (comme elle est là requise) sinon qu'elle feust appuyée sur sa verité immuable?...Finalement si toutes ses voyes sont misericorde,

uses the entire chapter to explain it, and he reinforces the list again at the end of the chapter. It is only with the second edition of Calvin's *Institutes*, that Calvin directly relates God's 'things' to salvation, which signifies sanctification and immortality.

The second edition of the *Institutes* has seventeen chapters and Calvin discusses *providentia Dei* in almost every chapter, except in those about penitence, the difference between the Old and New Testaments, sacraments, baptism, and the five false sacraments. Compared to the 1536 *Institutes*, Calvin discusses *providentia Dei* in relation to God's creation, the Apostolic Creed, prayers, ecclesiastical and civil appointment with greater elaboration in the 1539 *Institutes*. For example, he uses a few paragraphs to explain that everything happens not by fortune but by *providentia Dei*.[61] This explanation is not included in the 1536 *Institutes*. He also distinguishes two kinds of motions which both imply God's providence: '*generalis actio*'[62] (or '*universae motus*') governs the matters of the world and '*speciali Dei motioni*'[63] which guides humanity. In addition, Calvin uses '*singulari providentia*'[64] to argue that God maintains a non-general care[65] for some '*singulas*'.[66]

In the 1539 *Institutes*, when he discusses the function of singular providence, Calvin says, '*Qua in re singulari providentia Deus posterorum saluti consuluit*'.[67] God takes care of the salvation of the posterity with His singular providence. However, in the 1541 French edition, when Calvin translates the same sentence, he simply says, '*Enquoy le Seigneur a subvenu au bien de successeurs par une singuliere providence*'.[68] No meaning of salvation is given. In the 1539 *Institutes*, when Calvin added that

---

jugement et justice, en icelles pareillement reluyt sa saincteté." Calvin, *Institution de la Religion Chrétienne* 1541, 234–235.

61 "Quantum vero attinet ad ea quae praeter naturalis decursus ordinem quotidie eveniunt, quotusquisque non magis reputat, caeca potius fortunae temeritate rotari et volutari homines, quam Dei providentia gubernari?" *CO*1:290.

62 "…in conservando autem et moderando, generalem quandam actionem, unde vis motionis dependeat. At vero fides altius penetrat, et quem omnium creatorem esse didicit, statim perpetuum quoque moderatorem et conservatorem cogitat. Neque id, universali quadam motione tam orbis machinam…" *CO*1:511.

63 "…verum si aures tot testimoniis praebemus, quae Dominum in his quoque regere animos hominum clamant, arbitrium ipsum speciali Dei motioni subiiciemus." *CO*1:355.

64 *CO*1:292. Cf. "…quam singulas eius partes agitando; sed singulari quadam providentia, unumquodque eorum quae condidit, ad minimum usque passerem, sustinendo, fovendo, curando." *CO*1:511.

65 Non-general providence includes '*speciali providentia*' and '*praesentissima Dei*'. This will be discussed in the section about *De aeterna Dei praedestinatione* 1552.

66 *CO*1:511.

67 *CO*1:292.

68 Calvin, *Institution De La Religion Chrétienne* 1541, 217. Cf. "…mais elle comprend sa providence singuliere, par laquelle il maintient, conserve et vivifie toutes choses qu'il a creées, jusques aux plus petis oyseaux de l'air." Calvin, *Institution De La Religion Chrétienne* 1541, 605.

God was the source of '*sanctitatis*' in the first paragraph of chapter one, it seemed to convey the message that God's action is salvific. However, in the 1541 *Institutes*, which is supposed to be a direct translation from the 1539 Latin edition, Calvin kept the term '*saincetété*' in the first paragraph of chapter one, but he took out the emphasis on salvation in relation to special providence and returned to the interpretation of God as a source of '*bien*' only. Why does he do this? Calvin might have made a mistake in his interpretation of special providence in the 1539 *Institutes*, therefore he corrected it in the 1541 *Institutes*. Yet, this is not feasible as in his later works, he kept the step he took in 1539. Therefore, most probably Calvin was still developing his doctrine of special providence when he wrote the second edition of the *Institutes*. As we shall see, this is further confirmed by his sermons, commentaries and the 1559 *Institutes*.

Thus, is there a special kind of God's providence just for the faithful? The terms '*singulari providentia*'[69] and '*singuliere providence*'[70] are used in the 1539 and 1541 *Institutes*, respectively. Both terms have the meaning of particular, rare, and uncommon. However, these two terms seem to describe God's providence in human history, which is for general humans rather than describing a distinctive providence for a rare group of people, the Elect. According to Werner Krusche, the Holy Spirit is the author of the '*providentia specialissima*' and he argues that for Calvin, this very special providence is truly predestination.[71] It seems that even for special providence, Calvin suggests different kinds of special providence by distinguishing between '*singularis providentia*' and '*providentia specialissima*'. God's special action leads the faithful in their daily lives and His very special action endows the faithful eternal lives. However, it should be noted that Calvin did not make this distinction and there is no explanation of '*providentia specialissima*' to be found in the second edition of the *Institutes*. This topic of '*providentia specialissima*' will be explained in chapter 5.

As Calvin explained in *Psychopannychia* and in the 1536 *Institutes*, the fountain of all good is God's provision of life for those who believe, and it is found that there is a closer relationship between salvation and *providentia Dei*, which Calvin tries to

---

69 "Neque id, universali quadam motione tam orbis machinam, quam singulas eius partes agitando; sed singulari quadam providentia, unumquodque eorum quae condidit, ad minimum usque passerem, sustinendo, fovendo, curando." *CO*1:511.

70 "…mais elle comprend sa providence singuliere, par laquelle il maintient, conserve et vivifie toutes choses qu'il a creées, jusques aux plus petis oyseaux de l'air." Calvin, *Institution De La Religion Chrétienne* 1541, 605.

71 Werner Krusche, *Das Wirken des Heiligen Geistes nach Calvin* (Göttingen: Vandenhoeck & Ruprecht, 1957), 14. Also quoted in Charles Partee, *Calvin and Classical Philosophy*, Studies in History of Christian Thought 15 (Leiden: E.J. Brill, 1977), 135 & in Mark W. Elliott, *Providence Perceived: Divine Action from a Human Point of View* (Berlin/Boston: De Gruyter, 2015), 142.

argue in the 1539 *Institutes*.[72] God's action in this world shows His holiness and the people who are saved in special providence also shows God's holiness. In addition to this, Calvin's interpretation of *providentia Dei* in this edition of the *Institutes* consists of much of the discussion regarding the explanation of the reprobation aspect of double predestination, and he combines the examination of the doctrines of predestination and providence in the same chapter.

In the *Institutes* of 1539, Calvin first suggests that in God's eternal secret counsel, some people are predestined to eternal life, while the remainder are condemned to eternal death. Fundamentally, Calvin uses his interpretation of *providentia Dei* to explain his proposal of double predestination, and he assures the Elect that they are endowed with salvation, life, and immortality from the fountain of life in Christ: they are chosen by God's pleasure.[73] However, the Reprobate, by God's providence, are set apart for destruction, and although God permits and wills those, the condemned are responsible for their own sin. Furthermore, God is not the author of sin, but He predestines sinners to an eternal death to carry out His judgment.

Calvin uses providence to explain predestination[74] and to show that God's action is above everyone's actions[75] but humankind is condemned because of the corrupt nature of mortal beings.[76] The addition of holiness in the first paragraph of chapter one, the emphasis of special providence in relation to salvation, and the placement of the discussion of the doctrines of providence and predestination indicate that Calvin's doctrine of providence starts to show a sense of soteriology in the 1539 *Institutes*. The occasional withdrawal of the term 'salvation' in the 1541 *Institutes* when discussing special providence only shows that Calvin was developing the definition of special providence, because in another place when he discusses predestination and providence in the same edition, he retains salvation when discussing

---

72　The chapters about predestination and providence are the same in both the 1539 and 1541 editions. Therefore, the following discussion mentions only the 1539 *Institutes*, but the concerns also apply to the 1541 *Institutes*.

73　*CO*1:880. Cf. Calvin, *Institution de la Religion Chrétienne* 1541 Tome II, 1073.

74　"S'il y a donc pleincte aucune, ou juste ou de quelque apparence, elle s'adresse plustost à sa providence. Or ce que je dy ne doibt sembler advis estre estrange: c'est que Dieu non seulement a preveu la cheute du premier homme et en icelle la ruine de toute sa posterité, mais qu'il l'a ainsi voulu." Calvin, *Institution de la Religion Chrétienne* 1541 Tome II, 1058.

75　*CO*1:865. Cf. Calvin, *Institution de la Religion Chrétienne* 1541 Tome II, 1039.

76　"Parquoy contemplons plustost en la nature corrompue de l'homme la cause de sa damnation, laquelle luy est evidente, que de la cercher en la Predestination de Dieu, où elle est cachée, et du tout incomprehensible." Calvin, *Institution de la Religion Chrétienne* 1541 Tome II, 1061.

providence.[77] *Providentia Dei* is kept distinct, but it is not totally separated from salvation. This will be further demonstrated in chapters 3, 4, and 5 of this work.

In the 1536 *Institutes*, Calvin informs the rulers of countries that their appointment is by divine providence and that they are God's representatives to guide their citizens. In the 1539 *Institutes*, Calvin asserts explicitly that both leaders of church and country are representatives of God. Although humankind's corrupt nature is '*la cause*' of their destruction, as '*les causes inferieures*',[78] they do have a role in *providentia Dei*. Additionally, Calvin argues that it is necessary to honour '*ministres et dispensateurs de ses benefices*',[79] for he considers Church ministers to be God's representatives to distribute or extend His benefits to the faithful on earth, as they are the lawful instruments of God's providence.[80] Similarly, in the 1539 *Institutes*, Calvin continues to affirm that civil governors are God's instruments, and should therefore show an image of *providentia Dei* in care, goodness, kindness, and justice.[81] The issues concerning Calvin's interpretation of causality in *providentia Dei* will be discussed in chapters 3 and 4.

Commentarius in epistolam Pauli ad Romanos 1540

Commentary on the epistle to the Romans was published in Strasbourg in 1540, and Calvin dedicated this work to Simon Grynaeus[82] who was imprisoned because of

---

77 "Pourtant le cœur de l'homme Chrestien, veu qu'il a cela tout resolu qu'il n'advient rien à l'advanture, mais que toutes choses se font par la Providence de Dieu, regardera tousjours à luy comme à la principale cause de tout ce qui se fait, mais cependant il ne laissera point de contempler les causes inferieures, en leur degré. Davantage, il ne doubtera pas que la Providence de Dieu ne veille pour sa conservation et qu'elle ne permettra rien advenir qui ne soit pour son bien et salut." Ibid., 1103–1104.

78 Ibid., 1109.

79 "Brief, nous porterons ceste honneur à Dieu de le recongnoistre principal autheur de tout bien, mais nous honorerons aussi les hommes, comme ministres et dispensateurs de ses benefices, et penserons qu'il nous a voulu obliger à eulx puisqi'il s'est monstré nostre bienfaicteur par leurs mains." Ibid., 1109.

80 "Quant est des choses futures, nous prendrons pied principalement à ces causes inferieures dont nous avons parlé…Plustost, estimans que c'est Dieu qui nous presente à la main toutes creatures lesquelles nous peuvent porter proffit, nous les appliquerons en usage comme instrumens legitimes de sa Providence." Ibid., 1110. Cf. "…mais que toutes choses se font par la Providence de Dieu, regardera tousjours à luy comme à la principale cause de tout ce que se fait, mais cependant il ne laissera point de contempler les causes inferieures, en leur degré." Ibid., 1103.

81 "In summa, si se Dei vicarios esse meminerint, omni cura, sedulitate, industria, invigilent, oportet, qui hominibus quandam divinae providentiae, custodiae, bonitatis, benevolentiae, iustitiae, imaginem in se repraesentent." CO1:1104.

82 Reformer and teacher in Basel and south-west Germany (d. 1541).

his advocacy of Luther's doctrines.[83] In this work, Calvin similarly puts the doctrines of predestination and providence together, and explicitly uses 'God's hidden providence', describing it as the hidden fountain of God, to explain predestination. In the exegesis of Romans 9:17, Calvin confirms that Pharaoh's condemnation is God's predestination.[84] Why is that so? It is to glorify God by making His name known. To put it concisely, the predestination of Pharaoh proceeds from the hidden fountain of God's providence for the purpose of glorifying God's name,[85] and that of carrying out His judgment.

In the 1539 *Institutes*, Calvin used the image of the fountain to describe God's *'choses'* without referring to the Book of Baruch. In the commentary on Romans, Calvin directly links the image of the fountain to God's hidden providence to explain the controversial aspect of double predestination. Although this is probably the first time Calvin directly link *providentia Dei* to the image of the fountain, it seems that in this commentary on Romans, he uses this image of the fountain to 'describe' God as the source of the hidden providence. There are no theological explanations of the image of the fountain, (for instance God as the fountain of power, wisdom, etc.) as there were in the 1539 and 1541 *Institutes*.

When Calvin wrote the commentary on Romans in 1540, his interpretation of special providence continued to be soteriological,[86] and when commenting on Romans 10:14–15, he stresses that faith is being produced by the word of God which is preached by church ministers in God's special providence.[87] Thus, the action of

---

83 John Calvin, *Commentary on Romans*, translated by John Owen (Grand Rapids, MI: Christian Classics Ethereal Library, 1849), 12.

84 "Proinde duo sunt hic consideranda, praedestinatio Pharaonis in exitium: quae ad iustum quidem, sed arcanum Dei consilium refertur." Ioannis Calvini, *Commentarius in Epistolam Pauli ad Romanos,* Rom 9:17, CO49:183.

85 "Unde sequitur, frustra iam cum ipso disceptari, ac si ad reddendam rationem obstrictus foret, quum ultro prodeat ipse in medium, atque hanc obiectionem anticipet reprobos ex arcano providentiae suae fonte manare pronuntians, in quibus nomen suum celebrari velit." Rom 9:17, CO49:184. See also "Hunc nodum ita breviter solvas, quod origo impietatis, quae ita in se provocat Dei furorem, est perversitas naturae a Deo derelictae. Quare non abs re Paulus de aeterna reprobatione haec citavit, quae ex ea prodeunt ut fructus ex arbore et rivus a scaturigine. Impii quidem propter sua scelera iusto Dei iudicio caecitate puniuntur: sed si fontem exitii eorum quaerimus, eo deveniendum erit, quod a Deo maledicti nihil omnibus factis, dictis, consiliis suis, quam maledictionem accersere et accumulare possunt." Rom 11:7, CO49:216.

86 "…tam Iudaei quam gentes, nomen Dei invocando…Porro fides ex verbo Dei nascitur: verbum autem Dei nullibi praedicatur, nisi speciali Dei providentia et ordinatione." Rom 10:14, CO49:204.

87 "Hoc specimen esse et pignus divini amoris significat, ubi gentem aliquam evangelii sui praedicatione dignatur: neque ullum esse eius praeconem, quem non peculiari sua providentia suscitarit. Quare non esse dubium quin Deus nationem eam visitet, in qua evangelium annuntiatur." Rom 10:15, CO49:205.

church ministers has a part in God's special providence, and church ministers are God's instruments in his providence, as stated in the 1539 *Institutes*.

The 1543 and 1550 *Institutes*

After 1541, Calvin published two more editions of the *Institutes* before his definitive work of 1559. The 1543 edition is enlarged by four more chapters to make a total of twenty-one. The added chapters consider monasticism, a more comprehensive discussion on the Apostolic Creed, a detailed explanation of the relationship between the creed and church, and an extended elaboration of the theological foundation of the offices. In 1550, Calvin issued another even longer volume of the *Institutes*. He translated both editions into French and had them printed within two years. Although Calvin added some new topics to the original content for the 1539 *Institutes*, he did not make any changes on the doctrines of God's providence and predestination. These two editions still kept the discussions in one chapter.

De aeterna Dei praedestinatione 1552[88]

Prior to this work of 1552, Calvin wrote *Defensio sanae et orthodoxae doctrinae*[89] 1543, which responds to the first six chapters of Albert Pighius's ten books on human will and divine grace. Calvin intended to issue an answer to the remaining four books on providence and predestination in 1544.[90] However, as a result of Pighius's death, Calvin postponed the publication of the *De aeterna Dei pradestinatione* until 1552 in order not to insult the 'mad dog' Pighius.[91] Calvin published *De aeterna Dei pradestinatione* in Geneva and it aimed to refute the false teachings of Jérôme-Hermès Bolsec, Georgius Siculus, and Pighius concerning human freewill and God's secret counsel.

In *De aeterna Dei praedestionatione*, Calvin uses the hardening of Pharaoh's heart to demonstrate God's governing and His permission on all events.[92] This discussion

---

88 The full title for this work is *De aeterna Dei praedestinatione qua in salutem alios ex hominibus elegit alios suo exitio reliquit: item de providentia qua res humanas gubernat, Consensus pastorum Genevensis ecclesiae.*

89 The full title for this work is *Defensio sanae et orthodoxae doctrinae de servitute et liberatione humani arbitrii adversus calumnias Alberti Pighii Campensis.*

90 A.N.S. Lane, "Introduction", in John Calvin, *The Bondage and Liberation of the Will* (Grand Rapids, MI: Baker Books, 1996), xv.

91 Ibid., xv.

92 "Certe quum Solomon pronunciat (Prov 21:1), in manu Dei esse cor regis, ut quocunque visum fuerit ipsum inclinet, generaliter ostendit, non minus voluntatem quam externa opera Dei arbitrio

has been explored thoroughly. There is another important discussion in this treatise which is worthy of investigating because it shows that Calvin continues to use the term *fons* but it is not used to describe divine providence.

De aeterna Dei praedestinatione consists of two parts addressing predestination and providence, respectively. In the first part, Calvin uses the term *fons* to describe God as the fountain of grace.[93] Quoting support from Augustine,[94] Calvin argues that God is the source of grace and that He endows His people with grace just as He allows grace to flow through all His members. Yet, Pighius asserts that the ungodly are damned because their wickedness has provoked God's wrath, hence, Pighius concludes that their reprobation is not by God's decree. Calvin refutes this argument, stressing that humankind sin not by compulsion but by their own heart's inclination as human corruption is the 'fountain of all evil'.[95] To defend against the argument for God being a tyrant and exerting absolute power, Calvin declares that God's will is reasonable because he is the fountain of all justice.[96] The use of the image of the fountain is not exclusive for the illustration of God's 'things' but becomes a general description of everything meaning 'origin'.

Richard Muller reminds the scholars of Calvin studies to examine Calvin's doctrines historically, and so no study of Calvin should rely on only one work of Calvin.[97] This significance is shown in the study of Calvin's use of the image of the fountain in relation to *providentia Dei*. These works, *Psychopannychia*, the 1536 *Institutes*, the 1539 *Institutes*, *Commentarius in epistolam Pauli ad Romanos*, and

---

regi. Obduratum ab eo cor Pharaonis dicit Moyses (Exod 4:21 et 7:3). Frustra hic ad permissionem confugitur: quasi Deus fecisse dicatur, quod fieri tantum passus est. Clare enim duritiem illam Dei opus fuisse Moyses affirmat. Nec sane alio sensu hic Dei consilio adscribitur Pharaonis saevitia, quam alibi gratiam dare populo suo dicitur in oculis Aegyptiorum (Exod 3:21). " Ioannis Calvini, *De aeterna Dei praedestinatione*, CO8:357.

93 "Appareat igitur in capite nostro fons gratiae: unde, secundum cuiusque mensuram, se per cuncta membra diffundit. Ipsa est praedestinatio sanctorum, quae in sancto sanctorum maxime claruit. Et paulo post: Sicut praedestinatus est ille unus, ut caput nostrum esset: ita et multi sumus praedestinati, ut essemus eius membra." CO8:267.

94 Augustine, *De Praedest. Sanct.* xvii.

95 "Etsi autem non extrinseco impulsu, sed spontaneo cordis affectu, scientes ac volentes peccarint: quin tamen fons et origo malorum omnium sit naturae corruptio et vitiositas, negandum non est: nisi prima pietatis rudimenta convellere libeat." CO8:309–310.

96 "Deo immoderatum affingere licet, ut in eo, sicut in hominibus, exsultet libido: sed merito hoc honoris defertur eius voluntati, ut pro ratione valeat: quando omnis iustitiae fons est ac regula." CO8:310. Cf. CO8:311.

97 Richard Muller, *The Unaccommodated Calvin: Studies in the Foundation of a Theological Tradition* (Oxford: Oxford University Press, 2002), 4–6, 22. Cf. Richard Muller, "Ordo docendi: Melanchthon and the Organization of Calvin's Institutes, 1536–1543", in *Melanchthon in Europe-his work and influence beyond Wittenberg*, edited by Karin Maag (Grand Rapids, MI: Baker Books, 1999), 124.

De aeterna Dei praedestionatione, need to be read together to discern the early development of Calvin's formulation of *providentia Dei*.

The second part of the discussion in *De aeterna Dei praedestinatione* concerns God's providence. Calvin neither uses the term *fons* nor refers to where the idea appears, as he did previously to interpret *providentia Dei*, hence the use of the image of the fountain to describe *providence Dei* recedes to the background. However, the definitions of the three kinds of *providentia Dei*: '*generalis mundi gubernatio*', '*singulis Dei*', and '*praesentissima Dei*' are clarified probably for the first time, and subsequently he uses them to explain God's providence in his work. Firstly, there is a general government of the world so that everything is kept in its proper and natural state.[98] Secondly, there is a special government of particular parts of the world, but this aspect of care is especially for human beings.[99] Thirdly, God protects and guides the Church by His fatherly care and '*praesentissima Dei*'.[100] Calvin then gradually gives an elaboration of '*praesentissima Dei*' in his later works.

Conclusion

Calvin's historical context affects his understanding of *providentia Dei*. From 1534–1552, Calvin's interpretation of *providentia Dei* displays a development rather than a fixed doctrine. Theologically, his doctrine of *providentia Dei* is consistent, but Calvin gradually drops the usage of the image of the fountain and clarifies the definition of *providentia Dei*, which he subsequently uses to preach, to write commentaries and to finish his definitive edition of the *Institutes*.

At the time when Calvin wrote *Psychopannychia* in 1534, he had to defend his position against arguments for 'soul-sleep' and the mortality of the soul. Human beings are not separated from God's power, as they are remembered in God's providence. He argues that God is powerful because he is the fountain of everything, and He endows human beings with life through the death and resurrection of Christ. Calvin adopts the concept of '*virtute Dei*' from the Book of Baruch 3:14 and he uses the image of the fountain to illustrate God's power.

---

98 "Itaque, ut pro captu rudium crasse agamus, primo loco statuenda est ante oculos generalis mundi gubernatio, qua foventur et vegetantur omnia, ut stet incolumis naturae eorum status." *CO*8:349.

99 "Deinde considerandae sunt in singulis partibus regendis et curandis Dei excubiae: et quidem tales, ut nihil nisi nutu arbitrioque eius eveniat. Tum peculiaris generis humani cura in mentem nobis venire debet…" *CO*8:349. Cf. "Nunc in ista speciali providentia, quae currandis singulis Dei operibus privatim excubat…" *CO*8:348.

100 "Ultimo praesidium vere paternum, quo ecclesiam suam tuetur, cui praesentissima Dei ipsius virtus annexa est." *CO*8:349.

In the first section of chapter one in the 1536 *Institutes*, Calvin uses the quotation from the Book of Baruch 3:14 again but the term *fons* does not appear next to the source. He uses the term *fons* in the context of other chapters to state that the fountain of living water is in Christ. The interpretation of God's providence is not related to soteriological matters but the idea of God's power as the fountain of life does have a connotative sense of salvation.

In the first paragraph of chapter one of the 1539 and 1541 *Institutes*, Calvin uses the term *fons* and *fonteine* respectively to describe the benefits that God graciously gives to humanity: God is the fountain of all truth, wisdom, goodness, righteousness, judgment, mercy, power, and holiness, and he does not refer to the Book of Baruch 3:14. Calvin added 'holiness' in this list of describing God's actions, as compared to the shorter list in the 1536 *Institutes*, indicating that he initiated to the inclusion of salvation as one of the benefits God gives. Calvin has a clear definition of general providence but regarding the meaning of special providence, he was indecisive. In the 1539 *Institutes*, He wrote that in special providence, God gives salvation to the godly, but he skipped the term 'salvation' in the same place when translating the 1541 *Institutes*. However, in another place in the 1541 *Institutes*, Calvin kept the idea that God endows the faithful with all goodness and salvation. It seems that Calvin was still deciding the meaning of special providence during the period when he composed the second edition of the *Institutes*. Yet regardless of the fitful relationship of providence and salvation, based on the inclusion of holiness in the list of God's 'things' and the inclusion of salvation in special providence, Calvin, in the 1539 *Institutes*, formally discusses soteriological matters within the doctrine of *providentia Dei*.

In Calvin's *Commentarius in epistolam Pauli ad Romanos* 1540, he argues that the predestination of Pharaoh proceeds from the 'hidden fountain of God's providence', and in this work the linkage between predestination and God's providence becomes apparent. This is also the first time he uses the image of the fountain to describe the hidden providence of God.

Up to the time of the 1550 *Institutes*, Calvin did not change his explanation of *providentia Dei*. In *De aeterna Dei praedetinatione* 1552, Calvin uses the image of the fountain to describe God's grace, His justice, and human sin. The image of the fountain is used to describe everything which means origin. After dropping the reference to the Book of Baruch from 1539, Calvin's use of the heuristic key of the image of the fountain in relation to *providentia Dei* becomes less prominent. Instead, he made an effort to define three types of providence: '*generalis mundi gubernatio*', '*speciali providentia*', and '*praesentissima Dei*', which can be translated as general providence, special providence and providence for the Church. The providence for the Church is a fatherly care in which God as a father guides and protect His children. Calvin continues to gloss '*praesentissima Dei*' in his sermons, commentaries, and in the last edition of the *Institutes*.

Muller reminds Calvin scholars 'not to read Calvin's thoughts against a generalized background of the Reformation and Renaissance movements or of the Middle Ages but against a background of specific ideas, documents, and individuals that impinged on or influenced Calvin's thought'.[101] The arguments of this chapter align with Muller's assertion as it shows that Calvin's doctrine of *providentia Dei* is not fixed in his early works, and therefore it cannot be simply concluded that his thoughts about *providentia Dei* are influenced by humanism or scholasticism. Yet, this chapter does not agree with Muller's argument that the 1539 *Institutes* is a 'genuine *institutio*'[102] as it comprises the right theological *loci*.[103] This chapter recognises the important step which Calvin takes in the 1539 *Institutes* regarding the formulation of the doctrine of *providentia Dei*, and the relationship between the doctrines of predestination and providence. However, the definition of *providentia Dei* does not conclude with the 1539 *Institutes*, and this work argues that a significant change of the theological *loci* for the doctrine of divine providence is resulted in the 1559 *Institutes*.

101 Muller, *The Unaccommodated Calvin: Studies in the Foundation of a Theological Tradition*, 185.
102 Ibid., 186.
103 Ibid.

3. Calvin's interpretation of *providence de Dieu* in *Sermons sur le livre de Job* 1554 to 1555

Calvin preached a total of 159 sermons on Job in Genevan churches from Feb 1554 to March 1555. The congregation was comprised of Genevan citizens and French refugees who had fled from religious persecution in France. Although Calvin and his fellow pastors were eager to encourage the church to take care of the disadvantaged, such as the French refugees in their community, the influx of refugees created a great burden for the local hospital and this burden became the main complaint among Genevans during the 1550s.[1]

In 1554, when Calvin preached the sermons on Job, he was facing conflicts among different national groups, condemnation by his allies and attacks from those who opposed him. Calvin supported the French refugees both financially and spiritually but in 1554, a French refugee, Jérôme-Hermès Bolsec publicly refuted Calvin's doctrine of predestination, alleging that the doctrine implied that God was the author of sin. This doctrine was so controversial that it resulted in the 1554 burning of Calvin's writing in Bern, thus indicating that Calvin was considered heretical.[2] Furthermore, this same doctrine was questioned by other reformers, such as Heinrich Bullinger.

The Feburary 1554 writing of Calvin's *In defense of the Holy Trinity orthodox faith against the Spanish monster errors of Michael Servetus*[3] was released to defend his position against Sebastian Castellio's charges. Calvin condemned Servetus's deviation from orthodox Trinitarian teaching and explained his justification for executing a heretic, with support from Scripture and Church Fathers. Later in March 1554, Castellio, using a pseudonym, released a text *Heretics, whether they should be persecuted*,[4] to oppose the killing of heretics with justification from Church Fathers and the Reformers, including Calvin. Calvin himself was being condemned as a heretic when his opponents burned his writing in Bern, and ironically this was

---

1 William Naphy, *Calvin and the consolidation of the Genevan Reformation with a new preface* (Louisville, KY: Westminster John Knox Press, 2003), 121.

2 Bruce Gordon, *Calvin* (New Haven: Yale University Press, 2011), 202, 204, 209.

3 The full title is: *Defensio orthodoxae fidei de sacra Trinitate, contra prodigiosos errores Michaelis Serveti Hispani, ubi ostenditur haereticos iure gladii coercendos esse, et nominatim de homine hoc tam impio iuste et merito sumptum Genevae fuisse supplicium.* Wulfert. de Greef, *The Writings of John Calvin–an Introductory Guide,* translated by Lyle D. Bierma (Grand Rapids, MI: Baker Books, 1993), 176.

4 Sebastien Castellion, *De haereticis an sint persequendi,* introduction by Sape van der Woude (Genève: Droz, 1954).

around the same time as he defended for executing heretics. In a social context like this, how does Calvin interpret *providence de Dieu*?

This chapter contributes four arguments. Firstly, when Calvin discusses God's goodness, power, justice, and wisdom, he refers to the activities God carries out in both His general providence and His special providence.[5] Secondly, Job participates in both God's general and special providence. Thirdly, when Calvin discusses human participation in God's providence, his interpretations concern both providential and soteriological matters especially when the participatory activities are related to God's goodness. Fourth, apart from the primary cause, which is God's guidance, there is a genuine sense that the secondary cause, which is humankind, acts as a '*participant*' in God's providence.

The first chapter of the 1539 and 1541 *Institutes* is about the knowledge of God. Echoing the list Calvin displayed at the beginning of the first chapter,[6] and at the end of this chapter, Calvin reinforces that it is necessary for the faithful to grasp the knowledge of God through His mercy, righteousness, judgement, power, goodness, truth, and holiness, as a whole.[7] When Calvin preaches the sermons on Job, he consolidates this list into four: goodness, power, justice, and wisdom, and he uses them to explain the *providence de Dieu*.

The following discussion examines firstly, Calvin's interpretation of *providence de Dieu* and then it explores Job's participation in *providence de Dieu*.

---

5 Samuel Hopkins recognises Calvinist interpretation of holy providence in relation to God's actions in His power, goodness, justice, and wisdom. Samuel Hopkins, *The System of Doctrines: Contained in Divine Revelation, Explained and Defended. Showing Their Consistence and Connection with Each Other. To which is Added, a Treatise on the Millennium*, Volume I (Boston: Isaiah Thomas and Ebenezer T. Andrews, 1793), 135.

6 At the beginning of the first chapter in the 1539 *Institutes*: "Illa scilicet, quae non modo unum esse Deum ostendat, quem ab omnibus oporteat coli et adorari, sed simul etiam doceat, illum unum omnis veritatis, sapientiae, bonitatis, iustitiae, iudicii, misericordiae, potentiae, sanctitatis fontem esse, ut ab ipso et exspectare et petere universa ista discamus, praeterea cum laude et gratiarum actione accepta illi referre." Ioannis Calvini, *Institutio Religionis Christianae* 1539, CO1:279. Cf. At the beginning of the first chapter in the 1541 French *Institutes*: "Dont la premiere doibt monstrer non seulement qu'il est un seul Dieu, lequel il fault que tous adorent et honorent, mais aussi qu'iceluy est la fonteine de toute verité, sapience, bonté, justice, jugement, misericorde, puissance, et saincteté, afin que de luy nous aprenions d'attendre et demander toutes ces choses." Jean Calvin, *Institution de la Religion Chrétienne* 1541 Tome I, edited and translated by Olivier Millet (Genève: Librairie Droz S.A., 2008), 187–188.

7 "…c'est de me congnoistre le Dieu qui faictz misericorde, justice et jugement en la terre. Certes ces trois choses nous sont principallement necessaires à congnoistre…Neantmoins en cela faisant, n'est pas obmise ne sa puissance, ne sa verité, ne sa saincteté, ne sa bonté." Calvin, *Institution de la Religion Chrétienne* 1541, 234.

General providence

General providence is God's universal governance in the order of nature and there is a hidden dimension which human beings cannot fully comprehend until they receive God's personal revelation. In *Sermons sur le livre de Job*, Calvin continues using the definition of general providence, which he defined in *De aeterna Dei praedestinatione* 1552,[8] and he also suggests that God's providential actions are in His goodness, power, wisdom, and justice. When Calvin preaches on Job 37:14–24, he argues that God created everything by His power and maintains His creation through His goodness, wisdom, and justice.[9] Calvin describes the four kind of actions as follow. Firstly, God's infinite and mighty power upholds the world to a state which pleases Him. This power guides, preserves, and keeps the world in order.[10] Secondly, God's goodness is full of His rich blessings which manifest His fatherly love and mercy to all creation.[11] Thirdly, God's admirable wisdom sets this world in order.[12] Fourthly, God's justice governs the world by taking care of His creatures and judging the ungodly in His admirable fashion.[13] In the sermons on Job, Calvin defines general providence as God's actions in His power, goodness, wisdom, and justice towards all creation. God guides everything on earth in His

---

8 "Itaque, ut pro captu rudium crasse agamus, primo loco statuenda est ante oculos generalis mundi gubernatio, qua foventur et vegetantur omnia, ut stet incolumis naturae eorum status." Ioannis Calvini, *De aeterna Dei praedestinatione*, CO8:349.

9 "Mais de tous ceux qui ont eu quelque semence de religion, combien qu'ils ayent seu cela, que Dieu avoit creé le monde: toutes fois ils n'ont point entendu sa providence: en laquelle tout est contenu, d'autant que maintenant les choses qui ont esté creées par sa vertu, subsistent par sa bonté, et sagesse, et iustice." Jean Calvin, *Sermons Sur le livre de Job*, Sermon 146 Job 37:14–24, CO35:342. Cf. CO35:344.

10 "…il y a une vertu infinie en ce que Dieu maintient, et conserve ce qu'il a fait, et que le tout est sousteinu en son estat. Car il semble bien que ce soit chose impossible." Sermon 46 Job 12:7–16, CO33:572.

11 "Il y a aussi sa bonté. Car pourquoy a-il fait le monde? Pourquoy l'a-il rempli de tant de richesses? Pourquoy l'a-il ainsi orné? N'est-ce pas pour declarer son amour envers les hommes, et mesmes sa misericorde? comme il est dit aux Pseaumes, qu'elle s'estend iusques aux bestes brutes. Et que sera-ce donc de nous, qui luy sommes beaucoup plus prochains, et où il a mis plus de noblesse sans comparaison? Voila donc la bonté de Dieu qui se monstre et declare…" Ibid.

12 "Nous voyons que Dieu a si bien disposé le monde que rien plus. Voila une sagesse admirable, nous y devons estre ravis…" Ibid.

13 "Voila donc la bonté de Dieu qui se monstre et declare: nous voyons sa iustice, comme il veille sur ses creatures, qu'il a le soin de nous: et cependant nous voyons aussi d'autre costé ses iugemens, nous voyons qu'il gouverne le monde d'une façon si admirable, qu'encores que les meschans ne cerchent qu'à y mordre, si faut-il qu'ils demeurent là confus." Ibid.

pleasure and sometimes, He also guides with '*secret moving*'.[14] This secret moving is part of God's general providence, but it is beyond human comprehension.

Randall Zachman thinks that Calvin ascribes goodness, wisdom, and power to the Father, the Son, and the Holy Spirit, and so these attributes are in some way Trinitarian.[15] In the context of the 1559 *Institutes*, when Calvin talks about the nature of the Trinity, he emphasises that it is not wise to use analogy to describe the Trinity. Instead, he shows that the Son and the Holy Spirit are from the Father, just like wisdom and power are from the fountain of everything.[16] This image of the fountain is biblical,[17] as Calvin intends to illustrate that the Father, Son, and Holy Spirit, are inseparable and that the Son and the Holy Spirit come from the Father.[18]

Similarly, Calvin shows that God's wisdom and His power are inseparable, and that wisdom and power come from God, as He is the source of everything.[19] Hence, in the 1559 *Institutes*, the reason Calvin ascribes goodness, wisdom, and power, to the Father, Son and Holy Spirit, is because of their likeness. However, in Calvin's *Sermons sur le livre de Job*, Calvin shows that goodness, wisdom, and power together with justice, are God's action in His general providence, while power, goodness, wisdom, and justice categorise God's activities in the order of creation. No Trinitarian order is explicitly stated. However, one must ask from where did Calvin adopt the idea of God's actions in goodness, justice, power, and wisdom

---

14 "...que nostre Seigneur n'ait commandé, et que ces creatures (combien qu'elles soyent insensibles) n'ayent un mouvement secret de celui qui gouverne tout, et qui est par dessus tout...Voila donc d'un costé la providence de Dieu qui nous est ratifiee, afin que nous ne doutions point que tout se gouverne par sa volonté..." Sermon 146 Job 37:14–24, CO35:342.

15 Zachman states that Calvin ascribes goodness to the Father, wisdom to the Son and power to the Spirit. Randall C. Zachman, *Reconsidering John Calvin* (Cambridge: Cambridge University Press, 2012), 10. Cf. "Ea autem est, quod patri principium agendi, rerumque omnium fons et scaturigo attribuitur; filio sapientia, consilium, ipsaque in rebus agendis dispensatio; at spiritui virtus et efficacia assignatur actionis. Porro quanquam patris aeternitas, filii quoque et spiritus aeternitas est, quando nunquam Deus sine sapientia virtuteque sua esse potuit, in aeternitate autem non est quaerendum prius aut posterius, non est tamen inanis aut supervacua ordinis observatio, dum primus recensetur pater, deinde ex eo filius, postea ex utroque spiritus. Nam et mens uniuscuiusque eo sponte inclinat ut primo Deum consideret, deinde emergentem ex eo sapientiam, tum postremo virtutem qua consilii sui decreta exsequitur." Ioannis Calvini, *Institutio Christianae Religionis* 1559 1.13.18, CO2:105.

16 "Ea autem est, quod patri principium agendi, rerumque omnium fons et scaturigo attribuitur; filio sapientia, consilium, ipsaque in rebus agendis dispensatio ; at spiritui virtus et efficacia assignatur actionis." 1559 *Institutes*,1.13.18, CO2:105.

17 "Quam tamen scripturis notatam distinctionem animadvertimus, subticeri non convenit. Ea autem est, quod patri principium agendi, rerumque omnium fons et scaturigo attribuitur..." Ibid.

18 Ibid.

19 "...Deum esse primum agens, quia principium et causa est omnis motus; quum potius hoc solatio in rebus adversis se leniant fideles, nihil se perpeti nisi Dei ordinatione et mandato: quia sunt sub eius manu." Ibid., 1.16.3, CO2.146.

to explain general providence? Some clues are provided in Zwingli's sermon on providence.

Immediately prior to Zwingli and his companion, Johannes Oecolampadius holding their debate with Luther about the Lord's Supper at Marburg in 1529, Zwingli preached his *Sermo de providentia Dei*, which was regarded as part of the Colloquy of Marburg.[20] At the beginning of the sermon on providence, Zwingli affirmed that 'providence must exist, because the supreme good (*summum bonum*) necessarily cares for and regulates all things'.[21] Supreme good has the qualities of being true, simple, pure, complete, unchangeable, and powerful.[22] If power is good and 'divinity' (*numen*) is powerful, then 'divinity' is supreme good.[23] Here, Zwingli argues syllogistically[24] and suggests that 'divinity' also has qualities which

---

20 "On Sunday afternoon 3rd October, 1529, the penultimate day of the Marburg Colloquy, Luther and Zwingli admitted their failure to reach agreement on the Lord's Supper." Iren Snavely, "'The evidence of things unseen': Zwingli's Sermons on Providence and the Colloquy of Marburg", in *Westminster Theological Journal* 56 (1994), 399. Cf. "...Zwingli thundered from the pulpit, was not bodily present in the elements of bread and wine but through the Holy Spirit, and the proper response of the people was thanksgiving". Bruce Gordon, Luca Baschera & Christian Moser, "Emulating the Past and Creating the Present: Reformation and the Use of Historical and Theological Models in Zurich in the Sixteenth Century" in *Following Zwingli Applying the Past in Reformation Zurich* (Surrey: Ashgate Publishing Limited, 2014), 5.

21 "Providentiam necessario esse, ex eo quod, summum bonum necessario universa curat ac disponit."Ulrich Zwingli, *Ad illustrissimum Cattorum principem Philippum, sermonis de providentia Dei anamnema* (Tiguri: Zentralbibliothek Zürich, 1530), Chapter 1, 3. Cf. Ulrich Zwingli, *On Providence and Other Essays*. Edited by William John Hinke (Eugene, Oregon: Wipf & Stock Publishers, 1999), 130.

22 "...idcirco mutationi obnoxia, constat unum ac solum summum bonum, uerum, hoc est, simplex, purum ac integrum esse, quoniam idem solum est immutablie, constat solum uerum, hoc est, purum, syncerum... secondo, quod summum ac uerum est, potens quoquos omnium esse oportet. Nam quod ad summum attinet, facile uidertur summum esse enquire, ni ui ac potential primum ac summum sit." *Sermonis de providentia Dei anamnema*, Chapter 1, 4

23 "Hoc est, si uirtus atquos potentia bonum est, iam numen nostrum summe potens est : si ueritas bonum est, iam summe uerum est, & sic deinceps...si summum numen summum bonum est, & ueritas de ratione boni est, ut summum bonum esse nequeat nisi uerum sit, as prorsus ipsa ueritas." *Sermonis de providentia Dei anamnema*, Chapter 1, 4–5.

24 A.P. Martinich suggests that Duns Scotus' proof of God's existence shows a basic and simple syllogism. Martinich summarises his reasoning as follow: 'Some being is the primary efficient and final cause and the pre-eminent being in the universe. The primary efficient and final cause and the pre-eminent being in the universe is infinite. Therefore, some being is infinite.' A.P. Martinich, "Scotus and Anslem on Existence of God", in *Franciscan Studies*, vol. 37 (1977), 139–152. Cf, Bolliger argues that Zwingli adopts the theology of Scotus, and the interpretation of God's nature in Zwingli's sermon on providence does show Zwingli's reception of Scotus' theology, and syllogistic reasoning. Daniel Bolliger, *Infiniti Contemplatio. Grundzüge der Scotus- und Scotismusrezeption im Werk Huldrych Zwinglis. Mit ausführliclier Edition bisher unpublizierter Annotatione Zwinglis* [Studies in the History of Christian Thought 107] (Leiden/Boston: Brill, 2003).

are true, simple, pure, complete, unchangeable, and powerful. In the later part of his sermon, he concludes that the creation of the world is as a result of God's goodness, justice, wisdom, and power.[25] While this work does not further discus Zwingli, one significant issue needs to be highlighted. Calvin's interpretation of the doctrine of *providentia Dei* in his *Sermons sur le livre de Job* shows a line of continuity with Zwingli's interpretation of the same doctrine in his *Sermo de providentia Dei*.

Special Providence

God's special providence is His providential care specifically for individual creatures. Calvin continues to use the term, 'singular', which he defined in 1552, to describe God's special care for humanity when he preached his sermons on Job in 1554. Singular providence is also special providence, but it is especially for mankind.[26] However, to Calvin, this 'singular' is to describe a special group of people. In Sermon 146, Calvin announces that the philosophers are ignorant of God's actions in His goodness, power, wisdom, and justice in His general providence and that 'heathen men' do not understand these actions.[27] Yet, who can acknowledge this general providence? Calvin then argues that the people who are saved in Jesus Christ can confess this knowledge.[28] As it is briefly discussed, in God's very special providence, He draws people to Himself through the Holy Spirit, so that they are moved to believe in Him and be saved. Scholars of Calvin studies call this kind of God's very special providence, '*providentia specialissma*',[29] and Charles Partee asserts

---

25 "Nonne enim totius mun di creatione & sapientia illius proditur, & ipsa deinde cunctarum rerum facture admirabilior fit, cum ab infinita saipentia factas esse uidemus? Quamuis simul opitulatae sint bonitas, aequitas, iusticia, uirtus, prospicientia, propensio sive uoluntas?" *Sermonis de providentia Dei anamnema*, Chapter 6, 44.

26 "Ainsi donc cognoissons que ç'a esté une bonté singuliere de Dieu, de ce qu'il n'a point permis que son serviteur tombast iusques aux abysmes: et que par cela nous soyons admonnestez, qu'il est bon besoin que Dieu nous maintiene, et mesmes qu'il nous releve quand nous sommes cheus." Sermon 70 Job 19:13-16, CO34:108. Cf. Definition of special (singular) providence in Charles Partee, *The Theology of John Calvin* (Louisville, KY: Westminster John Knox Press, 2008), 114–115.

27 "Mais de tous ceux qui ont eu quelque semence de religion, combien qu'ils ayent seu cela, que Dieu avoit creé le monde: toutes fois ils n'ont point entendu sa providence: en laquelle tout est contenu, d'autant que maintenant les choses qui ont esté creées par sa vertu, subsistent par sa bonté, et sagesse, et iustice. Cela donc n'a point esté cognu des payens." Sermon 146 Job 37:14–24, CO35:342.

28 "Pour ceste cause retenons bien ceste doctrine qui est ici couchee, laquelle est conforme à ce que dit nostre Seigneur Iesus Christ (Iean 5:17), Que le Pere besongne tousiours, et lui avec, qui est ceste Sagesse de laquelle parle Salomon au huictieme chapitre. Ainsi donc voulons-nous bien cognoistre que Dieu est Createur du ciel et de la terre, comme nous le confessons?" Ibid.

29 Very special providence equals predestination. Werner Krusche, *Das Wirken des heiligen Geistes nach Calvin* (Göttingen: Vandenhoeck & Ruprecht, 1957), 14.

that "...providence is the doctrine of predestination applied universally to the world, and predestination is the doctrine of special (particular) providence applied directly to individuals."[30] Similarly, Mark Elliott argues, "Providence should really be understood in the first place as special providence".[31] Hence, when people are kept safe in special providence, they will then understand part of general providence and this general providence becomes special (providence) to them. The very special kind of providence is defined as the third kind of providence, which Calvin distinguished in 1552. He called it '*praesentissima Dei*' back then. In the sermons on Job, Calvin does not preach this kind of providence as '*praesentissima Dei*', or '*providentia specialissma*', but '*providence celeste*'.[32]

Furthermore, it should be highlighted that the terms general and special providence are used here for discussion purposes. However, when Calvin was preaching in the Genevan churches, he did not always distinguish different types of providence, but simply used *providence de Dieu* to describe God's many actions acted upon the world and His creation (Calvin's audience), to reinforce his assertion that only the faithful can make sense of providence. As he was preaching to a church community, it was not necessary to make the distinctions required in his polemical works.

Definition of human participation in divine providence from 1534 to 1554

In *Psychopannchia* 1534, Calvin's primary aim was to refute the idea of soul–sleep after the death of humankind. God created all the lives in the world and all creatures have the same living souls. Beasts have a living soul, but they live differently to human beings. Human souls consist of reason, intellect, and will, and do not perish with the body after death,[33] while every aspect of beasts will perish when they die. However, when Jesus Christ accepts humans into His glory, the dead bodies will also be kept and they will be resurrected and will become different people participating in the glory of God.[34]

---

30 Partee, *The Theology of John Calvin*, 116.

31 Mark W. Elliott, *Providence Perceived: Divine Action from a Human Point of View* (Berlin/Boston: De Gruyter, 2015), 142.

32 Calvin discusses '*providence celeste*' two times in the sermons on Job and this topic is examined in chapter 5.

33 Ioannis Calvini, *Psychopannychia*, CO5:202.

34 "Vides igitur nos non aliud futuros in resurrectione, sed tamen alios: detur verbo venia. Atque haec quidem de corpore dicta sunt, cui anima sub elementis huius mundi vitam administrat: ubi autem figura huius mundi praeterierit, participatio gloriae Dei id supra naturam evehet. Habemus verum ac germanum apostoli sensum." Ibid.

Humans are above all creations of nature. Although this text does not directly relate human participation to God's general providence, Calvin emphasises that God created humans differently to the rest of creation, and that God takes care of their lives after death. This kind of care towards humans is God's special providence, as Calvin defined it after 1534. Human beings take part in God's glory but exactly how they participate in God's glory and the kinds of activities in which they participate are not discussed.

Although human participation in God's providence is not one of the themes in Calvin's 1536 *Institutes*, Calvin still provides some explanations which he continues to elaborate on in his later works. The faithful are chosen by God's eternal providence and they become members of the church.[35] In this process, God firstly calls the chosen, draws them to Himself, and shows them that His role is as their God and Father. Then, He justifies them in the righteousness of Christ, and adorns them by covering up their own imperfections. Furthermore, He continuously cleanses the Elect's sins through the Holy Spirit day after day. When they are entirely sanctified, God's majesty is revealed in His kingdom, and finally, God will be glorified.[36] In this process, God's children benefit from His eternal care, and at the same time can join in glorifying God in His eternal providence.

In the 1541 *Institutes*, Calvin refutes Saint Gregory's saying: "although the faithful know their calling very well, they are uncertain of their election".[37] The uncertainty Gregory speaks of causes the faithful to fear that they do not have hope for salvation unless they labour to earn it. Calvin objects to the view that human work merits salvation and claims that Gregory's fallacy would prevent the Elect from having

---

35 "Sancta etiam est, quia quotquot aeterna Dei providentia electi sunt, ut in ecclesiae membra cooptarentur, a Domino omnes sanctificantur (Ioan 17; Eph 5)." Ioannis Calvini, *Institutio Religionis Christianae* 1536, CO1:73.

36 "Vocat, dum ad sese attrahit suos, illis se pro Deo et patre cognoscendum exhibens. Iustificat, dum eos Christi iustitia vestit, qua et pro sua perfectione ornentur et suam imperfectionem obtegant, ac sancti sui spiritus benedictionibus eos irrigat, quibus de die in diem a carnis suae corruptione expurgentur et in vitae novitatem regenerentur, donec plane sancti et immaculati in conspectus eius appareant. Glorificabit, cum maiestas regni sui in omnibus et per omnia manifestata fuerit. Itaque Dominus, dum suos vocat, iustificat, glorificat, nihil aliud quam aeternam suam electionem declarat, qua huc eos destinaverat, antequam nascerentur." Ibid.

37 "Ce a esté donc très mal parlé à Saint Gregoire de dire que nous sçavons bien de nostre vocation, mais que, de nostre élection, nous en sommes incertains. Et de cela il nous exhorte à terreur et tremblement, usant de ceste raison: que nous sçavons bien quelz nous sommes aujourd'huy, mais que nous sommes ignorans quelz nous serons demain." Jean Calvin, *Institution de la Religion Chrétienne* 1541 Tome II, edited and translated by Olivier Mille (Genève: Librairie Droz S.A., 2008), 1079. Cf. "qui utilise cet argument -et la crainte qu'effectivement il suscite - évidemment pour exhorter les fidèles à mener avec persévérance une vie chrétienne." Saint Gregory, *Homily* 38 (3.24.9).

a taste (*goust*) of God's goodness (*bonté de Dieu*)[38] since this '*bonté de Dieu*' is understood as the gratuitous grace which God eternally predestines for the Elect to enjoy.[39] Without any activities of merit, the faithful can enjoy a taste of God's goodness, merely from His gratuitous grace, which represents a pre-enjoyment of predestined eternal salvation. This taste of God's goodness, is a taste of the happiness of eternity: happiness not to be obtained by merit but through the '*principal autheur de tout bien*'.[40]

What does it mean to have a taste of God's goodness? In his sermons on Job, Calvin delivers a fuller definition where he asserts that the *providence de Dieu* is shown by God's actions in His goodness, power, wisdom, and justice. On the one hand, God's providence is displayed in God's action in these four 'things'. On the other hand, human beings can also participate in God's action.[41] Calvin uses the French term '*participant*' more than thirty times to describe the human role in God's activities.[42] Yet, what does it mean to participate in God's activities and how do human beings take part? Humans participate in God's providence by tasting

---

38 "Quoniam enim ab operum meritis electionem suspendebat, deiiciendis animis plus satis illi suppetebat causae: confirmare non poterat, qui a se ipsis ad divinae bonitatis fiduciam non transferebat. Hinc qualemcunque eius, quod initio posuimus, gustum habent fideles: praedestinationem, si rite cogitetur, non fidei convulsionem, sed optimam potius confirmationem afferre." CO1:883. Cf. "Ce a esté donc très mal parlé à Sainct Gregoire…Car pource qu' il fondoit l'eslection sur le merite des œuvres, il avoit assez de matiere à espoventer les hommes et les mettre en deffiance; de les confermer, il ne povoit, pource qu'il ne les renvoyoit point à la fiance de la bonté de Dieu. Par cela les fideles peuvent avoir quelque goust de ce que nous avons dit au commencement: à sçavoir que la Predestination, si elle est bien meditée, n'est pas pour troubler ou esbranler la Foy, mais plustost pour la confermer très bien." Calvin, *Institution de la Religion Chrétienne* 1541 Tome II, 1079–1080.

39 CO1:883.

40 "Brief, nous porterons ceste honneur à Dieu de le recongnoistre principal autheur de tout bien, mais nous honorerons aussi les hommes…" Calvin, *Institution de la Religion Chrétienne* 1541 Tome II, 1109. Cf. CO1:897.

41 Todd Billings's monograph on human participation mainly discusses the interaction between God and humankind in the attainment of eternal salvation for believers through Jesus Christ. Todd J. Billings, *Calvin, participation, and the gift: the activity of believers in union with Christ* (Oxford: Oxford University Press, 2009). Julie Canlis' monograph on Calvin's doctrine of participation suggests that the faithful have a relationship of κοινωνια with God. Julie Canlis, *Calvin's Ladder-a spiritually theology of ascent and ascension* (Grand Rapids, MI: W.B. Eerdmans Publishing Company, 2010). Human participation in God's providence is not the focus in either of these two works. Furthermore, no existing literature appears to discuss this topic.

42 For instance, Calvin ends his first sermon on Job by saying, "…mais que nous souffrions que Dieu nous purge de toutes nous ordures et infections, comme il nous l'a promis au nom de nostre Seigneur Iesus Christ, iusques à ce qu'il nous ait retirez des souillures et pollutions de ce monde, pour nous conioindre avec ses Anges, et nous faire participans de ceste felicité eternelle, à laquelle nous devons maintenant aspirer." Sermon 1 Job 1:2, CO33:33–34. Also, in Sermon 12, Calvin preaches, "Mais tant y a que les fideles sont desia participans de ceste ioye…" Sermon 12 Job 3:11–19, CO33:159.

God's greatness. God bestows on humanity a clear vision so they can perceive His justice, power, and wisdom in His works in the order of nature, and so to glorify Him.[43] Furthermore, God actively gives His people a small taste of His greatness in the created world, but there are still many aspects of nature that humankind can never comprehend.[44] This limited participation in God's action is described as tasting only with the tip of the tongue.[45] That means even if human beings can participate in God's providence, they can only partially understand God's actions. This human participation is initiated by God, and Calvin exhorts the congregation to be humble enough to enjoy this little taste of God's general providence and not to murmur at His hiddenness.[46]

Thus, can the faithful participate in God's hidden counsel? Calvin suggests if there is a need, God in His counsel, enables His people to know His goodness and wisdom through His word,[47] and Calvin explains that God's word is a looking glass offering a brief glance at His hiddenness.[48] In Sermon 146, Calvin asserts that human beings can have a little taste of God's actions in the order of nature

---

43 "Et pourtant toutes fois et quantes que nous verrons quelque raison en ce qui se fait par nature, que nous verrons par quel moyen Dieu besongne, et que nous apprehenderons sa iustice, sa vertu, et sagesse…" Sermon 146 Job 37:14–24, CO35:344. Cf. "…mais il y aura une humilité pour approuver tout ce que Dieu fait, et confesser qu'il n'y a que droiture, sagesse, bonté, equité, et iustice: en sorte qu'il ne nous reste sinon de le glorifier en tout et par tout." Ibid., CO35:347.

44 "…apprenons de faire tousiours ceste conclusion, Que tant y a que nous ne pouvons pas tout comprendre, non pas la centieme partie: c'est beaucoup que nous en ayons quelque petit goust pour lecher comme au bout de la langue: et encores ce goust-là nous ne pouvons l'avoir, qu'il ne nous soit donné d'en haut." Ibid., CO35:344–345.

45 Ibid.

46 "Et au reste que nous ne soyons iamais lassez d'appliquer nostre estude à la consideration des œuvres de Dieu: veu que nous pourrons acquerir un thresor inestimable, quand nous en aurons apprins quelque portion, voire pour entrer en goust comme nous avons dit…" Ibid., CO35:345.

47 "Mais cependant de l'autre costé cognoissons la bonté infinie de nostre Dieu, en ce qu'il nous esclaire au milieu des tenebres par sa parole: et que combien que nous ne comprenions pas en tout et par tout comment il a creé le monde, que nous n'appercevions pas les moyens par lesquels il besongne maintenant, il ne laisse pas de nous faire participans de son conseil entant qu'il nous est mestier. Et voila pourquoy il est dit, que la sagesse de Dieu luy a tenu compagnie quand il a basti le monde, qu'il a eslevé les montagnes, qu'il a abaissé les valees, qu'il a constitué cest ordre que nous voyons." Ibid., CO35:347.

48 "…qu'ils ne se fient pas en leur raison, et ne pensent point avoir assez d'industrie pour bien iuger: mais qu'ils sachent que c'est à Dieu de nous monstrer par sa parole ce que nous devons comprendre, et que c'est aussi par ce bout-la qu'il nous faut commencer…" Ibid., CO35:339. Cf. "Car il nous a fait contempler au miroir de son Evangile les secrets du ciel, tant qu'il nous estoit expedient. Or ie di entant qu'il nous estoit necessaire: car il n'est pas question de suivre nos appetits fols et desbordez: mais contentons nous de la revelation que Dieu nous donne (et ne soyons point curieux pour nous enquerir outre sa parole) contentons nous qu'il nous illumine par son sainct Esprit, afin que nous puissions iuger de ses œuvres comme il appartient." Sermon 149 Job 38:12–17, CO35:388.

through perceiving His work. Additionally, His children could have the privilege of knowing a little bit more in the order of nature through His word when the Holy Spirit inspires them.[49] That means in some special occasions, some of the Elect can taste more than this 'petit goust'.[50]

Therefore, how does humankind participate in special providence? Christians can have a taste of general providence through God's actions in His goodness, power, wisdom, and justice. Additionally, Christians feel that they are individually guided by God's special care. Elliott asserts, "Special providence -- that which concerns believers in their Christian lives -- takes precedence in Calvin's scheme".[51] In his *Sermons sur le livre de Job*, Calvin stresses that special providence for Christian lives is for both the present and for eternal lives. Following Elliott's analysis and Calvin's description of special care for the Elect, precisely, Calvin's assertion means that God takes special care of the faithful by granting them eternal life, but that in their present life, they can already have a taste of eternity, and that they as the faithful, are the only ones who can make sense of this taste.[52]

Calvin identifies two kinds of goodness: sweetness endowed by God and the created benefits offered by Papists. He argues that earthly benefits given by human beings cannot bring the faithful real happiness whereas the goodness and love from God which come together with the created benefits, will give them a taste of eternal happiness. Calvin describes that the goodness of God is like a true sauce to give meaningful flavour to the earthly food.[53] The flavour of good for the faithful and the unfaithful is different because God endows care upon the faithful's bodies and souls when they eat.[54] Hence, food or money will not bring eternal happiness, but our merciful Father blesses His faithful with material goods, and only God has the power to endow them with eternity.[55] If the faithful have experienced the 'goust de la douceur paternelle de Dieu', they are assured of God's mercy and fatherly love, and therefore they should not be afraid of God's judgements.[56] The faithful can

---

49 Ibid.

50 By reading the Scripture humbly, the faithful will submit to God's secret providence. See discussion in chapter 6.

51 Elliott, *Providence Perceived: Divine Action from a Human Point of View*,142.

52 "Providence should really be understood in the first place as special providence." Elliott, *Providence Perceived: Divine Action from a Human Point of View*, 142; cf. Sermon 146 Job 37:14–24, CO35:344–347.

53 Sermon 87 Job 22:23–30, CO34:326.

54 Ibid.

55 "...et qui nous fait sentir sa bonté, afin que nous soyons attirez plus haut, et que nous soyons tousiours tant plus certifiez de ceste amour paternelle qu'il nous porte: bref, que les biens corruptibles qu'il nous eslargit en ce monde nous soyent comme aides pour nous eslever au ciel, et que là nous apprehendions la vie eternelle à laquelle ce bon Dieu nous convie." Ibid., CO34:327.

56 Ibid., CO34:322.

then grasp this certitude of salvation while they are in the present life. Providence raises the believers' hearts to God.

In Calvin's *Sermons sur le livre de Job*, this teaching on the doctrine of God's providence is discussed in conjunction with the doctrine of salvation.[57] The doctrines of providence and predestination are discussed separately in Calvin's 1559 *Institutes* and some scholars of Calvin studies have given different explanations regarding this separation.[58] This research suggests that Calvin's doctrine of *providentia Dei* is consistently related to soteriological matters throughout his theological works, but the relationship becomes different in the last edition of the *Institutes*. This is shown in the subsequent chapters of this research.

Job's participation in *providence de Dieu*

Calvin preached a total of 159 sermons, and some sermons are chosen for discussion in this chapter because they all relate to Job and *providence de Dieu* in His goodness, power, justice, and wisdom. This selection of the sermons is also based on Calvin's use of the term '*participants*'. To highlight two examples of this usage, it is noticed that Calvin uses the term '*participans*' at the end of Sermon 1 to talk about the participation in God's eternal joy (*felicité eternelle*) by the faithful,[59] and then at the end of Sermon 159 (Calvin's last sermon on Job), he uses the term '*gout*' to teach that tasting God's goodness and mercy on earth is the human participation in eternal '*felicité*' prepared and confirmed through Jesus Christ.[60] Calvin ends his last sermon by saying that eternal life and pleasure are confirmed for the faithful to enjoy. This echoes Calvin's assertion about '*participans de cest felicité eternelle*' in

---

57 "The Holy Spirit is the author of providence and (since very special providence (providentia specialissima) equals predestination) the author of the doctrine of predestination." Krusche, *Das Wirken des heiligen Geistes nach Calvin* , 14. Cf. Charles Partee, *Calvin and Classical Philosophy,* Studies in History of Christian Thought 15 (Leiden: Brill, 1977), 135. Cf. Elliott, *Providence Perceived: Divine Action from a Human Point of View*, 142.

58 Richard A. Muller, "The Placement of Predestination in Reformed theology: Issue or Non-Issue?" *Calvin Theological Journal* 40, no. 2 (2005): 184–210. Cf. Paul Helm, "Calvin, the 'Two Issues', and the Structure of the *Institutes*", *Calvin Theological Journal* 42, no. 2 (2007): 341–348.

59 "...mais que nous souffrions que Dieu nous purge de toutes nos ordures et infections, comme il nous l'a promis au nom de nostre Seigneur Iesus Christ, iusques à ce qu'il nous ait retirez des souillures et pollutions de ce monde, pour nous conioindre avec ses Anges, et nous faire participans de ceste felicité eternelle, à laquelle nous devons maintenant aspirer." Sermon 1 Job 1:1, CO33:33–34.

60 "Nous avons desia declaré, que maintenant il ne nous faut plus longuement vivre pour sentir la bonté paternelle de nostre Dieu: que quand nous ne vivrions que trois iours en ce monde, il suffit pour gouster la bonté et misericorde de Dieu, et pour confermer nostre foi. Car puis que nostre Seigneur Iesus Christ est mort et ressuscité...et qu'il nous monstrera que nostre vraye vie et felicité permanente nous est apprestee là haut." Sermon 159 Job 42:9–17, CO35:514.

Sermon 1. The following discussion explores Job's situation and his participation in God's goodness, power, justice, and wisdom in his present life and eternal life.

Job's participation in God's goodness

Sermon 12 Job 3:11–19

Calvin reminds the congregation to think of God's goodness when they are sad and suffering, as doing so will assuage their sorrows.[61] Calvin explains his argument using the example of Job and stresses that although Job suffers, he should feel great honour as he is sent to the world as a reasoning creature different from other creations. Job has God's image and he is cared for by Him just like a son being protected by his father. Calvin describes this goodness of being God's child is inestimable,[62] thus, Job should feel privileged because he is honoured by God in such a gracious way. However, Job acts as if he had never tasted God's goodness,[63] and he despises all the fatherly goods from God.[64] It seems that other people witness Job's participation in God's providence, but he ignores everything that is obvious to others. Job's ignorance does not mean that he is not a participant in God's providence, only that he participates unknowingly. Job is not able to resist God's goodness, as evidenced by the example of the providential blessings given by God before Job's afflictions. At this moment, God's blessing to Job is no more than a taste.

This sermon also offers a discussion of people's second life, which is a joyful life after death. Calvin encourages the congregation by telling them that God endows the faithful with both benefits and difficulties in the present life, but that their hope should be in the second life, where God promises the faithful that there will be no more afflictions. Human beings will also be free from negative passions created by afflictions, and fleshly needs will not continue. Additionally, God adopts His

---

61 Sermon 12 Job 3:11–19, CO33:152–153.

62 "Et nous en voyons l'exemple en Iob, qui est le vray miroir de patience, car il devoit recognoistre, quelques maux qu'il endurast, qu'encores celuy estoit un grand heur, d'avoir esté mis en ce monde creature raisonnable, d'avoir porté l'image de Dieu, d'avoir esté nourri et substanté iusques en aage d'homme, afin qu'il cognust Dieu estre son pere. Voila des biens qui sont inestimables..." Ibid., CO33:153.

63 "Voila des biens qui sont inestimables: neantmoins tant s'en faut que Iob les prise, qu'il voudroit iamais ne les avoir gousté." Ibid.

64 "Or nous voyons que Iob les met ici en un faisseau, et despite tout. Par cela donc que nous soyons admonestez si tost que Dieu nous propose quelque benefice que nous aurons receu de luy, d'estre esmeus de sentir sa bonté paternelle, afin de le remercier..." Ibid., CO33:155.

children and gathers them in His joy,[65] which is not only for His pleasure, but a joy in which His people can also participate.[66]

Calvin assures the congregation that Job is one of those faithful participants who will enjoy God's joy, yet that Job speaks like a heathen who does not hope for eternal life or resurrection.[67] For when Job is overwhelmed by his misery, he is deeply affected by his passion, and cannot believe in the second life of eternity.[68] Calvin further describes Job as someone who 'does not know any of this',[69] as one of the partakers in everlasting life, while ignoring his participation. Sadly, Calvin's Job is not thankful for the '*biens*' given by God, and he does not consider himself as a participant appreciating the joy of '*seconde vie*'.

Sermon 13 Job 3:20-26

Calvin argues again that God lets the faithful taste His goodness even during the midst of afflictions, and that this goodness supports them through grievous suffering in the way that they can remember God's fatherly care in the past, pray to Him, and stop complaining.[70] However, Job is not one of these people. He does not taste God's goodness.[71] In addition, when Job asks why his life is hidden and why God has restricted him in this way, Calvin argues that Job does not submit himself to God's providence, "*car Iob monstre en quoy il a failli, c'est qu'il ne s'est point remis assez à la providence de Dieu*".[72] Certainly, Job is in God's providence, but he is desperate to know his state and what he will be, so he thinks that he does not have a taste of God's goodness, and he has not sufficiently trusted God's providence. Instead, Job focuses on his present problem, forgets about the goodness God has given him in the past, and has not hope for the future. Job truly believes that God's blessing is not with him.

---

65 Ibid., *CO*33:156, 159.

66 "Mais tant y a que les fideles sont desia participans de ceste ioye..." Ibid., *CO*33:159.

67 Ibid., *CO*33:155. Cf. "Voila un tesmoignage de la resurrection." Ibid., *CO*33:158.

68 Ibid., *CO*33:158.

69 "Or voici Iob qui ne cognoist rien de tout cela." Ibid.

70 Sermon 13 Job 3:20–26, *CO*33:171.

71 "Tant y a neantmoins qu'il nous faut bien condamner ceste infirmité ici en Iob: c'est à dire, ce qu'il s'est trouvé si abbatu de tristesse, qu'il ne pouvoit plus gouster la bonté de Dieu, pour avoir seulement quelque petite resiouissance, de laquelle il se soustinst." Ibid.

72 Ibid.

Sermon 29 Job 7:16-21

In this sermon, Calvin explains the meaning of being members in Jesus Christ, what benefits the members are entitled to, and what the members should do to enjoy their membership. By way of demonstration, Calvin makes a direct comparison between Job and David in the interpretation of Job 7:17 and Psalm 8:4.[73] Job's God positions His children high, but He also pulls them down like a wheel of fortune,[74] and Calvin's Job recognises that he himself is one of those children. However, Calvin strongly denies that the world is left to fortune because God governs actively with His sovereignty. Hence, Calvin stresses that Job misunderstands God's providence, and that he also turns it upside down by making everything the opposite.[75] In times of suffering, Job cannot recount God's infinite benefits like David could, and instead he passionately alleges and complains that God is against him.

Calvin reminds his audience that God is the *'garde des hommes'*.[76] Yet to Job, God is hardly his keeper as His providence is so far away. Job simply thinks that if God is a keeper of humankind, He should not cast His children into tremendous suffering without a cause. Calvin's Job interprets God as his *'garde'* in an ironic way because Job does not see God as his protector, but as a watcher, always checking to see if he commits sins. Although God is *'garde'*, Job considers that He is more like a spy.[77]

Sometimes, God's providence cannot be perceptible as there are some parts of nature which the average people cannot easily understand or experience.[78] Job is patient and he resists his fleshly emotions to control himself when afflicted but he also resists God's hidden providence.[79] In this sense, according to Calvin, David reacts better than Job because he recounts God's infinite goodness, and

---

73 A detailed discussion about David in relation to Job is in chapters 4 and 5. This chapter focuses on Job.

74 "…que Iob a voulu ici comme reprocher à Dieu, qu'il nous esleve comme si nous estions des petis Rois, qu'il fait semblant d'avoir un soin paternel de nous, et de nous preferer à toutes creatures: et apres il nous abbat, comme on a ceste peincture de le roue de fortune." Sermon 29 Job 7:16–21, CO33:359.

75 "Mais icy Iob le prend tout à l'opposite." Ibid., CO33:361. Cf. Nous voyons donc comme Iob tourne tout au rebours la providence de Dieu, qu'au lieu qu'il se devoit consoler et resiouyr en icelle, il voudroit que Dieu fust bien loin." Ibid.

76 Ibid., CO33:367.

77 "…que Dieu nous guette, qu'il veille sur nous, qu'il cognoist tout, comme si on veilloit quelqu'un, pour espier et pour observer tout ce qu'il fait et dit. Voila donc en quel sens Iob attribue ce titre à Dieu, qu'il est garde des hommes." Ibid., CO33:366.

78 Ibid., CO33:368.

79 Ibid., CO33:361 also in CO33:364.

does not understand God's providence by immediate experiences.[80] David is an example of a good member of Jesus Christ because he is able to honour God for His infinite goodness.[81] However, while all members are made '*participans de toutes ses richesses*',[82] Calvin believes that Job misunderstands this, and thus has no taste of God's goodness because he does not have any appetite for the 'good food' from God.[83]

Calvin includes God's richness in His goodness,[84] and thus people who participate in God's richness participate in God's providence through God's activities displaying His goodness. In this sermon, the activities include making people members in Jesus Christ.

Sermon 41 Job 10:18-22

Calvin explains in this sermon, how affliction can draw the believer closer to God.[85] Although human beings have sufferings on earth, God appoints His children to rule other creatures in the world, to enjoy God's fatherly love, and to be advanced to heavenly life.[86] Furthermore, God honours His children by appointing them to manage the world. Therefore, the present life of God's children is a testimony to their father, and eternal life is a promise of participation in "*gloire immortelle*" for His children.[87] God changes His children's life from that of miserable death to glorious immortality and He gives them a taste of this heavenly glory in their present lives.[88] However, Job does not perceive that God honours him and makes him a partaker of His glorious immortality. As one of God's children, Job understood that he was

---

80 Ibid., *CO*33:360.

81 Ibid., *CO*33:361.

82 "…et que nous sommes participans de toutes ses richesses…" Ibid.

83 "Mais icy Iob le prend tout à l'opposite. En quoy nous voyons quand les hommes sont desgoustez, que rien ne leur vient à propos: comme si un estomac estoit debiffé par maladie, les viandes qu'on luy presentera, les meilleures et les plus delicates n'auront nulle saveur…" Ibid.

84 Sermon 46 Job 12:7–16, *CO*33:572.

85 Sermon 41 Job 10:18–22, *CO*33:514.

86 Ibid., *CO*33:508.

87 "Et que cela soit pour nous faire aspirer à cest heritage du ciel, auquel Dieu nous appelle pour nous y faire participans de son immortalité glorieuse." Ibid., *CO*33:518.

88 "Car Dieu nous eust changez en immortalité glorieuse."Ibid., *CO*33:515. Also in: Or il ne faut point que nous pensions de la vie humaine simplement en soy: mais il faut regarder la fin où elle tend, c'est assavoir que nous soyons conduis à ceste esperance qui nous est encores cachee au ciel: combien que Dieu nous en donne icy quelque goust, voire entant que selon nostre rudesse nous le pouvons comprendre." Ibid., *CO*33:509.

honoured by God to rule other creatures, but he could not believe that God created him in His own image nor that he would taste everlasting life.[89]

Job feels that he has no part in tasting the goodness of God because he only perceives his sorrows and is overwhelmed by them.[90] Calvin dislikes Job's speech because he sounds like a faithless person who does not believe in the immortality of the soul and resurrection.[91] However, Calvin still argues that Job has faith and hope for eternal life but that when facing difficulties, Job is wholly confused.[92] Calvin argues that when humankind are afflicted, it is a time for them to ponder their mistakes and sins so that they may have a taste of the heavenly life.[93] Furthermore, when sinners repent by calling upon God, they are drawn near to Him for help and forgiveness.[94] However, in this case, Job is far away from God's succour and heavenly life.

Does Job participate in God's goodness?

Instead of fixing his eyes on God's providence, Job focuses excessively on his sorrows, and therefore becomes so blind that he cannot see God's care anymore. This blindness includes mistrusting God, misunderstanding God's providence, and walking away from Him. Certainly, Job participates in God's providence through enjoying His earthly blessings, however, when Calvin declares that Job sounds like a non-believer, having no taste of God's goodness, he truly thinks that Job is not saved, is not a member of Jesus Christ, nor a participant in eternal life. Calvin believes that if the faithful trust in God's care while experiencing good and bad times, they participate in God's providence both in their present lives by tasting God's goodness and in their future lives by tasting eternal happiness. Following this analysis, it is noted that Calvin's interpretation of human participation in God's providence is linked to soteriological matters.

---

89 "Tant y a que Iob revient là, qu'il voudroit n'estre iamais nay. Et pourquoy ? D'autant qu'il estoit en tel trouble, son esprit estoit si confus, qu'estant ainsi saisi et preoccupé de fascherie, il ne peut avoir ceste consideration que Dieu toutesfois l'a creé à son image, qu'il l'a tenu au monde comme l'un de ses enfans, qu'il lui a fait gouster la vie eternelle à laquelle les hommes sont conviez." Ibid., CO33:508.

90 Ibid.

91 "Iob parle ici comme un homme qui n'avoit nulle esperance ne de l'immortalité des ames, ne de la resurrection qui nous est promise." Ibid., CO33:515.

92 "Iob avoit eu et foy et esperance de la vie eternelle: mais pour un peu de temps il est saisi d'une telle frayeur, qu'il ne conçoit en la mort sinon toute confusion et desordre: car quand il regarde le sepulchre, il voit l'enfer ouvert pour l'engloutir." Ibid., CO33:518.

93 Ibid., CO33:510, 516.

94 Ibid., CO33:514.

Job's participation in God's power

Sermon 53 Job 14:1–4

Calvin offers the congregation an explanation of original sin in this sermon, where Adam was created in the image of God, with the expectation that he would show God's perfectness, righteousness, and soundness. However, because of sin he was condemned and cut off from the fountain of wellspring that is full of God's goodness.[95] Human beings are descendants of Adam and inherit this original sin, with the result that people's lives become shortened and miserable. Furthermore, people do not have '*une seule goutte de bien*'[96] in them and because they are so deprived of power to do the right thing, they fail to call upon God and instead, they complain.[97] It seems that there is a play on words between '*goutte*' and '*goust*', connoting that although people do not have 'a single drop of goodness', God let them 'taste his goodness'. How do they do that? When they pray to God, He will make them the '*participans de ses benefices*' by letting them taste His '*bonté*'.[98]

In this sermon, Calvin uses the terms goodness and benefits interchangeably, and he emphasises that the faithful can enjoy bliss in them,[99] as God is both Father and saviour. Thus, He lets his people participate in His goodness to taste His mercy,[100] and draws them to Him to taste His power.[101] Likewise, sometimes Calvin discusses the idea of God's power under the topic of God's goodness, and it seems that tasting God's power is the activity in which the faithful participate to have a role in God's

---

95 Sermon 53 Job 14:1–4, *CO*33:660.

96 "Le mal croist et s'augmente: il n'y a pas une seule goutte de bien." Ibid., *CO*33:657.

97 Ibid., *CO*33:655, 657.

98 "Pour exemple: en premier lieu, combien que nostre vie soit miserable, si est-ce neantmoins que Dieu nous y fait gouster sa bonté en tant de sortes, que nous pouvons conclure que nous sommes bien-heureux, d'autant qu'il nous fait participans de ses benefices."Ibid., *CO*33:662.

99 Ibid.

100 In the 1541 *Institutes*, Calvin discusses God's mercy in relation to salvation. He says, "Certes cei troi choses nous sont principallement necessaires à congnoistre: sa misericorde, en laquelle consiste le salut de nous tous; son jugement, lequel journellement il exerce sur le iniques, et lequel il leur reserve plus rigoureux à confusion eternelle; sa justice, par laquelle se fideles sont benignement entretenuz." Calvin, *Institution de la Religion Chrétienne* 1541, 234.

101 "Pour exemple: en premier lieu, combien que nostre vie soit miserable, si est-ce neantmoins que Dieu nous y fait gouster sa bonté en tant de sortes, que nous pouvons conclure que nous sommes bien-heureux, d'autant qu'il nous fait participans de ses benefices. Nostre vie est brefve: mais elle n'est pas si brefve, que Dieu ne nous donne le loisir de cognoistre qu'il est nostre Pere et Saveur, et de gouster quelle est sa vertu en nous, et qu'il nous appelle à soy." Sermon 53 Job 14:1–4, *CO*33:662. Cf. "…mais si est-ce que cependant Dieu nous donne quelque goust de sa misericorde, quand nous voyons qu'il nous supporte, et que s'il lui plaist nous affliger, ou il nous donne patience, ou il modere sa rigueur, tellement que tousiours nous sentons sa bonté." Ibid., *CO*33:663.

goodness. Calvin suggests that the faithful can taste God's power in themselves, yet what does it mean to taste God's power? Tasting God's power is to get to know that God is Father and saviour and that in life after death, God makes the Elect the participants in eternal life.[102]

The definitions of the four descriptors, goodness, power, wisdom, and justice that Calvin offered in Sermon 46 do not explicitly refer to salvation. However, Calvin stresses that God's power maintains and preserves the things He created. Returning to Sermon 53, Calvin discusses the ideas of God's power and mercy under the topic of God's goodness. God's power shows that He as saviour, has the authority to endow people with eternal life, that is, to correct the 'shortness' of their lives and restore them to endless life.[103] Hence, the explanation of God's power in Sermon 53, is an extension of the explanation in Sermon 46 and it entails that God's power brings salvation.

In Sermon 53, Calvin shows that God's actions in His goodness and power work together to show His mercy as Father and saviour, and to give people life on earth and in eternity. Accordingly, God as Father and saviour, must have mercy on His people. Therefore, if the faithful fall into their own fleshly affections and lust because of adversities, they should bridle their complaints but confess their sins instead.[104] Job however, complains frequently that God is his adversary, not his saviour, and although Job admits that he is guilty, Calvin believes that he talks in a contrary way.[105] Calvin's Job speaks with a lot of passion and wants to vindicate his claim to his own cleanness from sin. In contrast, Calvin points to David as one who admits that he has offended God, that he is a sinful man, and was so even in his mother's womb. In this respect, Calvin encourages his congregation to deal with their sins as David did,[106] by humbling themselves and being eager to glorify God,[107] for God's power has life giving ability in which the sinners can be saved and restored when they repent.

---

102 "Il n'est point question là que nous ayons une vie egale à ceste-ci en longueur de temps: mais Dieu nous fait participans de sa vie propre, qui est immortelle." Ibid., *CO*33:664.

103 "Nostre vie est brefve: mais elle n'est pas si brefve, que Dieu ne nous donne le loisir de cognoistre qu'il est nostre Pere et Sauveur, et de gouster quelle est sa vertu en nous, et qu'il nous appelle à soy." Ibid., *CO*33:662. Cf. Ibid., *CO*33:661 and "Et pourtant consolons-nous quand nous avons dequoi nous resiouir en la brefveté de nostre vie, que nous avons matiere d'estre patiens, et de ne nous point fascher par trop. Et pourquoi? Car si nous avons ceste esperance de la vie celeste, alors nous cognoistrons que ce monde n'est rien." Ibid., *CO*33:664.

104 Ibid., *CO*33:664.

105 Ibid., *CO*33:657, 666.

106 Ibid., *CO*33:666.

107 "Quand donc nous penserons à cela, nous aurons dequoi nous humilier et donner gloire à Dieu." Ibid., *CO*33:667.

Sermon 54 Job 14:5–12

From Sermon 53, one knows that God shows His power through His role as a life-giving saviour. In continuing this analysis, Calvin suggests in Sermon 54, that the faithful sustain their lives through God's power.[108] At the same time, God, as Father, blesses the faithful with food: for example, meat, drink, and remedies for illness in their transient life.[109] Yet this life is transitional, God still promises that He guides His children through good and bad times when they live on earth. However, ultimately, the hope for the faithful should be in eternal life,[110] and Calvin argues that Job forgets about this kind of hope because he passionately talks about human torments and sufferings as if he did not recognise God's promise of eternal life.[111] Therefore, Job's mistake is in focusing on the created world and things happening in it. Hence, how can the faithful recognise eternality when they are still in their present transition?

Calvin argues that the faithful are made to sense everlasting life by experience and by faith,[112] where through experience and faith, they can become '*participans de sa vie*'. The lives of the faithful continue in God after death and these lives will be fully restored to '*vie cacheé*', which is in God's glory and immortality.[113] They participate in God's own eternal life by praying and calling upon God. This participation for which the faithful hope for is a participation in God's glory,[114] modelled by the participation of Jesus in His father's life. Therefore, the faithful in eternity also become members in Jesus and participate in everything that Jesus is given by His father.[115]

---

108 Sermon 54 Job 14:5–12, *CO*33:670.

109 Ibid., *CO*33:672.

110 Ibid., *CO*33:676.

111 "Or notons en premier lieu, que quand Iob parle des hommes, il en parle en ses passions et tourments (comme desia nous avons veu) et puis il ne regarde qu'à ceste vie presente..." Ibid., *CO*33:673.

112 "...et d'autrepart toutes fois il nous monstre et nous fait sentir par experience, et par la foi que nous sommes vivans, voire en lui, que nous sommes participans de sa vie, il nous fait voir comme en un miroir ceste immortalité que nous attendons..." Ibid., *CO*33:676.

113 "...l'homme apres sa mort persiste en Dieu, et qu'il a une vie cachee, et que ceste vie–la a une bonne semence, afin que nous soyons pleinement restaurez en une perfection, de laquelle nous sommes maintenant bien loin: cest assavoir, en sa gloire celeste et en son immortalité glorieuse." Ibid., *CO*33:674. Cf. "Que nous revenions à ce que dit sainct Paul aux Colossiens (Col 3:3), c'est assavoir, que nous sommes morts, mais nostre vie est cachee en nostre Seigneur Iesus Christ, et Dieu la manifestera quand il sera temps." Ibid., *CO*33:675.

114 "... qu'ils doivent estre participans de cest gloire de Dieu...mesmes que nous devions estre unis au Fils de Dieu? Ibid., *CO*33:677.

115 "...que nous soyons membres de son corps pour participer à tout ce qui lui est donné..." Ibid.

Furthermore, although the bodies of the godly weaken on earth, Calvin offers consolation by saying that the frailties of human beings ought to lead them to magnify God's goodness (*magnifier la bonté de Dieu*) and that at the same time God will humble them and bring much of His goodness to them (*magnifier sa bonté*).[116] This goodness involves the Holy Spirit dwelling in the bodies of the faithful, and though the bodies of the faithful will decay, God will restore them to life one day.[117]

Calvin believes that Job does not intend to conclude that God exterminates people when they finish this earthly life,[118] but that Job murmurs as if he realised nothing about resurrection because he forgets that life continues on in God's glory.[119] Moreover, Job has turned to a '*mauvais usage*'[120] expressing his agony, but ignoring God's power and His goodness, and forgets that God has prepared an everlasting place in heaven for him.[121]

Does Job participate in God's power?

God as Father and saviour, shows His power and goodness, and this power shows that in His mercy, He is able to endow the faithful with eternal life. Calvin shows that God's actions in His power and goodnesswork together in His providence and this providence shows His mercy to His faithful. However, Job is not able to appreciate the lifegiving God, so when he is afflicted, he believes that God becomes his adversary. Job's fleshly passion becomes his lust which Calvin considers as sin, yet Job does not seem to admit his sins. In this case, the more Job continuously vindicates himself, the more Calvin thinks that Job is far away from God's providence, as Job does not believe in resurrection, and he has no taste of God's goodness and His power. Calvin's interpretation of human participation in God's providence is related to soteriological matters.

---

116 Ibid., *CO*33:676.

117 Ibid.

118 "Vray est que Iob ne peut estre accusé là, comme s'il concluoit que Dieu exterminast les hommes du tout, quand il les retire de la terre." Ibid., *CO*33:673.

119 "Iob donc n'a pas eu ceste apprehension-la, voire pour s'y arrester, mais pour un temps il a esté esbloui en ses passions." Ibid., *CO*33:674. Cf. Ainsi donc notons bien, que Iob, quand il parle ici de la vie humaine comme un homme qui n'a point d'esgard à la resurrection à venir, ne s'est point arresté là du tout (car il avoit bien prevue ce qui en est) mais il a voulu exprimer quelle passion il a senti..." Ibid., *CO*33:679–680.

120 Ibid., *CO*33:677.

121 Ibid., *CO*33:674.

Job's participation in God's wisdom

Sermon 95 Job 26:1-7

The Holy Scriptures are an exposition of God's law and they have healing and strengthening power over human feebleness,[122] so when His word is preached, His people will be drawn to Him and be strengthened.[123] They also have the power of drawing people out of eternal death to revitalisation because human beings do not have a *'goutte de vie'*.[124] Therefore, God dwells among the faithful in the power of His word so that the faithful can live in God one day. In this sense, God makes them *'participans de soi et de ses graces'*, and they can participate in Him and His grace. For when people participate in God's power, they participate in God's goodness as well. This participation entails a current meaning: the feeble people are strengthened; and a future meaning: the faithful are pulled out of eternal death. Thus, the guidance of the Holy Scriptures contains the perfection of wisdom, and all the faithful can trust in this,[125] for both the power and wisdom of God are shown in the Holy Scripture.

Job acknowledges the power of God's word and he strongly despises Bildad's ignorance of God's wisdom[126] and power.[127] Calvin's Job claims that it is necessary to respect God's power in the order of creation and in His governance.[128] However, Calvin also stresses that some people claim to know all of these but they are 'morons'.[129] Calvin despises people who claim to know God's providence, but never feel God's glorious power in them, and describes this behaviour as pretentious.[130] Calvin indirectly suggests that Job is one of these hypocrites as Job does not honour God's work in this world although he claims to know God's power and wisdom.

---

122 "Notamment il est dit de la Loy de Dieu, qu'elle est pour instruire les ignorans, et les petis: et cela s'estend à toute l'Escriture saincte, qui n'est qu'une simple exposition de la Loy." Sermon 95 Job 26:1-7, *CO*34:421.

123 Ibid., *CO*34:427.

124 Ibid., *CO*34:426. See also "Le mal croist et s'augmente: il n'y a pas une seule goutte de bien." Sermon 53 Job 14:1-4, *CO*33:657.

125 Ibid., *CO*34:421-422.

126 Ibid., *CO*34:421.

127 "Voila donc en quoi Bildad est redargué par Iob: c'est que quand il a disputé de la puissance de Dieu..." Ibid., *CO*34:428.

128 Ibid.

129 "Car nous verrons beaucoup de gens sauvages, qui à grand' peine ont iamais conceu qu'il y a un Dieu au ciel qui gouverne tout: ils sont là abbrutis." Ibid.

130 "Voire, mais iamais n'ont senti que c'est de sal gloire, iamais n'ont apprehendé ceste vertu admirable qui est en lui. Il leur faut aussi monstrer que le service de Dieu est spirituel, et qu'il faut venir à lui en integrité et rondeur, et que nous soyons purgez de toute feintise." Ibid.

Calvin argues that Job eloquently explains God's works in the created world and that Job 'understands' God's providence better than unbelievers.[131] Job does participate in God's providence but how much does he understand it? Perhaps only a little better than unbelievers do.

Sermon 102 Job 28:10-28

Calvin argues that Job tries to show that true wisdom is in God's hiddenness, and that Job acknowledges that this wisdom is humanly untouchable,[132] for understanding God's secret is a special gift and it is God's will to enlighten whoever delights in Him.[133] Furthermore, God's wisdom is known by nobody but Himself and therefore, people should be silent before His hiddenness.[134] Yet, although Job knows that God has the authority to reveal Himself, he also desperately wants to know the hiddenness of His judgement in His wisdom.[135] In respect to the hiddenness of God, Calvin suggests a solution. Having fear of God is the way to honour God's wisdom and it is also because of this fear that, when God sends secret judgement to the faithful, they can be patient and wait for God's revelation in the future in His will.[136] Calvin warns His congregation not to search for the reason for God's judgements as they are in His wisdom, and hints that Job does not appreciate God's hiddenness.

Does Job participate in God's wisdom?

Calvin discusses God's wisdom together with His power and justice, declaring that God's actions in His wisdom, power, and justice are inseparable. Job claims to understand God's wisdom and His power, yet because his behaviour does not show that he has hope for God's glory in eternity, Calvin concludes that Job is a hypocrite. Calvin stresses that even if Job trusts in God's revealed wisdom and justice, he still desperately searches for God's hiddenness. This evidence proves that Job is not

---

131 "Ainsi maintenant nous voyons comme Iob nous propose les œuvres de Dieu, pour nous testifier que do son costé il n'a point vescu au monde comme les gens prophanes et contempteurs qui ne portent nulle reverence à Dieu, qui ne cognoissent point sa puissance et vertu pour l'adorer..." Sermon 96 Job 26:8–14, CO34:441.

132 Sermon 102 Job 28:10–28, CO34:510.

133 Ibid., CO34:512.

134 Ibid.

135 "Maintenant nous voyons l'intention de Iob ou plustost du sainct Esprit. Et ainsi apprenous de ne plus lascher la bride à ceste folle cupidité et fretillante qui est en nous, de savoir ce qui ne nous peut de rien servir, et d'entrer au conseil estroit de Dieu, de vouloir examiner la raison de tous ses iugemens: ce n'est point là où il nous faut occuper, et appliquer nostre estude." Ibid., CO34:516.

136 Ibid., CO34:514, 516.

hopeful for God's revelation in the future. Calvin's Job participates in God's wisdom and justice, but he probably does not appreciate the way he can participate. Calvin's interpretation of human participation in God's wisdom and justice is related to soteriological matters.

Job's participation in God's justice

Sermon 56 Job 14:16-22

Calvin argues that humans are poor sinners who deserve greater punishment than they encounter from God, but that Job still complains that God's judgement is too excessive.[137] Job identifies himself as a sinner, yet he still complains passionately and argues that God's hand and sternness are heavy on him.[138] Calvin refutes this kind of complaint and exhorts the audience to think upon God's benefits bestowed on them by God their father in their previous experiences in life, and to trust God's provision in both the present and future times.[139] The faithful are participating in God's riches in the present life already, however, the richness the faithful experience now is temporary, but He will make them the partakers of His riches and immortal glory.[140]

Sermon 87 Job 22:23-30

In the present life, God punishes sinners and faithful alike, as God can punish the faithful by His higher and hidden justice. Calvin encourages his congregation, telling them that past experiences of enjoying God's goodness offers a way for the faithful sufferers to deal with God's judgement in the present life. If the faithful have experienced the '*goust de la douceur paternelle de Dieu*', they are assured of God's mercy and fatherly love, and therefore they should not be afraid of God's judgements.[141]

---

137 Sermon 56 Job 14:16–22; *CO*33:695.

138 Ibid., *CO*33:698, 699.

139 Ibid., *CO*33:704.

140 "...d'autant que Dieu par ce moyen-la nous retire des povretez de ce monde, pour nous faire participans de ses richesses, et de son immortalité glorieuse." Ibid., *CO*33:706.

141 Sermon 87 Job 22:23–30, *CO*34:322.

Does Job participate in God's justice?

In the 1541 *Institutes*, Calvin defines God's judgements as His daily practices upon the wicked where they are strictly assigned for eternal condemnation. However, God's righteousness is His preservation of the faithful. In his sermons on Job, the justice Calvin mentioned focuses on the judgement and God's goodness comes to maintain the faithful, as stated in Sermon 87. Hence, God's judgement is also against the godly, but His goodness can help them to face judgement.

While Job admits his sin, he argues that God's judgement on him is too heavy and that when he complains, he forgets the taste of God's goodness, implying that Job is not a participant in God's riches and His immortal glory, for if Job had tasted God's goodness, he would not be afraid of God's judgement. Calvin discusses God's justice together with God's power and His goodness, entailing that human participation in God's providence is related to soteriological matters.

Does Job participate in God's providence?

Job's participation in God's providence depends on the confession of his own sins. Now to consider Job's course of repentance.

Job's pseudo repentance

Sermon 53 Job 14:1–4 and Sermon 63 Job 16:10–17

In Sermon 53, Job admits that he is guilty, but Calvin believes that he means the opposite: Job thinks that he is treated unfairly, and that he is not guilty.[142] Calvin's Job speaks with a lot of passion and wants to vindicate his claim to his own cleanness from sin. In Sermon 63, Calvin states that Job works on some of the activities which Calvin mentioned to signify a person's participation in God's providence. For example, Job feels sorrow, weeps, and clothes himself with sackcloth. These are gestures of repentance longing for God's forgiveness.[143] Job declares that he is clean, and his prayers are pure, however, Calvin argues that everyone in the world is effected by sin, including Job.[144] Job is too confident of his own '*intégrité*'[145]

---

142 Sermon 53 Job 14:1–4, CO33:657, 666.

143 Sermon 63 Job 16:10–17, CO34:21.

144 Ibid., CO34:26.

145 Ibid., CO34:24. Cf. Calvin agrees with Elihu's argument by saying that Job places himself above God's righteousness. "Quand le sainct Esprit prononce que tous ceux qui se despitent et murmurent

rather than relying on God's '*bonté*',[146] and according to Calvin, people with this kind of attitude will have difficulty in praying to God.[147] Furthermore, Calvin even says that these people will gradually go further away from God. Therefore, Calvin advises his congregation that when they are undergoing afflictions, they have to examine their lives and admit that if they were punished according to their sins, they should actually be scourged a hundred times more,[148] as God never punishes without a cause.

Although Calvin does not seem to consider Job's sufferings as a punishment from God,[149] he has a negative impression of Job for not trusting in providence, not believing in second life or resurrection, not recounting blessings, for talking like an unbeliever, and complaining when he suffers. These are all sinful attitudes, therefore, Calvin encourages his church to examine their life and to ask God for forgiveness when He afflicts them.[150]

Calvin claims in Sermon 58 that God reveals His hiddenness through His spirit, His words and prayers of the faithful.[151] The Holy Spirit inspires the faithful by the Holy Scriptures, and hence helps them understand God's 'things'.[152] Additionally, the faithful can pray daily to God for His revelation, but they should learn from David's prayer as David is patient enough to wait for God's full revelation in the

---

en leurs afflictions, tous ceux qui ne se peuvent assuiettir à la main forte de Dieu pour confesser que tout ce qu'il fait est iuste et raisonnable, que tous ceux-la se font iustes par dessus Dieu…" Sermon 119 Job 32:1–3, *CO*35:8.

146 Sermon 63 Job 16:10–17, *CO*34:17, 18.

147 "…il est impossible que nous approchions de lui: nous le fuirons, et quand nous en serons eslongnez une fois, encores tascherons-nous de nous en retirer d'autant plus." Ibid., *CO*34:18.

148 Ibid., *CO*34:23, 24.

149 "Mais prenons le cas que Dieu ne nous traitte point ainsi pour nos pechez: comme à la verité il n'a point eu ce regard en Iob, qu'il l'affligeast pource qu'il l'avoit ainsi desservi." Ibid., *CO*34:24.

150 "Et de fait quand Dieu nous afflige, voila qu'il nous faut faire, d'entrer en nous-mesmes, et d'examiner nostre vie: et là dessus quand nous aurons offensé, que nous gemissions devant Dieu pour dire…" Ibid., *CO*34:23.

151 "Combien donc que nous ne soyons point conseillers de Dieu, toutes fois si nous a-il fait la grace et cest honneur, de nous reveler ce qui nous est incognu et caché. Comment cela? Il n'y a nul qui cognoisse ce qui est en l'homme, que l'esprit qui habite en lui…Voila donc comme nous sommes faits participans des choses qui estoient du tout separees de nous…car quand Dieu nous veut reveler ses secrets, il ne nous envoye point seulement de inspirations, mais il parle à nous…Mais de nostre costé cognoissons aussi qu'il nous ouvre les yeux, afin que ce qui est contenu en l'Escriture saincte ne nous soit point comme un langage estrange…Et au reste, d'autant qu'il a pleu à Dieu de nous faire participans de sa volonté, que nous comprenions son conseil, selon qu'il nous le monstre…Et au reste, encores que nous n'entendions pas la dixieme partie de ce qui est en l'Escriture saincte, prions Dieu que de iour en iour il nous revele ce qui nous est auiourd'hui caché…" Sermon 58 Job 15:11–16, *CO*33:719–720.

152 Ibid.

later days.[153] David's prayer is different from Job's kind of prayer mentioned here, for Calvin implies that prayers expressing the urge to be cleansed by God from sin should be a lot humbler than those asking for God's revelation. If it pleases God to accept the prayers of sinners, He will make them perceive His goodness, and then He will also make them partakers of His everlasting glory.[154]

It is not clear if Calvin suggests that Job is not a partaker of eternal glory because Calvin seems to imply that Job's prayer does not show his humility and he moves away from God's goodness. It is not until Calvin preaches on Job 40:5 in Sermon 154, that he acknowledges that Job sincerely repents.

Job's participation in *providence de Dieu*

Sermon 154 Job 39:36-38 to 40:1-6 and Sermon 157 Job 42:1-5

Calvin considers that Job becomes a humble person, following God's revelation to him in Job 40:4-5. Calvin describes that Job is as tame as a little lamb, showing his humility by not making noises anymore. In Job 40:4, when Job admits that he is unworthy, Calvin encourages his congregation to follow this as their example.[155]

---

153 "Car il faut que les plus advancez, et les plus parfaits cognoissent que ce n'est point encores à eux de savoir tous les secrets de Dieu: car sela est reservé au dernier iour. Et de fait, ce n'est point sans cause que David s'escrie (combien qu'il fust un Prophete si excellent) que c'est une chose admirable que des conseils de Dieu." Ibid., CO33:721.

154 "...nous faire participans de sa gloire immortelle." Sermon 63 Job 16:10-17, CO34:26.

155 "L'exemple de Iob condamnera une telle stupidité et obstination. Et pourquoy? Combien que Iob eust esté impatient pour un temps, et qu'il y eust eu en luy quelques esmotions qui le transportoyent: si est-ce en la fin qu'il a ouy ceste voix de Dieu bruyante, que ce tourbillon luy a causé en luy quelque frayeur, tellement qu'il s'est corrigé, s'imposant silence." Cf. "...mais qu'à l'exemple de Iob nous disions, Seigneur, me voici de basse condition." Sermon 154 Job 39:36-38 to Job 40:1-6, CO35:441. Maarten Wisse argues that Calvin uses two opposite hermeneutic strategies to explain the Book of Job: the 'positive hermeneutic' and the 'negative hermeneutic'. He supports his argument by showing that Calvin encourages the faithful to follow Job as an example in Sermon 26 but not to do the same in Sermon 27. Maarten Wisse, "Scripture between Identity and Creativity A Hermeneutical Theory Building upon Four Interpretations of Job-John Calvin Perspective of Job", in *Ars Disputandi Supplement Series*, Volume 1, edited by Marcel Sarot, Michael Scott and Maarten Wisse (Netherlands: Utrecht University Library, 2003), 51-76. Wisse misinterprets Calvin's meaning as in Sermon 26, Calvin says, "Et c'est ce que Iob traitte en ce passage. Car il proteste que quand il sera enseigné il se taira, il demande qu'on luy monstre en quoy il a failli. Il n'y a nulle doute qu'ici Iob en sa personne ne donne une regle commune à tous enfans de Dieu: c'est que quand il nous sera monstré que nous avons failli, il ne faut plus que nous ayons la bouche ouverte pour amener des excuses frivoles...D'autant plus devons nous bien noter ce qui est ici dit: car combien que Iob traitte ici de sa vertu, si est-ce neantmoins que l'Esprit de Dieu nous la met ici devant les yeux comme un miroir et exemple que nous devons ensuyvre...Apprenons de nous taire en premier lieu, c'est que

Job has already repented once in Job 40:4–5 but Calvin considers that Job is touched by God's revelation more in Job 42, and therefore Calvin stresses in Sermon 157 (Job 42:1–5) that Job's second repentance is more '*parfait*'.[156] This perfection is a process in which God continuously trains the faithful. In this process, they have to repent continuously, and in each repentance, they will have a small taste of God's goodness.[157]

Calvin emphasises that when Job acknowledges God's power in his second repentance, he wholly submits to God,[158] and finally understands that he cannot judge God's work or wisdom by his own foolishness.[159] Job further realises that he participates in God's general providence after God reveals part of His plan to him. Calvin also stresses that God makes His faithful the partakers of His life when they die. Certainly, faithful partakers include Job, although Calvin makes this point very implicitly.[160] At various stages of Job's life, he participates differently in God's providence. Calvin encourages the faithful to pray actively when they are confused

---

nous n'empeschions point la grace de Dieu quand elle nous est offerte: mais que nous escoutions, et que nous ayons la bouche close pour ne point repliquer." Sermon 26 Job 6:24–30, CO33:319–321. Calvin does not regard Job as a good example to follow as Job brags about his previous merits and complains too much when he is afflicted. Calvin emphasises that the godly should be quiet, wait for God patiently, and follow the example the Holy Spirit shows them. It is only when Job repents in Job 42, that he sets a humble example, however, Wisse misses this part of the sermon.

156 "En somme nous voyons que la penitence ne se parfait point du premier coup, mais qu'il faut que Dieu apres nous avoir rabottez nous polisse: comme quand on voudra faire une piece d'ouvrage sur un bois ou sur une pierre, il faudra marteler beaucoup." Sermon 157 Job 42:1–5, CO35:477.

157 "Et au reste quand nous aurons ouy quelque bonne instruction pour nostre salut: si nous l'avons receuë, sachons que ce n'est qu'un goust: que nous ne sommes point encores droitement repeus, et qu'il nous y faut retourner." Ibid.

158 "Voila donc les disputes de Iob, où il est entré. Et pourquoy? Car il s'est fourré trop avant aux conseils de Dieu. Maintenant pour se corriger il dit, que ces choses ont esté admirables par dessus luy." Ibid., CO35:482.

159 "Qui est celui qui cache le conseil sans science? Dieu avoit auparavant reproché ceci à Iob. Et semble bien que Iob vueille confesser qu'ainsi est: c'est assavoir qu'il a enveloppé la sagesse de Dieu en ses fols propos: car si nous disputons des œuvres de Dieu selon nostre portee, et que nous en vueillions estre iuges: c'est cacher le conseil, c'est le barbouiller (comme on dit) voire sans science: car nous voulons estre trop sages, parlans ainsi sans avoir esté enseignez." Ibid., CO35:481.

160 Sermon 159 Job 42:9–17, CO35:510.

by God's hiddenness[161] and in this way they can truly taste and participate in God's secret providence.[162]

Job and David

As shown in the previous sections concerning Job's participation in God's goodness and power, Job's poor attitude and deficiencies in dealing with afflictions, resulted in Calvin's suggesting to his congregation to follow the example of David instead. In Sermon 29, Calvin reminds his audience that when David suffers without understanding the reason for the suffering, he recounts God's goodness, and respects God's hidden providence. In Sermon 53, Calvin praises David for his humility because he reflects on his sin when he suffers without complaining to God. Calvin especially has high regard for David's willingness to confess and to repent, because this gesture shows humility, and Calvin illustrates this gesture through David's prayer.

In Sermon 30, Calvin encourages the faithful to do three things when God chastises them. Firstly, they must run to God without any delays.[163] Secondly, they should pray to God, confess their sins, and ask for His forgiveness and mercy.[164] Thirdly, they should pray with a pure and righteous heart.[165] Who can demonstrate

---

161 "Notons bien donc quand nous venons à Dieu, et qu'il est question de parler de ses œuvres, que nous devons sentir que ce sont des secrets trop hauts pour la debilité de nostre esprit. Or ie di qu'il nous faut avoir ceste persuasion-là tant de la providence de Dieu en general, que de ce qui appartient à son royaume spirituel." Sermon 157 Job 42:1–5, CO35:482. Cf. "Voila donc ce que nous avons à retenir pour le premier en ce passage: c'est que les œuvres de Dieu, et sur tout les promesses du salut eternel qui sont contenues en l'Evangile, sont choses admirables par dessus nous: qu'il ne faut point donc que nous y venions à la volee avec audace ni presomption: mais qu'en toute crainte nous prions Dieu qu'il nous face gouster ses secrets entant qu'il nous est utile: et qu'il nous clarifie de iour en iour ce qui nous est obscur: et qu'il ne permette point que nous passions nos bornes: mais que ce qu'il nous aura revelé nous profite, en attendant qu'il nous augmente la foi. Et par ainsi que nous ne parlions iamais, et ne pensions de ses secrets qu'avec toute reverence et humilité." Sermon 157 Job 42:1–5, CO35:483–484.

162 "…mais qu'en toute crainte nous prions Dieu qu'il nous face gouster ses secrets entant qu'il nous est utile: et qu'il nous clarifie de iour en iour ce qui nous est obscur…" Ibid., CO35:484.

163 "Or en somme il y a ici trois choses que nous devons bien noter, l'une c'est, que si tost que Dieu nous visite, nous recourions à luy en nous hastant, et n'attendant point du iourd'huy à demain. Voila pour un item." Sermon 30 Job 8:1–6, CO33:380.

164 "La seconde est, que nous y venions avec prieres, nous condamnans en nos fautes afin d'obtenir pardon et merci de luy." Ibid.

165 "La troisieme c'est que nos oraisons ne soyent point faites en hypocrisie : mais que nous apportions un coeur droit et pur." Ibid.

these three? Calvin suggests that David can model the above and the congregation should learn from this example.[166]

In Sermon 63, Calvin again uses Job as an example, encouraging the congregation to learn from Job's different behaviour. Calvin encourages the congregation to follow Job's example of repentance where Job longed for God's forgiveness,[167] as demonstrated by his weeping in sackcloth and ashes. However, Calvin urges his congregation not to follow Job's example where he declares that he is clean, and his prayer is pure. Calvin argues that everyone in the world is affected by sin, including Job,[168] and that Job is too confident of his own integrity[169] rather than relying on God's goodness.[170] Although Calvin encourages his audience to follow Job, as he shows outward signs of repentance,[171] he truly appreciates people who are humble enough to run to God, confess their sins, and beg for His pardon.[172] Thus, the true essence of the gesture of repentance is confession of sin. Calvin considers the significance of both the inward and outward expressions of repentance, and this is one of the reasons he prefers David's example to Job's. To Calvin, David shows his willingness to repent physically and spiritually, through the act of prayer. This is discussed in the next chapter.

---

166 "Mais sur tout sachans que Dieu nous convie, que nous venions à luy, voire de matin: et puis que ce soit y apportans un coeur pur et droit pour le supplier qu'il nous pardonne nos fautes: et qu'à l'exemple de David (Pseau 51:4) nous luy requerions qu'il nous nettoye de toutes nos macules, comme il faut que nous soyons lavez par luy, afin que nous puissions nous presenter devant sa face en telle pureté comme il commande." Ibid., CO33:380–382.

167 Sermon 63 Job 16:10–17, CO34:21.

168 Ibid., CO34:26.

169 Ibid., CO34:24.

170 Ibid., CO34:17, 18.

171 "Et pourtant quand telle chose adviendra, que nous ensuivions l'exemple de Iob, c'est qu'apres avoir pleuré, voire iusques à ternir nostre face de larmes, nous venions faire confession de nos fautes, et que nous demandions à Dieu qu'il nous soit pitoyable." Ibid., CO34:20. Cf. "Et ainsi les fideles ont eu ces signes exterieurs de repentance quand Dieu les affligeoit, et qu'ils ont confessé leurs pechez pour obtenir pardon..." Ibid., CO34:21.

172 "Toutes fois que nous advisions de recourir à nostre Dieu, lui demandans qu'il lui plaise de nous purger de toutes nos iniquitez, qui sont cause des maux que nous endurons en ceste vie presente..." Ibid., CO34:26. Calvin also illustrates this point using the example of ancient father (Joel 2:13): "Maintenant donc nous voyons comme les Peres anciens ont usé du sac et de la poudre:quand il a esté question de protester leur repentance devant Dieu...Si donc les Peres anciens ont eu besoin de s'humilier en cognoissant leurs pechez..." Ibid., CO34:22.

Conclusion

In Calvin's *Sermons sur le livre de Job*, he describes God's general and special providence as God's activities shown in His goodness, power, wisdom, and justice. These four kinds of God's activities act upon the order of nature and human history inseparably, and they also relate to soteriological issues.

Calvin identifies four categories of God's providential activities in which human beings can participate: God's goodness, power, justice, and wisdom. Job participates in all these categories, especially the category of His goodness, although Job ignores this participation at the beginning by acting as a non-believer. Since heathens do not understand God's goodness, power, wisdom, and justice, and therefore Calvin considers Job as one of the heathens. Although Job is a partaker in God's activities on earth where he has tasted God's providence and especially His goodness, he is confused by God's secret providence, and uses his limited reason to search for God's judgement and His wisdom, thus in this way Job acts like a non-believer. However, when Job receives God's revelation, he repents and then he acknowledges that he has tasted God's special and general providence, and enjoys a taste of eternal life on earth.

Human participation in God's providence shown by Calvin in *Sermons sur le livre de Job* is both part and an extension of divine providence. A '*vir providus*' is a secondary cause, which acts as an instrument used by God in *providentia Dei*.[173] Calvin affirms that apart from the primary cause, which is God's governance, there is a genuine existence of secondary cause, where a believer, acts as a '*participant*' in God's providence.

---

173 "Et pensons-nous donc qu'il appelle maintenant un compagnon pour lui aider à disposer de ses creatures? Vrai est que Dieu usera bien de moyens inferieurs pour gouverner le monde: mais si est-ce que ce n'est point pour amoindrir son autorité, ce n'est pas pour avoir quelque compagnon: car il domine tousiours par dessus… Si un homme tient une scie, ou qu'il tienne un cousteau, qu'il en couppe, et qu'il s'en serve selon sa volonté: et l'instrument se peut-il dresser sur l'homme? Nenni: mais c'est pour monstrer que l'homme non seulement se peut aider de ses mains, et de bras: mais qu'il a aussi les choses qui sont hors de soy à son commandement…Cognoissons donc quand Dieu use des moyens de ce monde, et qu'il se veut servir des hommes comme d'instrumens…si est-ce que Dieu toutes fois les induit avec une puissance violente pour executer ce qu'il a ordonné en son conseil. Et ainsi maintenant nous voyons comme il nous faut considerer la providence de Dieu…" Sermon 130 Job 34:10–15, *CO*35:152–153. Cf. "Quemadmodum contra neglectu et socordia, quae illis iniunxit mala, sibi accersunt. Qui fit enim ut vir providus, dum sibi consulit, imminentibus etiam malis se explicet, stultus inconsulta temeritate pereat, nisi quod et stultitia et prudentia divinae sunt dispensationis instrumenta in utramque partem? Ideo nos celare futura omnia voluit Deus, ut tanquam dubiis occurranmus…" 1559 *Institutes* 1.17.4, *CO*2:157. Cf. 1.17.6, *CO*2:159.

4. Calvin's interpretation of *providentia Dei* in *Commentarius in librum Psalmorum* 1557

Calvin's *Commentarius in librum Psalmorum*[1] was published in 1557. In the same year, a French edition was released but it did not follow the Latin original accurately, so Calvin wrote another edition and issued it in 1561. Calvin also discussed the Book of Psalms in weekly sermons, which began from 1555, the same year that Calvin completed *Sermons sur le livre de Job*, and the weekly sermons on Psalms continued until 1559.[2]

The previous chapter has explained Job's role in Calvin's account of *providentia Dei*. In *Sermons sur le livre de Job*, Calvin's Job does not deal with life's suffering in a godly way and thus Calvin recommends the '*exemplum Davidis*' to the congregation as he considers David as a better model to follow. It is quite unusual to mention a different figure with such a high degree of frequency when David is not even a character in this biblical book. However, Calvin has his reasons. In *Sermons sur le livre de Job*, Calvin uses the biblical figure of Job to illustrate a glorious God in *providentia Dei* in His goodness, power, wisdom, and justice, but he also leads believers to attend to the role of David in *providentia Dei*. This role is related to the prayer of Calvin's David that he discussed in *Commentarius in librum Psalmorum*,[3] for humans are not passive, and there is a genuine existence of human agency as a secondary cause in *providentia Dei*. Through prayer, human beings can understand some parts of divine providence.

To offer a brief comparison of David and Job in Calvin's *Sermons sur le livre de Job*, it should be noted that when Calvin preaches on Job 8:7–13, he uses David to illustrate that past experiences cannot help the faithful to fully comprehend God's infinite goodness. However, these experiences remind them of the fatherly goodness they taste in the present life even when they are afflicted, and they can thus recall that they are cared for by God their father. David is led to God through all those

---

1 Calvin also preached sermons on the Book of Psalms from 1549 but only 26 sermons were preserved and they are kept in the CO. Wulfert de Greef, *The Writings of John Calvin-an Introductory Guide*, translated by Lyle D. Bierma (Grand Rapids, MI: Baker Books, 1993), 112, 115.
2 From February 1554 to March 1555, Calvin preached 159 sermons on the Book of Job at the Genevan churches.
3 Ioannis Calvini, *Commentarius in librum Psalmorum*, CO31–32. Cf. John Calvin, *Commentary on Psalms*, Volume 1–5, translated by James Anderson (Grand Rapids, MI: Christian Classics Ethereal Library. 1571).

previous encounters and so he is moved to call upon God for His succour.[4] When God hears David's prayers of repentance, He forgives his sins, and makes him feel His goodness in blessings.[5] Therefore, if the faithful honour God's goodness, are thankful for God's grace, and pray to God for His help, God will maintain them just like His watering of a plant. This is because when the faithful do all these activities, it is as if they plant themselves by God, and so they will never wilt.[6] However, Job is different. Job is not like David who remembers the goodness he tasted in the past, but instead he is emotionally confused in his sufferings.[7] Calvin believes that prayer can help the sufferer to overcome sorrows,[8] and apparently, he does not think that Job prays with the right attitude. The reason is Job claims that his prayer is pure, and that is the issue. Calvin argues that nobody's prayer is pure because even the faithful are sinners.[9] Therefore, Calvin encourages the churches in Geneva to follow David's example when they encounter life's afflictions, as David confesses his sin, and prays for God's pardon. Calvin considers David's prayer as

---

4 "Et voila mesmes pourquoy David proteste, qu'estant affligé, il luy est souvenu des iours lointains, qu'il les a reduits en memoire (Pseau 143:5). Mais si faut-il pourtant, que nous ayons ce principe, de bien mediter les œuvres de Dieu, et non seulement celles que nous avons veu de nostre temps, mais aussi de ce qui nous est raconté. Dieu a voulu encores, qu'il y eust des histoires, et que la memoire des choses fust conservee par ce moyen-la. Or cependant les hommes prendront plaisir à lire, mais ce sera un esbat de vanité, pource qu'ils n'appliquent point à leur instruction les histoires de tout le temps passé, qui sont une vraye escole pour savoir regler nostre vie." Jean Calvin, *Sermons Sur le livre de Job*, Sermon 31 Job 8:7–13, CO33:385.

5 "Venons y donc avec prieres, comme il en est ici parlé, qu'il nous faut supplier le Seigneur…Dieu n'est pas ainsi: mais quand ils declare que nos pechez nous sont pardonnez, il adiouste quant et quant l'effect, qu'il nous fait sentir sa bonté en nous benissant, et en nous faisant prosperer." Ibid., CO33:382–383.

6 "Notons bien donc que Dieu procure nostre salut par ce moyen, quand il dit (Ier 2:13), Ie suis la fontaine d'eau vive, ie suis le vray ruisseau, il faut que vous soyez arrousez continuellement de ma grace, où il n'y a que seicheresse en vous: et encores que vous verdoyez, cela n'est rien: vous flestrirez." Ibid., CO33:390.

7 "Tant y a neantmoins qu'il nous faut bien condamner ceste infirmité ici en Iob: c'est à dire, ce qu'il s'est trouvé si abbatu de tristesse, qu'il ne pouvoit plus gouster la bonté de Dieu, pour avoir seulement quelque petite resiouissance, de laquelle il se sousinst." Sermon 13 Job 3:20–26; CO33:171.

8 "Or voyans que cela luy est advenu, d'autant plus devons nous estre soigneux à prier Dieu, que la tristesse ne domine en nous, en sorte que nous soyons du tout opprimez." Ibid.

9 "Apprenons donc quand il est ici dit, que Iob a esté traitté d'une telle rigueur, combien qu'il eust ses mains pures, et que son oraison fust droite devant Deiu: que quand tout le monde seroit ainsi affligé, il ne s'en faudroit point esbahir…Car qui est celui qui pourra dire qu'il ait cheminé en telle integrité, qu'il puisse protester à la verité qu'il a ses mains pures devant Dieu? Helas! Il s'en faut beaucoup. Puis qu'ainsi est donc, cognoissons que c'est pour nos pechez que Dieu nous punit quand nous endurons quelques afflictions: et pourtant que nous les portions patiemment, cognoissans mesmes, que nous en avons merité d'avantage." Sermon 63 Job 16:10–17; CO34:25–26.

pure and righteous, without any hypocrisy.[10] Calvin's deep affection for David is apparent in his *Sermons sur le livre de Job*, but what about his *Commentarius in librum Psalmorum*? *Commentarius in librum Psalmorum* demonstrates that Calvin prefers using David as a pious model because of Calvin's own personal experience and historical context.

This chapter presents two arguments. Firstly, Calvin argues that through prayers, human beings can understand some parts of *providentia Dei*. Secondly, there is a genuine existence of secondary cause in *providentia Dei*. The following discussion will first explore Calvin's personal experience and the historical context in relation to his fondness for David.

Calvin and David

In *Commentarius in librum Psalmorum*, David's situation reflects the images of the godly who have suffered, yet who can also be encouraged by David's positive reaction and consoled by his merciful God. Calvin pushes the exegesis further to a subjective level by suggesting that his own situation resembles David's and in the mirror of the psalms, he sees himself in David. Therefore, he shows a deep affection for both the psalmist[11] and the content of the Psalms.[12] Calvin describes the Psalms as a book which embraces every possible emotion of man. He terms

---

10 "Or en some il y a ici trois choses que nos devons bien noter, l'une c'est, que si tost que Dieu nous visite, nous recourions à luy en nous hastant, et n'attendant point du iourd'huy à demain. Voila pour un item. La seconde est, que nous y venions avec prieres, nous condamnans en nous fautes afin d'obtenir pardon et merci de luy. La troisieme c'est que nos oraisons ne soyent point faites en hypocrisie: mais que nous apportions un coeur droit et pur…Mais sur tout sachans que Dieu nous convie, que nous venions à luy, voire de matin: et puis que ce soit y apportans un coeur pur et droit pour le supplier qu'il nous pardonne nos fautes: et qu'à l'exemple de David (Pseau 51:4) nous luy requerions qu'il nous nettoye de toutes nos macules, comme il faut que nous soyons lavez par luy, afin que nous puissions nous presenter devant sa face en telle pureté comme il commande." Sermon 30 Job 8:1–6, *CO*33:380–382.

11 Does Calvin mean that he has deep affection for all the psalmists: David, Asaph, Heman, Solomon, the sons of Korah, Moses, Ethan the Ezrahite and other unknown writers? It is not clearly stated but the psalmists do get positive comments from Calvin. He states in the comment on Ps(s) 1:1, "Haec (ut nuper attigi) praecipua est sententia, bene semper fore piis Dei cultoribus qui assidue in eius lege proficere student." Ps(s) 1:1 *CO*31:37.

12 "Quam varias ac splendidas opes contineat hic thesaurus, verbis assequi difficile est: equidem quidquid dicturus sum dignitate longe inferius fore scio. Sed quia praestat gustum aliquem tantae utilitatis vel tenuem dare lectoribus, quam prorsus de ea tacere: breviter attingere licebit, quod rei magnitudo non patitur plane explicare." Author's Preface, *CO*31:15.

the Book of Psalms 'an Anatomy of all the Parts of the Soul',[13] and reinforces that the Book of Psalms is like a '*speculum*' and that the images reflected "*in speculo*"[14] constitute an analysis of human emotions. These emotions certainly belong to David, the principal author of the Book of Psalms, but quite possibly they bear some relationship to Calvin's emotions created by the difficulties he encountered during the Reformation.[15]

Calvin seldom writes in any of his works about his conversion to the evangelical movement, or about his religious faith. Nevertheless, in the preface to Calvin's *Commentarius in librum Psalmorum*, he shares his own personal testimony in some detail.[16] In addition, Calvin also discusses David's life situation and while he acknowledges there are resemblances in their lives, he also recognizes that as a person he falls short of equalling David.[17] In terms of personal qualities, Calvin aspires to attain the same standard as David when facing life's difficulties, but he admits there is no way that he can fully compare himself to David. Calvin humbly says that his personality is far from approaching David's in terms of conscience and virtues.[18] Although Calvin does not want to steal any of David's glory, he does see himself in David, especially in David's life encounters. For instance, when he

---

13 "Librum hunc non abs re vocare soleo ἀνατομήν omnium animae partium: quando nullum in se affectum quisquam reperiet cuius in hoc speculo non reluceat imago." CO31:15, Jas 1:23. Also quoted in Sujin Pak, *The Judaizing Calvin: Sixteenth-Century Debates over the Messianic Psalms* (New York: Oxford University Press, 2010), 5.

14 CO31:15.

15 "Sed quando haec Davidis fuit conditio, ut de populo suo bene meritus gratis tamen exosus multis esset, sicuti Psal. 69:5 queritur: Se solvisse quod non rapuerat: mihi non levi solatio fuit, dum gratuitis eorum odiis impetor, quorum officiis sublevari me decebat, ad tale tamque praeclarum exemplar me formare. Atque etiam ad Psalmos intelligendos non parvo mihi adiumento fuit haec peritia, ne velut in regione incognita peregrinarer." Author's Preface, CO31:33.

16 See also Heiko A. Oberman, "Subita Conversio: The Conversion of John Calvin", in Oberman and others (eds), *Reformiertes Erbe*, vol. 2, edited by Heiko A. Oberman et al (Zürich: Theologischer, Verlag, 1993), 279–295.; William J. Bouwsma, *John Calvin: A Sixteen-Century Portrait* (USA: Oxford University Press, 1987); Alexandre Ganoczy and Joseph Lortz. *Le Jeune Calvin: Genese Et Evolution De Sa Vocation Reformatrice* (Wiesbaden: Franz Steiner Verlag GMBH, 1966); Bruce Gordon, *Calvin* (New Haven: Yale University Press, 2011).

17 "Et quum inter eos praecipuus sit David, ut eius querimonias de intestinis ecclesiae malis plenius cognoscerem, mihi non parum profuit, eadem quae ipse deplorat aut similia perpessum esse ac domesticis ecclesiae hostibus. Neque enim, quamvis ab eo longissime distem, imo ad multas quibus excelluit virtutes aegre lenteque adspirans contariis vitiis adhuc laborem: si quid tamen mihi cum ipso commune est, conferre piget. Ergo quamvis inter legenda fidei, patientiae, ardoris, zeli, integritatis documenta merito innumeros mihi gemitus dissimilitudo expresserit..." Author's Preface, CO31:19, 21.

18 "...magnopere tamen profuit, quasi in speculo cernere tum vocationis meae exordia, tum continuum functionis cursum: ut quidquid praestantissimus ille rex ac propheta pertulit, mihi ad imitationem fuisse propositum certius agnoscerem." Author's Preface, CO31:21.

compares his divine calling to David's, he identifies some similarities,[19] where he considers that he resembles a young David in terms of the nature of the original plans designed by their fathers.[20]

Calvin embraces the similarities between himself and David. Heiko Oberman argues that Calvin, after his sudden conversion, sees himself as a prophet for the Church as implied in his commentary on Psalms.[21] Jon Balserak asserts that Calvin does not elaborate the nature of the prophetic office in *Commentarius in librum Psalmorum*, but instead does so in the exposition of the Books of the Minor Prophets.[22] Balserak argues that Calvin identifies himself as one of the Minor Prophets[23] because 'Calvin believed himself to be God's mouthpiece'.[24] Hence, according to his preface to Psalms, what did God call Calvin to accomplish?

Although Calvin does not directly say that God calls him to be a prophet in the Preface to the commentary on Psalms, he does assert that he is called to be a preacher and a minister of the gospel.[25] He also thinks that he is in the position to accept this offer as 'God has reckoned him worthy of being invested'[26] in, thus Calvin is certain that God has chosen him because of God's confidence in him. Calvin believes that his relationship with God is exceptional, and he finds similarities between his suffering and David's adversity, so when Calvin speaks of David facing life's agonies, he is often speaking of himself.[27] For example, David was banished

---

19 "Conditio quidem mea quanto sit inferior, dicere nihil attinet. Verum, sicuti ille a caulis ovium ad summam imperii dignitatem evectus est, ita me Deus ab obscuris tenuibusque principiis extractum, hoc tam honorifico munere dignatus est, ut evangelii praeco essem ac minister. Theologiae me pater tenellum adhuc puerum destinaverat. Sed quum videret legum scientiam passim augere suos cultores opibus, spes illa repente eum impulit ad mutandum consilium." Ibid.

20 Gordon, *Calvin*, 35.

21 "Calvin sees himself as a prophet and Oberman affirms that his *'subita conversione'* is not a private affair but an act of the Church, which reveals God's calling on individuals." Heiko A. Oberman, 'Subita Conversio: The Conversion of John Calvin', in Oberman and others (eds), *Reformiertes Erbe*, 281.

22 Jon Balserak, *John Calvin as Sixteenth-Century Prophet* (Oxford: Oxford University Press, 2014), 76.

23 Ibid., 125.

24 Ibid., 96, 182.

25 "Verum, sicuti ille a caulis ovium ad summam imperii dignitatem evectus est, ita me Deus ab obscuris tenuibusque principiis extractum, hoc tam honorifico munere dignatus est, ut evangelii praeco essem ac minister." Author's Preface, CO31:21.

26 Author's Preface, CO31:21. Also in Calvin, *Commentary on Psalms*-Volume 1, 25.

27 "Hence, when Calvin speaks of David, he is often speaking of himself. This circumstance opens the door to a rich source of information about Calvin. From the remark of Calvin quoted above it is no wonder that this biographical information is most of all to be found in the Psalms written by David." Herman J. Selderhuis, *Calvin's Theology of the Psalms* (Grand Rapids, MI: Baker Academic, 2007), 32.

from Jerusalem and his life was threatened first by Saul and later by his son,[28] so like David, Calvin was forced to flee. Calvin's afflictions and difficulties came from all directions, including from his allies. First, he fled France and settled in Geneva, but later he was expelled from this city, before returning to it several years later.

In his years as a fugitive, Calvin stresses that by following David's footsteps, he experienced great consolation.[29] In addition to the similarities of their young lives and the resemblance of their relationship with God, their life encounters are also very similar, in that Calvin followed the '*exemplum Davidis*' closely. Yet what is so special about David?

The '*exemplum Davidis*' during difficult times

Providence concerns the creator and creation, and while the content of the Book of Psalms is about God and God's people, the doctrine of *providentia Dei* is one of the main themes of this Book.[30] Calvin uses the Book of Psalms to explain his theological views concerning *providentia Dei* and he recommends that Christians read the Book of Psalms and follow David's faith in order to face life's problems, especially when dealing with disaster.[31] There are many comments in *Commentarius in librum Psalmorum* that Calvin clearly makes to illustrate David as a great and faithful servant. In the comments of Psalms 3, 4, and 6 for example, Calvin describes David's faithfulness in his attitudes towards despair, adversity, and repentance.

In Psalm 3:2, Calvin stresses that '*exemplum Davidis*' reminds the faithful to listen to God when they are driven to despair and that they should be assured of His promise of salvation.[32] In the argument of Psalm 4, Calvin states that '*exemplum Davidis*' teaches the importance of meditating upon God's promises when weighed

---

28 Ps(s) 126:2, CO32:318.

29 In the Latin edition, Calvin uses a double negative to describe David's influence on him: is no small consolation,' In the French edition, Calvin firmly asserts that David gives him wonderful reliefs. "...quum mihi suis vestigiis viam monstraret David, non parum inde solatii me fuisse expertum." Author's Preface, CO31:27; cf. "...qu'en considerant tout le discours de la vie de David, il me sembloit qu'à chacun pas il me monstroit le chemin, et que cela m'a este un merveilleux soulageuent." Author's Preface, CO31:28

30 Selderhuis, *Calvin's Theology of the Psalms*, 89.

31 "David is often presented to his readers as an example, and from Calvin's choice of his words it is indeed clear that David is an admirable model. All of the faithful can learn a great deal from this king." Ibid., 33.

32 "Docet igitur suo exemplo David, quamvis una voce totus mundus nos ad desperationem impellat, Deum unum potius audiendum esse, ac spem salutis ab eo promissae semper esse intus fovendam: et quia animas nostras confodere tentant impii, precibus esse confirmandas." Ps(s) 3:2, CO31:53.

down by adversity.[33] These two kinds of perceptual practices: listening and meditating, are suggested by Calvin to believers so that by following these practices they might understand the promise of divine providence. In Psalm 4:2, this promise is shown, and 'exemplum Davidis' teaches believers that although their uprightness might be misunderstood, the ones who accuse them await God's judgement,[34] for God will judge the world's righteousness with His own justice.

In Psalm 6, Calvin suggests the congregation to follow 'exemplum Davidis' in dealing with afflictions. David does not grumble about adversities because he has a special understanding of his afflictions and that is why he does not complain to God as if He were his enemy.[35] David sees life's suffering as a reparation for his sins[36] and therefore with this thought of 'I deserve a judgment', he can actively invoke honest confession and earnest prayers to God for His forgiveness.[37] David knows that he will be justly punished by God but as soon as he confesses his sins, he asks God not to deal with him in His justice because he is afraid of God's wrath.[38] David prays for God's mercy, forgiveness of sin, and a restoration of a favourable relationship with Him.[39] Although Calvin does not say directly that the life agonies of the faithful are the result of sin, this inference can be drawn from the incidents David encountered and he feels that he deserves a judgement. That is the reason Calvin clearly exhorts the faithful to have a humble attitude when dealing with suffering and this is the same attitude they should show, when they ask for God's pardon for the evil deeds they committed. David shows this attitude, and when David asks for judgement for

---

33 "Itaque suo exemplo nos docet, quoties res adversae urgent, vel extremae angustiae premunt, meditandas esse promissiones Dei, quibus spes salutis ostenditur ut hoc clypeo obiecto omnes tentationum motus perrumpere liceat." Argumentum, Ps(s) 4, *CO*31:57.

34 "Ergo iustitia pro bona causa capitur, cuius testem Deum constituens David conqueritur homines sibi malevolos esse et iniquos: suoque exemplo nos docet, si quando non appareat coram mundo nostra integritas, non decere tamen nos animis frangi, quia in coelo est vindex noster." Ps(s) 4:2, *CO*31:58.

35 "Non enim expostulat cum Deo, quasi infestus saeviat absque causa..." Ps(s) 6:2, *CO*31:74. Whereas for Calvin's Job, sometimes he talks as if God was his adversary.

36 "Sed quia saepe fit ut homines, dum coguntur sentire iratum sibi esse Deum, potius ad impias querimonias prosiliant, quam se ipsos incusent, ac sua peccata: notandum est, Davidem non simpliciter quidquid sustinet malorum Deo ascribere, sed fateri iustam rependi mercedem suis peccatis." Ps(s) 6:2, *CO*31:74.

37 "Non enim expostulat cum Deo, quasi infestus saeviat absque causa: sed arguendo et castigandi partes ei tribuens, tantum optat poenis statui modum, quibus verbis declarat iustum esse scelerum ultorem. Caeterum, ubi confessus est iure se corripi, summum ius vel rigorem deprecatur." Ibid.

38 "Neque enim poenam omnino refugit, quod iniquum esset, atque ei quoque noxium magis esset quam utile: sed tantum iram Dei exhorret, quae interitum peccatoribus minatur." Ibid.

39 "Nos vero quoties rebus adversis prememur, discamus, exemplo Davidis, ad hoc remedium confugere ut Deo reconciliemur: quia minime sperandum est ut nobis bene sit ac prospere, nisi ipso favente. Unde sequitur nunquam defore malorum congeriem donec peccata nobis remittat." Ibid.

the ungodly who inflicted him, he is in fact asking God for the forgiveness of his own sins.[40] David cries for divine righteousness indirectly and fatherly love directly but the merciful God has granted him both.[41] In respect of this behaviour, Calvin focuses on David's willingness to repent rather than on his sin.

It is certainly unquestionable that David's sin of adultery is not a model to follow. Nevertheless, Calvin treats this repented sinner in a very special way. Not only does Calvin not despise David's fall, but when commenting on Psalm 51, he also uses distinctive positive wording to describe this incident and David's repentance.[42] These favourable words include: 'pray daily', 'divine worship', 'conforming his life to law', and 'having fear of God'.[43] The reason for Calvin's positive attitude towards David's repentance is the same view of fear that he shares with David. Calvin stresses that the act of asking for God's pardon stems from fearing God. If people enjoy committing sins, they will provoke God's wrath, and then God will severely punish them. Therefore, if they fear God, they should humbly admit their transgressions before God and then, repent.[44]

In the discussion on Psalm 6:1, Calvin does not focus on David's sin but David's willingness to confess his sin to God, for David fears the Lord. The positive language used by Calvin is stronger in his comments on Psalm 51:3 than his *Argumentum* at the beginning of Psalm 51, showing that Calvin truly sees 'fearing God' as the first perceptual virtue the faithful should possess before asking for God's pardon. For example, Calvin affirms in Psalm 51:3 that the prayer is 'a deep inward feeling', 'said in keenest anguish', and 'different from a hypocrite'.[45] Calvin's heart-felt appre-

---

40 "Quamvis malum forte ab hominibus inflictum esset, prudenter David sibi cum Deo negotium esse reputat." Ibid., *CO*31:73.

41 "Dicitur quidem irasci Deus peccatoribus, quoties illis poenas infligit, sed improprie: quia non modo aliquam gratiae suae dulcedinem aspergit, quae dolorem mitiget, sed poenas temperans, et clementer manum suam sustinens, se illis propitium esse demonstrat." Ibid., *CO*31:74.

42 "Neque tamen putandum est, sic caruisse omni sensu, quin Deum in genere agnosceret mundi iudicem: quotidie precaretur: nec modo se exerceret in eius cultu, sed vitam quoque et officia sua ad legis normam exigere studeret. Sciamus ergo, non omni Dei timore fuisse penitus vacuum, sed excaecatum in una specie, ut sensum irae Dei perversis blanditiis sopiret." Argument, Ps(s) 51, *CO*31:508.

43 Calvin, *Commentary on Psalms*-Volume 2, Argument, Ps(s) 51, 239.

44 "Tunc ergo serio a Deo petimus ut nobis ignoscat, dum scelerum atrocitas oculis nostris se ingerens, horrorem simul incutit. Unde sequitur, quamdiu sibi indulgent homines, magis in se accendere Dei vindictam, ut severius ipsos puniat. Ideo discamus, non modo ore nos damnare, sed rigidum et formidabile examen habere de peccatis nostris, si cupimus a Deo absolvi." Ps(s) 51:5, *CO*31:510.

45 "Neque enim David se apud homines fateri peccata dicit, sed intus sentire, et quidem non sine diro cruciatu: quum hypocritae a tergo secure proiiciant, vel prava oblivione sepeliant quidquid vitiorum eos pungit." Ibid. Cf. Calvin, *Commentary on Psalms*-Volume 2, Ps(s) 51:3, 242.

ciation[46] is dedicated to David's confession of the plurality of his sins.[47] He values David's consciousness about the sins he has committed and David's knowledge of his offence against God, knowing he will be under God's judgement because of these sinful acts. Calvin believes that the fear of the Lord moves David to long for God's forgiveness so badly that a state of peace is just insufficient.[48] It seems that David prefers to be in a fearful state so that he is always aware not to sin against God.[49] Because David is constantly in this state, he also continuously prays for God's pardon.

The beginning of this section argues that David is more concerned about his sins being forgiven by God rather than seeing the judgment of his enemies, because he believes that his suffering is the result of his sin. Intrinsically, David also wants deliverance from his sufferings,[50] however, he considers that the urge to ask for God's forgiveness is a lot greater and therefore he desperately prays for the restoration of his favour with God.[51] The original Latin does not have the meaning of "favour" but James Anderson (translator in 1571) adds this for his own understanding.[52] This addition is perceptive as in some places in Calvin's *Commentary on the Book of Psalms*, Calvin stresses that David desperately wants to resume his close relationship with God.[53] The profound supplication expressed in Psalm 51 moves Calvin, and

---

46 "Fear plays an important part in Calvin's theology..." Gordon, *Calvin*, 35.

47 "Ac iterum notandus est in Peccatis pluralis numerus. Quanquam enim ex uno fonte omnia manabant, multiplex tamen eius culpa erat, quod adulterio adiunxerat perfidiam et crudelitatem: nec unum hominem modo prodiderat vel paucos, sed totum exercitum, pro salute ecclesiae Dei pugnantem. Itaque non abs re in uno scelere multas species agnoscit." Ps(s) 51:3, *CO*31:510.

48 "Nam utcunque se ad tempus demulceant qui neglectis promissionibus, conscientiae terrores pacare vel effugere conantur, certum est caecis tormentis intus semper uri. Verum utcunque illi obtorpeant, quisquis serio Dei timore tangitur, non aliud inquietudinis suae remedium optabit quam auditionem istam laetitiae, dum scilicet promittit Deus, abolito nostro reatu, se nobis esse propitium." Ps(s) 51:9, *CO*31:516.

49 "Porro, quum sancto prophetae et praestantissimo regi obrepserit tam bruta socordia, nemo est qui non ad eius exemplum expavescere debeat. Quod autem ad prophetae vocem statim perculsus est, ac deposita omni contumacia docilem se ac morigerum praebuit, hinc colligimus non fuisse exstinctum in eius animo pietatis sensum: quia non tam facile nec subito erumperet in illam vocem, Peccavi Domino, quid faciam? 2 Sam 12:13 nisi retinuisset aliquod pietatis semen, licet absconditum. Docemur autem hoc exemplo, non esse exspectandum, ubi peccavimus, dum e coelo tonet Deus, sed placide et libenter obtemperandum esse eius prophetis, quorum ore ad poenitentiam nos invitat." Ps(s) 51:2, *CO* 31:508–509.

50 Ps(s) 3:7–8, *CO*31:56–57.

51 "Deinde quia aeternam abdicationem meritus erat, ut merito spoliandus esset omnibus spiritus sancti donis, sollicite precatur in integrum restitui." Argumentum, Ps(s) 51, *CO*31:508.

52 "But being persuaded that he was not utterly cut off from the favour of God, and that God's choice of him to be king remained unchanged, he encourages himself to hope for a favourable issue to his present trials." Calvin, *Commentary on Psalms*-Volume 1, Ps(s) 3:3, 59.

53 For example: Ps(s) 7:3, *CO*31:80 & Ps(s) 7:8, *CO*31:83.

he affirms that David sets an example for all people who have sinned against God,[54] and that they should pray, like David, to ask for His forgiveness.

In contrast, the exposition of Psalm 51 in Calvin's sermons on 2 Samuel 12:13 suggests that Calvin's presentation of David is not as positive as he is in *Commentarius in librum Psalmorum*. From the year 1562, (seven years after he preached the sermons on the Book of Job and five years after he commented the Book of Psalms) Calvin preached 87 sermons on the Book of 2 Samuel, in which a total of six sermons were about David's adultery,[55] and five of them are about the condemnation of David's heavy sin. In the first four sermons, Calvin ironically states that believers should learn from 'David's example to go in the opposite direction'.[56] The last sermon is an exception. This sermon was supposed to be on 2 Samuel 12:13 but Calvin refers to David in Psalm 51 rather than in the Book of 2 Samuel, and David's image is more positively described. Calvin shows a deep appreciation for David because of two reasons: David confesses his sin, and he is not a hypocrite.

In this sermon, Calvin on one hand praises David because he is 'silent'[57] in the sense that he does not defend himself when he is condemned. Calvin sees this silence as a gesture of humility. Also, Calvin reproaches the papists' use of impressive words when confessing, and he despises this pretence.[58] As in *Sermons sur le livre de Job* discussed in the previous chapter, here in Calvin's sermons on 2 Samuel, he also warns his congregation not to follow the ostentatious prayers of the papists.[59] After many years of preaching sermons on Job, Calvin still showed enormous concern about the hypocritical prayer. That might be one of the reasons

---

54 "Hoc ergo simpliciter voluit David, efficax et ratum in se fore quod Deus populo suo testatus fuerat." Ps(s) 51:7, *CO*31:515.

55 John Calvin, *Sermons on 2 Samuel Chapters 1–13*, translated by Douglas Kelly (Edinburgh: The Banner of Truth Trust, 1992), 476–564.

56 "Quand donc nous voyons que nous sommes si enclins et adonnez a ces deux vices, apprenons, a l'exemple de Dauid, d'aller a l'opposite, cest ascauoir d'esleuer (incontinent que nous aurons failli) les yeux en haut; non pas auec orgueil et presomption, mais pour estre abbatu puis apres, comme il est requis." Johannes Calvin, *Supplementa Calviniana Sermons inédits* Volumen I (Neukirchen Kreis Moers: Verlag der Buchhandlung des Erziehungsvereins, 1961), Sermon 33, 2 Sam 11:5–13, 287.

57 "Ainsi Dauid pouuoit faire du reuesche. Quand, de son bon gré, il est ainsi abbatu, c'est qu'il a tousiours sa bouche close, c'est plus que s'il parloit beaucoup...Ainsi donc la confession de Dauid a plus de vertu au silence, qu'elle n'auoit point en l'impression des motz...Mais le contraire est en Dauid; en se taisant, il donne liberté au Prophete de le condamner tant qu'il voudra, et est là pour souffrir confusion et honte; quand chacun luy cracheroit au visage, il scait bien qu'il le merite." Ibid., Sermons 37, 2 Sam 12:13, 321.

58 "Car nous verrons ordinairement les hypocrites qui se confesseront, afin que nul n'adiouste mot puis apres." Ibid.

59 "Car en la Papauté, encores qu'ilz viennent se frapper en leur poictrine et quilz voysent a vn prestre, pour auoir la croix sur le dos, si est-ce quilz ne vueillent point estre repris, mais qu'on aille comme par dessus et qu'on ne face que leur chatouiller les oreilles au lieu de leur gratter la roigne." Ibid.

Calvin switched to David's example in Psalms 51 to exhort the church believers to pray with a humble heart, when he was in fact preaching 2 Samuel 12.

David's prayers are highly regarded in this sermon on 2 Samuel 12:13 but the emphasis is not on the emotional expression of David's fear of God. Calvin is concerned about how believers deal with sin.[60] David knows that he sinned against God and his sin was so serious that it could never be justified in God's righteousness. Therefore, he asks for God's pardon according to His goodness. It seems that in this sermon, Calvin stresses a two-fold petition from the human point of view. Firstly, the believer confesses sins honestly and continuously pleas for mercy. Secondly, God's sovereignty in judgement and salvation is still the primary cause and to a certain extent, it is the same as David's hope in Psalm 51, where David does not ask for a fair judgement for his enormous sin as he deserves everlasting condemnation, but he prays for God's mercy, and God grants him both eternal salvation and earthly blessings.

Although Calvin uses different approaches to interpret Psalm 51 and 2 Samuel 12, he aims to emphasise that David is aware of his sin. Does this mean that David is in a state of penance without wavering when he constantly fears God and continuously prays to Him? In Calvin's sermons on 2 Samuel 13, he argues that the origin of the horrendous incidents that happened to David's sons and daughter is because of his free-minded decision of marrying multiple wives,[61] and his undisciplined life.[62] That means, David has not stopped sinning regardless of his fear of God's wrath. Therefore, God chastises David using His rod (punishment) to compel him to confess his sins.[63] God's life chastisement given to David is indeed His delayed punishment for the sin he committed in his life.

Calvin sees David as an exceptional biblical figure from the way how God calls David and how David deals with sufferings and sin, hence Calvin depicts David as

---

60 "Et ainsi faut il que nous soyons tousiours attentifz et soigneux a prier Dieu qu'il luy plaise nous purger en telle sorte, que ce, en quoy nous l'auons offensé, soit effacé et qu'il continue tellement sa grace en nous, que nous cheminions en sa crainte, iusques a ce que nous ayons paracheué nostre course, afin qu'il soit purement serui et honnoré de nous, et soyons du tout siens." Ibid., 328. Cf. "C'est en somme pour cognoistre qu'il estoit maudit et qu'il seroit retranché de toute esperance de salut, sinon que Dieu luy fist merci." Ibid., 326.

61 "Et cependant, que nous facions nostre proffit de ce chastiment qui est aduenu a Dauid. Car il s'est donné trop de liberté, voire sans fin et sans cesse de prendre telle multitude de femmes, aussi le salaire luy est rendu et le payement, Dieu l'a puni." Sermons 41, 2 Sam 13:1–14, 364.

62 "...car a la fin, Dauid permet a sa fille, souz ombre d'aller apprester viande a Amnon, qu'elle soit corrompue." Ibid., 359.

63 "Et ainsi notons la cause, pourquoy Dieu a ainsi puni Dauid, combien qu'il luy eust pardonné son offense...si est-ce qu'encores faut il qu'il prenne les verges en main, pour nous chastier, et que, par ce moyen la, nous soyons domptez, que nous soyons tant plus incitez a nous rendre deuant luy comme coulpables, pour obtenir pardon de noz pechez..." Ibid., 356.

godly. Selderhuis's book titled *Calvin's Theology of the Psalms* highlights the importance of relating Calvin's theology to his biography in the historical context.[64] In view of this, one can acknowledge that David's temperament and his life experiences affect Calvin's theology. For instance, Selderhuis suggests that 'David is a God-given mirror in whom we can see what must incite us to prayer and what must move us to praise him when he answers our prayer'.[65] According to Calvin's interpretation, David's prayer is an indispensable part of *providentia Dei*.

Providentia Dei

Calvin's *Commentarius in librum Psalmorum* was published in 1557, and in the same year, Calvin responded to the calumnies from Castellio, which was not published until 1558.[66] From 1555 to 1559, the Psalms were studied at the Genevan church where Calvin ministered. It was around the time Calvin preached the *Sermons sur le livre de Job* in 1555 and when he was in the process of finishing his 1559 *Institutes*, that Calvin dedicated himself to teach and comment upon the Book of Psalms.

From *Sermons sur le livre de Job*, to *Commentarius in librum Psalmorum*, to the 1559 *Institutes*, Calvin consistently uses the definitions of *providentia Dei* that he formulated in *De aeterna Dei praedestinatione* 1552[67] to help him to preach, and to comment upon and to defend his position against his opponents. In *Sermons sur le livre de Job*, Calvin focuses on God's general and special providence in His goodness, power, wisdom, and justice. In the *Commentarius in librum Psalmorum*, he dedicates a significant portion to discuss the human role in three kinds of *providentia Dei*: general providence, special providence, and providence for God's Church.

Three kinds of providentia Dei

Calvin identifies three kinds of *providentia Dei*, termed *providentia universalis/ generalis*, *providentia singularis/ peculiaris/ specialis*, and providence for His church. His teachings on the topic are presented in works including disputations, treatises,

---

64 Selderhuis, *Calvin's theology of the Psalms*, 43.

65 Ibid., 23.

66 See chapter 5.

67 "Itaque, ut pro captu rudium crasse agamus, primo loco statuenda est ante oculos generalis mundi gubernatio, qua foventur et vegetantur omnia, ut stet incolumis naturae eorum status." Ioannis Calvini, *De aeterna Dei praedestinatione*, CO8:349. "Nunc in ista speciali providentia, quae currandis singulis Dei operibus privatim excubat..." Ibid., CO8:348. "Ultimo praesidium vere paternum, quo ecclesiam suam tuetur, cui praesentissima Dei ipsius virtus annexa est." Ibid., CO8:349.

commentaries, and sermons. In most of these works, Calvin dedicates a great deal of effort to defending God's sovereignty using the doctrine of *providentia Dei*, responding to the charges from different groups of opponents and some individual theologians or philosophers. In the *Commentarius in librum Psalmorum*, however, this argument is given less weight in a defence of God's sovereignty using the doctrine of *providentia Dei*.[68] Calvin still discusses God's general and special providence which God prepares for the faithful. He still stresses God's sovereignty and human sinfulness clearly, to refute his opponents' claim about God as the watcher from heaven and God as the author of sin, but he also brings readers' attention to the prayer of God's servant.

In addition, Calvin discusses the evidence and experience of God's providence towards His Church, and the final attainment of eternal salvation by His children in the Church community.[69] Furthermore, he emphasises the positive aspects of the Christian life in respect of the teaching in the Book of Psalms. As Sujin Pak has argued, Calvin reads some Psalms in reference to David as the supreme exemplar of Protestant piety,[70] and he also uses Psalms to teach, especially the doctrine of God's providence.[71] That is, Calvin adopts a particular form of biblical exegesis to support his theological advocacy. This can be seen in his interpretation of *providentia Dei* when he preaches the sermons on Job. However, Pak has not done any analysis on David's prayer in relation to different providential situations. The following discusses the role of David's prayer in three kinds of providence.

---

68 "Itaque non modo simplex docendi ratio ubique a me servata est, sed quo longius abesset omnis ostentatio, a refutationibus ut plurimum abstinui, ubi liberior patebat plausibilis iactantiae campus. Neque unquam contrarias sententias attigi, nisi ubi periculum erat ne tacendo dubios ac perplexos relinquerem lectores. Nec me latet quanto suaviores multissint illecebrae, ex multiplici congerie sugerere materiam ambitiosi splendoris: sed nihil pluris fuit, quam ecclesiae aedificationi consulere." Author's Preface, *CO*31:33, 35.

69 "Atque adeo quidquid ad nos animandos facere potest, ubi orandus est Deus, in hoc libro monstratur…Neque id modo, sed per haesitationes, metus, trepidationes nitamur tamen ad orandum, donec solatii nos non poeniteat…Et multis in locis animadvertere licet servos Dei ita fluctuantes inter orandum, ut alternis vicibus fere oppressi palmam arduo conatu obtineant…Quia tamen quae ad rationem rite precandi valent toto opera sparsa reperientur…Nusquam magis luculenta tum singularis erga ecclesiam Dei beneficentiae, tum omnium eius operum praeconia leguntur, nusquam tot narrantur liberationes, vel tam splendide ornantur paternae erga nos ipsius providentiae et curae documenta…ut nihil prorsus desit ad scientiam aeternae salutis." Ibid., *CO*31:17, 19.

70 Pak, *The Judaizing Calvin: Sixteenth-Century Debates over the Messianic Psalms*, 78.

71 Ibid., 127.

General providence and prayer

God created the world according to His own will and He continues to guide, rule, and maintain His creations in the way He fashioned them in general providence. In this government of the material universe, David sees the wonderful power and glory of God in creation.[72] As Sung Sup Kim asserts, the operation of universal providence (meaning general providence), '*operation universelle*' is the order of nature,[73] and God's attention to order in creation reveals His general providence in action for humanity.

Susan Schreiner suggests that the order of nature for Calvin is not to be understood on the hierarchical level but rather as a stabilizing, regulating, and continuing force.[74] In addition, she emphasises that Calvin speaks of a strong doctrine of creation out of nothing establishing providence as the ground of creation's dependence on God.[75] Kim and Schreiner talk about Calvin's interpretation of *providentia Dei* with reference to God's sovereignty and that God intervenes, maintains, and preserves.[76] This assertion, showing that God continuously guides and actively preserves in His general providence, is one of Calvin's most important theological convictions.

Calvin unreservedly rejects the concept of a distant God, a teaching promoted by the Epicureans, who believe that God as a *primum agens* (source of movement) created this world but is a distant God who sits idly in the sky, observing incidents which simply happen by chance. God's judgement seems to depend on human will and thus the world is left to the organisation of secondary causality.[77] Calvin, however, refutes the idea that God is only a source of movement as implied by the

---

72 "Proponit quidem sibi David ante oculos miram Dei virtutem et gloriam in toto mundi opificio et gubernatione: sed hanc partem leviter tantum perstringens, in consideratione summae erga nos bonitatis insistit." Ps(s) 8:1, *CO* 31:88.

73 *Contre la secte des Libertins, CO*7:186; John Calvin, *Treatises Against the Anabaptists and Against the Libertines* (Grand Rapids, MI: Baker Book House, 1982), 242–43. Also quoted in Sung-Sup Kim, *Deus Providebit-Calvin, Schleiermacher, and Barth on the Providence of God* (Minneapolis: Fortress Press, 2014), 27.

74 "Calvin did not adopt Augustine's rather 'fluid' hierarchical schemes in his understanding of the order of nature because Augustine equated God's immutability with supreme existence above the realm of time and change. Calvin on the other hand, interpreted divine immutability in terms of reliability in nature and salvation." Susan Schreiner, *The Theater of His Glory* (Grand Rapids, MI: Baker Books, 1995), 22.

75 Ibid., 22.

76 Kim agrees with Schreiner and states, "The world, especially after the fall, is in constant peril and needs to be preserved by God every moment." Kim, *Deus Providebit*, 28. Cf. "This disorder is only be rectified by God's providence in his active power of preservation." Schreiner, *The Theater of His Glory*, 29.

77 Calvin discusses this topic briefly in Ps(s) 10:5–6, *CO*31:112.

term *primum agens*[78] and uses the doctrine of general providence to argue against the charge of God's passivity. Hence, general providence cannot be just an initiative power by God as God's determination is involved, and it is impossible that God only watches, without any knowledge of what is going to happen. While it is important to understand that God has a sovereign role, in Psalm 8, Calvin's focus is not on defending God as an active ruler for a disputation context. Rather, in the context of human spiritual growth, Calvin considers humankind as a secondary cause has a part in general providence.

General providence in Psalm 8

Calvin sees David as a wonderful teacher of theology and doctrine, because David expounds the doctrine of God's providence in Psalm 8 in an exceptional way so that when the faithful read this Psalm, they are stirred to celebrate and praise the undeserved kindness of God.[79] God's kindness and goodness cannot be comprehended by fallen humankind, but through God's action in His power on earth, the faithful can understand part of this process.[80] God's creation is a mirror and if human beings contemplate it, they will see God's glory in His providence. In Psalm 8:1, Calvin speaks of David's exclamation[81] concerning God's creation because David has a lack of words to best describe God's wondrous works.

Regardless of David's limitation in words, he still has an urge to celebrate the incomprehensible goodness which God has lavished upon him, and Calvin considers that David's exclamation is a contemplation of God's greatness using a '*tota humani ingenii facultas*'.[82] The celebration is dedicated to God through David's tongue, body, and mind, in that his whole body uses to praise His providence. While David does not know how to use words to admire God's work, Calvin asserts that the Holy Spirit guides David's tongue to deliver the right speech, so that he is not merely content with the benefits God has given him, but rather David invests his whole

---

78 Schreiner states, "Calvin's polemics against the identification of God as a source of movement, then, may be directed against the rationalist movement influenced by Averroes. The belief that God's immediate creative and causal activity was restricted to the production of the first separate intelligence resulted in the denial that God knew or governed singulars and specific human action." Schreiner, *The Theater of His Glory*, 20.

79 Pak, *The Judaizing Calvin: Sixteenth-Century Debates over the Messianic Psalms*, 85–86.

80 "Nam hoc ad opera aut virtutes ex quibus cognoscitur, potius quam ad essentiam referri debet." Ps(s) 8:1, *CO*31:88.

81 "Mirum tamen est cur ab exclamatione incipiat, quum res ipsa prius narrari soleat, quam extolli eius magnitudo." ibid.

82 "Nam hoc epiphonema quo usus est David declarat, ubi intenta ad hanc cogitationem fuerit tota humani ingenii facultas, longe infra subsistere." Ibid.

effort in pursuing a holy and pious life.[83] This celebration is a spiritual appreciation of *providentia Dei* by humankind.

When Calvin comments on Psalm 8:9 which has the exact same wording as 8:1, he continues to reinforce his argument about the pursuit of the faithful, but God is the guide for this pursuit. God shows grace and fatherly love towards His people despite them being almost entirely ruined by sin.[84] This can be seen in how God graciously endows humankind with food and clothing, and how God has honoured them in *providentia Dei*. The reason humankind can enjoy God's providence is because of God's grace.[85] In the commentary for Psalm 8:1 and 8:9, Calvin describes the roles of the primary and secondary causes in *providentia Dei*: regardless of human sinfulness, the gracious God demonstrates His actions in this world in order that His people might enjoy God's providence.

Calvin claims that humanity is the mirror which lets us see the glory of God most clearly,[86] and Psalm 8:1 and 8:9 gives a procedure for this observation. God shows His power in His wonderful works in the world and when human beings experience this marvel, they are speechless, so they praise God with their whole body. This is because God's Spirit guides His people to join in God's admirable providence and He also leads them to aspire for everlasting goodness from God. Thus, all of humanity reflects God's glory.

There is an interaction between the divine and the humanity in *providentia Dei*, where humankind has a special role in glorifying God, but Calvin also says that one can observe His glory through 'all the subjects'[87], meaning all of creation, and not by observing humanity alone. Most importantly, Calvin further motivates the faithful not to overly focus on the temporal goodness benefiting life on earth. Although God

---

83 "Adde, quod spiritus sanctus, qui Davidis linguam direxit, non dubium est quin communem hominum torporem in illius persona excitet, ne immensum Dei amorem, et innumera quibus fruuntur beneficia parce tantum et frigide suo more laudent: sed potius nervos omnes intendant ad hoc pietatis exercitium." Ibid.

84 "Huc autem spectat summa, Deum in homine creando specimen immensae erga eum gratiae et plus quam paterni amoris edidisse, quod merito nos omnes reddere debeat attonitos. Iam quamvis hominis defectione conditio illa fere pessum ierit, manere tamen adhuc quasdam illius divinae liberalitatis reliquias, quae ad creandam nobis admirationem sufficiant." Ps(s) 8:9, *CO*31:95

85 "Nemo enim tam hebeti vel tardo est ingenio, qui si aperiat oculos, non videat mirabili Dei providentia fieri ut equi et boves hominibus sua obsequia praebeant: ut ad eosdem vestiendos lanam producant oves, ut iisdem alimentum ex propria carne omne genus animalia suppeditent. Quo magis visibile est dominii huius documentum, quoties vel cibo vescimur, vel fruimur reliquis commodis, divinae gratiae sensu nos magis decet affici. Non ergo simpliciter intelligit David, omnibus Dei operibus praefectum esse hominem, quia se lana et pellibus vestiat, quia animalium carne vescatur quia eorum laborem ad sua commoda applicet: sed tantum demonstrat in hoc spectaculo dominium illud quo ipsum Deus ornavit." Ibid., *CO*31:94–95.

86 Ps(s) 8:1; *CO*31:88. Also quoted in Selderhuis, *Calvin's Theology of the Psalms*, 76.

87 "...quia hoc est maxime illustre speculum in quo perspicere licet eius gloriam." Ps(s) 8:1, *CO*31:88.

gathers them under Christ and blesses them with all His goodness, they should focus on the eternal treasure benefiting their spiritual life in the kingdom of heaven.[88] Humanity's role is shown in two stages: to enjoy God's goodness physically, and to admire His goodness spiritually. Prayer helps to achieve both, and although Calvin does not mention the term prayer here, the act of praise using both body and spirit implies this meaning.

Special providence and prayer

Although God exercises His power over all of creation, as an ultimate judge in general providence, His special providence shows a higher level of care for people.[89] This concerns God's *providentia specialis* throughout human history. However, this divine care is often obscure and is not fully understood or comprehended by people. As with the order of nature, the reason for this obscurity is because of the disturbed order after the fall of Adam.

Calvin gives an objective theological definition of special providence in many of his works, but only in the Preface to *Commentarius in librum Psalmorum*, does he adopt a subjective approach using his own long story[90] to explain the hiddenness of special providence for God's people. Calvin narrates his story in times of affliction when he was a student, a fugitive, a reformer, and a church minister.[91] He describes that when humanity suffers without any reasons, it is intolerable,[92] and yet Calvin confesses in the Preface to *Commentarius in librum Psalmorum* that these common encounters by the faithful are governed by '*arcana Dei providentia*'.[93] Calvin is one of the faithful ones, and his suffering is governed by God's secret providence, but he cannot comprehend this providence. In *Commentarius in librum Psalmorum*, Calvin uses his own and David's testimony to explain the hiddenness in special providence.

---

88 "Esti autem David tantum in temporalibus Dei beneficiis subsidit, nostrum tamen est altius progredi, et inaestimabiles coelestis regni thesauros, quos in Christo explicuit, et quaecunque ad spiritualem vitam pertinent dona, reputare, ut haec consideratio corda nostra ad pietatis studium accendat, nec torpere nos sinat in celebrandis eius laudibus." Ps(s) 8:9, *CO*31:95.

89 Ps(s) 9, *CO*31:99–108.

90 Author's Preface, *CO*31:27.

91 Previously in this chapter, some of Calvin's life's agonies are discussed and they will not be repeated here.

92 "…quin ipsi quoque convicti probrose iaceant: ubi tamen centies purgatus quis fuerit a crimine, absque ulla causa repeti, toleratu acerba est indignitas." Author's Preface, *CO*31:29.

93 "Quia arcana Dei providentia mundum gubernari assero, insurgunt protervi homines, ac Deum hoc modo fieri peccati autorem causantur." Ibid.

Calvin usually uses secret providence in an argumentative sense when resisting those who claim that the doctrine of God's providence implies God to be the author of sin.[94] He affirms that God is not idle, and in His providence, every single incident in the world is under His rule, and in God's hidden providence, he works through Satan and the ungodly.[95] Calvin's argument about God not only permitting but also ruling over everything including sinful acts by using His hidden providence cannot settle the queries from many parties, including other Protestant Reformers[96] because it creates the charge of God being the author of sin.

Melanchthon argued that Calvin's teaching has a resemblance to Stoicism, and he directly referred to Calvin as Zeno, the founder of Stoicism.[97] Calvin's link to the Stoics, however, was not simple and direct,[98] and although he did not align himself with Stoicism, he did concur with much of their affirmation of divine providence. Schreiner argues that in Calvin's eye, the philosophy of Stoicism is superior to Epicureanism,[99] because the Stoics describe the nature of *providentia Dei* in a better way than other philosophical teachings due to their recognition of divine sovereignty. However, in the commentary on Psalms, while Calvin highly regards the Stoics' idea of a total submission to God during affliction,[100] he also

---

94 Refer to Calvin's polemic work such as the 1559 *Institutes*.

95 Calvin, *The Institutes 1559*, 1.17.1, CO2:153–154.

96 Heinrich Bullinger urged Calvin to write a book to make clear that God is not the author of sin because many people were annoyed by Calvin's teaching on predestination. Philip Melanchthon likened the subject of the controversy to Stoic understandings of necessity or fate. Barbara Pitkin, "The Protestant Zeno: Calvin and the Development of Melanchthon's Anthropology," *The Journal of Religion*, vol. 84, no. 3 (July 2004), 345–378.

97 "But see the madness of this age! The Genevan battles over Stoic necessity are such that a certain person who disagreed with Zeno was thrown into prison." Philipp Melanchthon, *Opera quae supersunt omnia*, ed. C.G. Bretschneider and H.E. Bindseil, Corpus Reformatorum, vol. 1–28 (Halle, 1834–52; Brunswick, 1853–60) CR7:930; also quoted in Pitkin, "The Protestant Zeno: Calvin and the Development of Melanchthon's Anthropology," 346.

98 "Nous voudrions montrer que, si l'on prend en compte le mouvement complet des textes de Calvin, les choses sont un peu plus complexes : ni pure adhésion, ni simple rejet, son attitude à l'égard du stoïcisme se présente comme le résultat d''une série de démarcations, dont le dessin entier permet de mieux comprendre la forme spécifique de réception qui est la sienne, et son insertion dans une stratégie philosophique déterminée." Pierre-François Moreau, "Calvin: fascination et crique du stoïcisme", in *Le Stoïcisme au XVI et au XVII siècle – Le retour des philosophies antiques à l'Âge classique*, ed. Pierre-François Moreau (Paris: Albin Michel S.A., 1999), 51–52.

99 "Yet those philosophers who assign the supreme authority to nature are much sounder than those who place fortune in the highest rank." John Calvin, *Commentary on the Book of Daniel*, translated by Thomas Meyers (Grand Rapids, MI: Christian Classics Ethereal Library, 1852), Dan 2:21, CO40:576. Also quoted in Schreiner, *The Theater of His Glory*, 17.

100 "Unde etiam colligimus, verae tolerantiae nihil esse magis adversum, quam altitudinem illam de qua garriunt Stoici: quia non prius vere humiliati censemur, quam dum cordis afflictio coram Deo nos prosternit, ut iacentes erigat." Ps(s) 34:19; CO31:344. Cf. "Et sane haec vera est patientiae ratio,

despises their belief in destiny and their thought of fatalism being a result of God's sovereignty.[101]

The Libertines interpreted Calvin's saying about the 'active ruling' of God wrongly: God is like a tyrant and He has power over everything including wicked deeds. Calvin considered the Libertines as the wicked because they said the above calumny to justify the liberty they requested at church.[102] The Libertines' detraction implies that all things in the world are done by one single Spirit[103] and that God exhibits absolute power in determining everything, including sin. They refute Calvin's idea of suggesting that humankind does not have any part in whatever has happened in this world, and therefore there is no genuine existence of secondary cause even in wicked deeds. Calvin considers that the Libertine's position is calumny, and he strongly refutes their allegation of 'determinism'. To further resist any ideas of God as the author of sin, and God's absolute power, Calvin stresses that there is a positive presence of divine power over all acts or events including evil deeds but since humankind provides secondary causes, they cannot evade responsibility.[104] This idea, now commonly known as divine concurrence, originally emerged in the seventeenth-century and was termed '*concursus*'.[105] Divine concurrence claims that 'the providence of God concurs with all secondary causes and especially with the human will; yet the contingency and liberty of the will remain unimpaired'.[106]

---

non contumaciter resistere rebus adversis (sicuti praefractam duritiem Stoici pro virtute laudarunt) sed nos libenter subiicere Deo..."Ps(s) 94:12, *CO*32:24.

101 "Stoici quum de fato disputant, vel potius balbutiunt, non modo spinosis anfractibus se involvunt et rem ipsam, sed verum principium: quia complexum causarum fingentes, eripiunt Deo mundi gubernacula. Impium hoc figmentum est, causas inter se perplexas nectere, quibus alligatus sit ipse Deus."Ps(s) 105:19, *CO*32:107.

102 "Totis quinque annis, quum nimia potentia instructi essent perversi homines, et pars etiam plebis eorum illecebris corrupta effraenem licentiam appeteret, pro disciplina, tuenda nobis absque intermissione pugnandum fuit." Author's Preface *CO*31:27.

103 *Contre la secte phantastique et furieuse des Libertins qui se nomment spirituelz* 1545 Par I *CO*7:149–248. Also quoted in Schreiner, *The Theater of His Glory*, 18.

104 John Calvin, *The Bondage and the Liberation of the Will: a defense of the Orthodox Doctrine of human Choice Against Pighius*, edited by A.N.S. Lane, translated by G.I. Davies (Grand Rapids, MI: Baker Books, 1996), 2.280; 69.

105 It was not until the seventeenth century, that a threefold distinction of '*conservatio*', '*concursus*' and '*gubernatio*' started to form. Heinrich Heppe, *Reformed Dogmatics Set Out and Illustrated from the Sources*, ed Ernst Bizer, trans. G.T. Thompson (London: Allen, 1950), 256. Also quoted in Kim, *Deus Providebit*, 29.

106 Turretin asserts, "But how these two things can consist with each other, no mortal can in this life perfectly understand. Nor should it seem a cause for wonder, since he has a thousand ways (to us incomprehensible) of concurring with our will, insinuating himself into us and turning our hearts, so that by acting freely as we will, we still do nothing besides the will and determination of God." Francis Turretin, *Institutes of Elenctic Theology Volume 1*, translated by Gorge Musgrave Giser, edited by James T. Dennison (Phillipsburg, NJ: P&R Publishing, c1992–1997), 511.

For Calvin, things seemingly most fortuitous are still subject to God, and nothing happens by chance or by contingency.[107] It is observed that Calvin does not adopt the terms divine conservation, divine concurrence, or divine governance but his interpretation of the interaction between primary and secondary causes bears the meaning of these terms. Human beings, as the secondary cause, have responsibility in the sinful acts and that is the reason why Calvin claims that *providentia Dei* must not be identified with a single divine Spirit which works in all things.[108] Although Calvin discusses the philosophical false teaching when he explains secret providence in his disputations and treatises, it is really not his focus in the commentary on Psalms.

In the Preface to *Commentarius in librum Psalmorum*, Calvin expresses that in God's secret providence, he himself had a sudden conversion and became an obedient servant,[109] caring for his congregation with deep love.[110] He sincerely confesses that he avoids refutations by teaching the truth[111] for the edification of the Church.[112] However, Calvin also makes sure that in this commentary, he explains clearly all the related principles and doctrines to avoid any misunderstanding. Calvin's confession shows that he has determined to move from public debates among non-believers to church pastoral care. In addition, he testifies of God's secret providence in an optimistic way.

From one perspective, it can be claimed that God judges sinners in His secret providence, yet from another perspective, Calvin suggests that the believer is aided by God's secret providence. This is an optimistic expression of secret providence in relation to Calvin's personal experience and the same positive treatment by Calvin is apparent when he comments on David's situation in Psalm 9.

Special providence in Psalm 9

Calvin confirms that David's life history shows God's special providence. In Psalm 8, Calvin suggests that in God's general providence, David enjoys the material benefits with which God endowed him. In Psalm 9, Calvin praises David on a higher level

---

107 Calvin does not like the term 'fortune' although he says that 'fortune' is regulated by a secret providence. The term is not recommended as when people claim that incidents happen because of 'fortune', it is a denial of God's providence. Calvin, *1559 Institutes*, 1.16.6–8, CO2:149–152.

108 Ibid., 1.16.2–3; CO2:145–147.

109 CO31:21.

110 CO31:33, 35.

111 "Itaque non modo simplex docendi ratio ubique a me servata est, sed quo longius abesset omnis ostentatio, a refutationibus ut plurimum abstinui, ubi liberior patebat plausibilis iactantiae campus." CO31:33.

112 CO31:35.

because David did not only receive wonderful benefits from God, but was also the beneficiary of God's special power that is above the ordinary, and so David receives 'those more signal and memorable deliverances'.[113] These are the moments of the execution of God's judgment among the sinners through His secret providence to exemplify His glory.[114] The godly in these situations tend to be pessimistically and passively awaiting judgements to happen. In this passage, Calvin suggests two solutions when humankind gets 'stuck' in God's silence: to trust God's secret providence by faith and also to pray.

Calvin emphasises that God sometimes delays aid for a lengthy period of time because He manifests Himself *tempestive*.[115] However, God succours the faithful at the right time. Calvin encourages readers that when God seems to be taking no notice of His faithful, and does not immediately remedy the evils they face, then by faith the godly might realize His secret providence.[116] Some parts of God's action can be seen in His revelation in this universe as Calvin suggests in Psalm 8.

In the comment on Psalm 9:9, Calvin states that some parts of God's action might be sought by the faithful through invocations, prayer, and by living an upright life.[117] Here, Calvin proposes that a spiritual revelation comes by way of faith, prayer, and a holy life, and he further stresses that these criteria are inseparable. In addition, only the faithful can invoke spiritual revelation as God's secret providence protects them.[118] It is also suggested by some scholars of Calvin studies that '*providentia*

---

113 "Ergo perinde est ac si testetur David se non vulgari modo fuisse a Deo servatum, sed conspicuam illic fuisse De virtutem, quia manum suam supra communem et usitatum ordinem mirabiliter extulerit." Ps(s) 9:1, CO31:97.

114 "Imo quum dissimulat, nec statim medetur malis nostris, fidei sensu apprehendere convenit occultam eius providentiam...dicit enim non ideo tantum regnare, ut sublimis emineat eius maiestas et gloria, sed ut mundum iuste gubernet." Ps(s) 9:6, CO31:99–100.

115 "...rebus vero ita confusis tempestive apparuerit Deus." Ps(s) 9:6, CO31:99.

116 Ibid.

117 "Porro, quamvis Dei nomen multi simpliciter pro Deo accipiunt, ego tamen (ut iam alibi dixi) amplius aliquid exprimi arbitror: nam quia occulta et incomprehensibilis est eius essentia, quatenus se nobis patefacit, maiestas eius in nomine statuitur...Fit autem hoc duobus modis, vel invocatione et precibus, vel studio sancte recteque vivendi." Ps(s) 9:9, CO31:101.

118 "...Deo curae esse res hamanas, continua inquietudine nos vexari necesse erit, sed quia plurimi ad Dei iudicia caecutiunt, profectum hunc David ad solos fideles restringit, et certe ubi nulla est pietas, nullus est operum Dei sensus." Ibid. Cf. "Quanquam David cum illis non disceptat: quin potius recta se ad Deum confert, et machinis illis quae duriter eius animum quatefacere poterant, Dei providentiam instar valli opponit...Ergo ut rite composita sint vota nostra, fulgeat in cordibus nostris primum necesse est fides providentiae Dei: nec tantum ordine praecedat omnes affectus, sed etiam temperet ac dirigat." Ps(s) 35:22, CO31:356. Cf. "Special providence -that which concerns believers in their Christian lives- takes precedence in Calvin's scheme. God can withhold sun and rain for the sake of special concerns. Providence should really be understood in the first place as special providence...the basic understanding of God's providence is not a neutral common

specialissima' is the same as predestination because both are moved by the Holy Spirit[119] and that '*providentia specialissima*' and predestination are God's care for the Elect. The implication of this claim is that only the faithful can enjoy secret providence.

Selderhuis probably does not think the faithful have an active role in secret providence because of the limitation of human nature that he considers.[120] He tries to stress that God is always in a revealed state but because human beings are created with limitation, then from the human point of view, God is considered as hidden. Thus, God is hidden in a passive way. Selderhuis stresses that in Psalm 9:18, Calvin writes about the hidden work of God's hand which can invisibly oppose the enemies of God's people.[121] He argues that this hiddenness is not attributed to sin nor to any deliberate concealment by God but that hiddenness is inherent in the original nature of the creature made by the creator. To put it precisely, Selderhuis suggests that because of the condition of humanity, people cannot understand divine providence.[122] This point concerning human limitation can explain the perceived hiddenness of God, however, the faithful can have an effect on the revelation of *providentia Dei*.

Selderhuis suggests that because human beings are not able to understand some parts of God's secret providence by default, therefore, they can only passively wait for God. Selderhuis overlooks the fact that Calvin suggests that through active prayer, one can see part of God's secret providence.[123] In addition, Selderhuis does not take note of Calvin's comment on Psalm 9:18 that there is a reason God seems to be slow to respond to our suffering, that is, God wants the faithful to awake Him with their prayers.[124] Although humanity is limited by the Fall, they can still

---

grace, but the conviction that God has power to protect the faithful." Mark W. Elliott, *Providence Perceived: Divine Action from a Human Point of View* (Berlin/Boston: De Gruyter, 2015), 142. Cf. "The purpose of Calvin's discussion of universal providence is not to define a common ground or territory between the believer and unbeliever, but to insist that the whole order of nature is the result of the special providence of God." Charles Partee, *Calvin and Classical Philosophy*, Studies in the History of Christian Thought 15 (Leiden: Brill, 1977), 129–130.

119 Partee, *Calvin and Classical Philosophy*, 15, 135; cf. Krusche, *Das Wirken des Heiligen Geistes nach Calvin*, 14. Cf. Charles Partee, *The Theology of John Calvin* (Louisville, KY: Westminster John Knox Press, 2008), 116.

120 Also, He is hidden in an active sense because God deliberately conceals himself from man. Selderhuis, *Calvin's Theology of the Psalms*, 180.

121 Ibid., 180–181.

122 Ibid., 180.

123 "Docemur autem hac precandi forma, quantumvis impotenter superbiant hostes nostri, tamen in manu Dei esse, nec plus posse, quam illis permittit..." Ps(s) 9:20, CO31:106–7.

124 "Quare sciamus nobis hac lege Dei auxilium promitti, ut tamen non praeveniat nostras afflictiones: sed ubi nos diu cruce domuerit, tandem succurrat. Et de spe vel exspectatione nominatim loquitur David, ut nos ad preces hortetur. Ideo enim ad nostras aerumnas connivet Deus, quia vult precibus

understand some parts of God's secret providence through His revelation by means of their prayer. This is an active way in dealing with God's hiddenness from the human point of view.

In the 1559 *Institutes*, Calvin argues that God the father will reveal Himself if the faithful pray to Him,[125] and he confirms that Christians can pray to God for His revelation of universal and special providence. Certainly, God decides how much He is going to reveal but here Calvin suggests that there is a genuine presence of secondary cause in the operation of *providentia Dei* through the prayer of the faithful.

The human role in both universal providence and special providence is active. Calvin emphasises this by stressing an optimistic view of secret providence in which believers' prayer plays an important role, in revealing God's 'hidden presence'.[126] Calvin does not explain specifically who can understand or enjoy general and special providence. Sometimes he explains that special providence is directed to 'people', and sometimes he points to the faithful. Yet, as he has shown in the Preface to *Commentarius in librum Psalmorum*, Calvin suggests that the Book of Psalms is a handbook for the faithful to practise their piety. Therefore, when Calvin discusses the situation of the 'people', he is in fact referring to those showing themselves to be godly at any point as a collective. Additionally, only the godly can understand providence, as Calvin clarified in *Sermons sur le livre de Job*, and only the godly can understand God's providence through prayer, as he specified in *Commentarius in librum Psalmorum*.

God's providence for the Church and prayer

Calvin discusses the topic of church in more than fifty Psalms and he also asserts that Psalm 149 is exclusively dedicated to the discussion of God's providence for the Church.[127] The Book of Psalms is a book for the faithful and Calvin encourages the faithful to read it to seek God's consolation as he claims that the Psalms show

---

nostris expergefieri, nam ubi vota nostra exaudit, quasi memor nostri esse incipiat, manum suam potentia instructam ad nos iuvandos porrigit." Ps(s) 9:18, *CO*31:106.

125 "Iam vero quam necessaria sit et quot modis utilis sit precandi exercitatio, nullis verbis satis potest explicari. Non abs re est profecto quod coelestis pater unicum in sui nominis invocation salutis praesidium esse testatur, qua scilicet praesentiam et providentiae eius, per quam rebus nostris curandis advigilet, et virtutis, per quam nos sustineat imbecilles et prope deficientes, et bonitatis, per quam misere peccatis oneratos in gratiam recipiat, advocamus: qua denique totum ipsum, ut se nobis praesentem exhibeat accersimus." 1559 *Institutes* 3.20.2, *CO*2:626.

126 Ibid.

127 "Si Psalmum hunc cum superioribus, et cum proximo qui ultimus erit, conferre libeat, hoc solum est discrimen, quod antehac peculiarem gratiam qua Deus ecclesiam suam fovet ac tuetur, generali

God's care especially for His children of the Church.[128] Calvin elevates the role of the Church as the 'orchestra' of God's theatre in the world to demonstrate His goodness, wisdom, justice, and power.[129] The Church is also His theatre to display His providence, thus if the Church features as the main character in God's theatre, He should always watch over His people, show them His guidance and keep them safe.[130]

Yet, why do His people suffer? God allows His children to suffer as a divine chastisement.[131] Selderhuis believes that according to Calvin's understanding, the adversities of the godly are not God's punishment but chastisements, which prevent sin from strengthening its hold on them when they have committed a particular offence.[132] In his comments on Psalm 34:17, Calvin explains that the godly suffer because of God's chastisement. When Calvin comments on Psalm135:13–15, he continues to explain that God has mercy towards His children and He will show them His sweet love.[133] Therefore, His people have to trust God, pray to Him for the manifestation of His grace and wait for their restoration in eternity.[134] Praying is a human action in response to divine chastisement.

God's providence for the Church in Psalm 51 and Psalm 122

Pak states that Calvin's David prays for the coming kingdom and the restoration of the Church, and that David is an example to teach the Church how to pray.[135] For

providentiae qua mundum sustinet, permiscuit propheta quisquis fuerit Psalmi autor: nunc tantum de beneficiis disserit quibus ecclesiam suam prosequitur." Argumentum Ps(s) 149, CO32:436.

128 Ps(s) 135:13, CO32:361.

129 It is found that in *Sermons sur le livre de Iob*, Calvin defines God's general providence as God's actions in His goodness, power, justice and wisdom. This definition is extended to providence for the Church in Calvin's *Commentarius in librum Psalmorum*: "Et certe sicuti totus mundus theatrum est divinae bonitatis, sapientiae, iustitiae, virtutis: pars tamen illustrior, instar orchestrae, est ecclesia…" Ibid.

130 Ibid.

131 "Nam dolorem quem ex Dei flagellis sensurus erat populus Moses lenire volens, Deum fore iudicem populi sui denuntiat…" Ibid.

132 Serlderhuis, *Calvin's Theology of the Psalms*, 101. "Deus autem simul ac lapsi sunt, ne peccata in *ipsis radices agant,* statim eos castigat, et quidem durius quam reprobos, quibus indulget in exitium". Ps(s) 34:17, CO31:343. It can be translated: "At the same time as they fell, lest sins take root in them, he punishes them immediately and rather more harshly than the Reprobate, whom he indulges with destruction."

133 "…suaviter fovere quos pro filiis agnoscit." Ps(s) 135:13, CO32:362.

134 "Dicit autem e Sione, quia quum pollicitus esset Deus se illinc exauditurum suorum vota, ac odorem gratiae suae inde diffunderet, simul etiam laudum materiam suggerebat." Ps(s) 135:15, CO32:363.

135 Pak, *The Judaizing Calvin: Sixteenth-Century Debates over the Messianic Psalms*, 88.

Calvin's David, prayer is also an extension of the repentance from his personal sin to the repentance of the whole Church.

In Psalm 51, Calvin describes David's sin as immensely detrimental, for he committed multiple sins.[136] David realised that the sin he committed hinder the salvation of the Church of God as he was considered as the pillar of the Church, but now that the support of the Church embarrassingly fell,[137] and David understood that he deserved an everlasting destruction, but he also sought God's pardon. Yet, how does David attain God's pardon? Calvin's David prays that God will direct his tongue so that he can sing something acceptable to God,[138] and God's acceptance of this praise is a gesture of divine forgiveness.

Finally, in Psalm 51:19, Calvin's David assures himself of God's pardon because he knows that he can do nothing, hence he comes before God's mercy with faith, a broken heart and a confession of his helplessness.[139] Calvin believes that when David feels that he is delivered again, he immediately prays for the deliverance of 'totam ecclesiam' because David knows that his sin not only destroys his own life but may also ruin the Church of God.[140] Thus, Calvin's David, in his prayer in Psalm 51, asks for God's mercy to restore the Church, and protect her until the coming of Christ's kingdom.[141] David prays with a heart of faithfulness, and with tears, humility, and regret, to invoke God's providential acts over himself and the Church.

In Psalm 122, David prays asking God to protect Jerusalem and to keep the holy city prosperous both externally and spiritually.[142] Calvin believes that David

---

136 "Ac iterum notandus est in Peccatis pluralis numerus. Quanquam enim ex uno fonte omnia manabant, multiplex tamen eius culpa erat, quod adulterio adiunxerat perfidiam et crudelitatem: nec unum hominem modo prodiderat vel paucos, sed totum exercitum, pro salute ecclesiae Dei pugnantem." Ps(s) 51:5, CO31:510.

137 Ps(s) 51:6, CO31:512.

138 "Eodem spectat proximus versus, ubi precatur labia sibi aperiri: quod tantundem valet ac praeberi laudis materiam. Scio locum hunc ita solere exponi, quasi David linguam suam dirigi optaret a spiritu Dei, ut idoneus sit ad canendas eius laudes, et certe nisi Deus verba nobis suppeditet, prorsus muti erimus. Sed aliud voluit David, se nunc quodammodo obmutescere, donec veniam adeptus, ad gratiarum actionem vocetur." Ps(s) 51:16, CO31:521.

139 Ps(s) 51:19, CO31:523.

140 "Iam non pro se uno privatim orat, sed totam ecclesiam adiungit, neque immerito: quia per eum non steterat quominus concideret totum Christi regnum…Quamvis ergo sua culpa everterit Dei ecclesiam quantum in se erat, petit tamen eam gratuita Dei misericordia restitui." Ibid.

141 "Adde quod non tantum de unius mensis vel anni aedificio hic agitur, sed ut Deus statum ecclesiae suae incolumem usque ad Christi adventum tueatur…Hic cert videmus, simulac reconciliati sumus Deo, non tantum liberam cuique pro salute sua precandi fiduciam permitti, sed nos etiam pro aliis admitti suffragatores: imo quod magis honorificum est, regni Christi gloriam, quae magis pretiosa est quam totius mundi salus, commendare licet." Ibid.

142 Ps(s) 122:7, CO32:307.

encourages all the children of God to pray for the preservation of the sacred community because the salvation of the holy city and the salvation of the whole Church are inseparable.[143]

Barbara Pitkin's newly published monograph, *Calvin, The Bible, and History* delivers a chapter on David, faith, and the confusion of history. She asserts that Calvin's exegesis of faith reflects 'his theological assumption of the unity of the covenant and also certain tensions inherent in this doctrine.'[144] Calvin does not stress that David has faith in Christ and that David's faith is similar to the faith of the Christian believers.[145] However, when Calvin formulates his doctrine of providence, he firmly emphasises that Christians in the difficult times of the sixteenth century, should be equipped with this similar faith in Christ and trust in God's providence. Faith rectifies the noetic effect of sin, helps believers to understand some aspects of divine providence,[146] and gives voice to prayer![147] The findings in this chapter concerning Calvin's explanation of the relationship between God's providence for the Church and prayer echoes Pitkin's arguments.

Prayer and faith: Psalm 3

It has been discussed that when the godly pray by faith, there is a possibility that they will understand some of God's providence. While some scholars concentrate on the noetic sense of human faith in relation to Calvin's doctrine of divine providence in this commentary on Psalms, Calvin's David in the Book of Psalms is also expressing a faith in action. In Psalm 3:1, David by faith, cries out to God for His help because he is facing a multitude of enemies, and his faith is shown by his action after his prayer when he is able to enjoy sound sleeps. Psalm 3:5 tells us that Calvin's David sleeps peacefully because he is in a state of mind that is well ordered.

In Psalm 3:7, David flees[148] to God for deliverance and salvation. Calvin stresses that David has experienced the assistance of God and this represents the answer of his prayers in Psalm 3:1. It seems as if faith and the prayer form a cycle of a

---

143 "...nempe quia in regno et sacerdotio inclusa erat totius ecclesiae salus. Iam vero quum necesse sit, collapsa communi salute, unumquemque nostrum misere perire, non mirum si David hanc curam et hoc stadium omnibus Dei filiis commendet. Itaque si rite ordinare volumus preces nostras, hoc sit exordium, ut Dominus ecclesiae corpus conservet." Ps(s) 122:6, *CO*32:306.

144 Barbara Pitkin, *Calvin, the Bible, and History-Exegesis and Historical Reflection in the Era of Reform* (New York, NY: Oxford University Press, 2020), 119.

145 Ibid.

146 Ibid., 105.

147 Ibid., 113.

148 Calvin likes to use these terms to describe David's act of prayer: flees, betakes, remains, etc. *CO*31:76, 85, 101, 104.

manifestation of faith by humanity: from experience of God's revelation through prayer, to a sense of faith, to an act of prayer, to experience of God's revelation, to a sense of faith, and to an act of prayer again. This cycle of a 'manifestation of faith' starts at the point when God lets human beings experience Him, and the result of this cycle is a regulated human mind in a peaceful state of sound sleep.[149] Calvin explains the cycle of faith in the 1559 *Institutes*, and also affirms the human role in *providentia Dei*:

> By so doing we invoke the presence both of his providence, through which he watches over and guards our affairs…through which he sustains us…through which he receives us…it is by prayer that we call Him to reveal Himself as wholly present to us. Hence comes an extraordinary peace and repose to our consciences.[150]

This signifies a similar cycle as in Psalm 3, and it emphasises the sovereignty of God. From prayer, God reveals Himself and when believers have come to understand some of God's revelation, they have extraordinary peace. Both works, the 1559 *Institutes* and *Commentarius in librum Psalmorum* stress that the cycle is prayer driven and a peaceful state of mind is attained in God's providence. It is agreed that prayer does have an active role in *providentia Dei*. Believers pray by faith but this faith is born from the Gospel and through God's Word (revelation of God), where their hearts are trained to call upon His name.[151] While *providentia Dei* initiates the human heart to pray, human prayer in turn has an active role in *providentia Dei*.

Therefore, what exactly is the role of human prayer in *providentia Dei*? In the commentary on Jonah, Calvin compares Jonah's situation in Jonah 2 to David's situation in Psalm 39:9 when David cries out, 'God, you are the one who has done it!' When Calvin's Jonah experiences God's revelation, he is so amazed and acts as

---

149 The description of a cycle of manifestation of faith is also shown in Calvin's commentary on Jonah. "In hac igitur desperatione animum etiam colligit Ionas, et potest sese recta ad Deum conferre: hoc est admirabile, et fere incredibile exemplum fidei. Ergo discamus expendere quod hic dicitur: quia quum Dominus duriter nos affligit, hoc est legitimum et opportunum orandi tempus. Scimus autem, ut maior pars animos despondeat, nec soleat libere preces suas offerre Deo, nisi quietis animis…" Ioannis Calvini, *Praelectionum in Duodecim Prophetas Minores*, Jonah 2:1, CO43:236.

150 "Non abs re est profecto quod coelestis pater unicum in sui nominis invocatione salutis praesidium esse testatur, qua scilicet praesentiam et providentiae eius, per quam rebus nostris curandis advigilet, et virtutis, per quam nos sustineat imbecilles et prope deficientes, et bonitatis, per quam misere peccatis oneratos in gratiam recipiat, advocamus: qua denique totum ipsum, ut se nobis praesentem exhibeat accersimus. Hinc eximia conscientiis nostris requies ac tranquillitas nascitur. " 1559 *Institutes* 3.20.2, CO2:626. Cf. John Calvin, *Institutes of the Christian Religion* 1559, translated by Ford Lewis Battles (Albany, OR: Books For The Ages, The Ages Digital Library, 1998) 3.20.2.

151 Calvin, *1559 Institutes*, 3.20.1, CO2:625.

if he was David, by crying out that God was the one who sent the things against Jonah to turn him back.[152] When Jonah calms down inside the bowel of the fish, he prays faithfully and asks earnestly for God's pardon, and finally in His special grace, God raises him again.[153] Therefore, the role of the prayer of the faithful is truly to invoke God's revelation,[154] so that the faithful are influenced to act to change.

'Coelestis pater' and 'coelestis iudex' in His providence for the Church

In Psalm 8:5 and Psalm 72:11, Calvin states that God as the Heavenly Father bestows on His children in His Church a fullness of blessings and eternal salvation through Christ.[155] This is an assurance for the children from their father that there is a place for them in the kingdom of God.[156] In Psalm 38:6, Calvin states that David humbly calls the Heavenly Judge to have mercy on him and that David is entirely submissive to the result of the judge's trial.[157] In Psalm 79:6, Calvin stresses that God as the Heavenly Judge, separates the Reprobate from the Elect because some people are not willing to repent in Christ and so they deserve to be condemned.[158] God as the Heavenly Father, bestows goodness and eternal salvation upon the Elect while God as the Heavenly Judge, condemns some people to reprobation. This special care for

---

152 "Hic pluribus verbis prosequitur Ionas quam multa potuerint occurrere, quae animum eius terrore obruerent, et procul retraherent a Deo, et tollerent omne. studium orandi. Semper autem memoria tenendum est quod iam diximus, fuisse ei cum Deo negotium. Et hoc ponderandum nobis est, quemadmodum quum Psalmo 39 dicit David, Tu fecisti tamen. Nam postquam conquestus est de hostibus suis, deinde animum reflectit ad Deum. Quid ego ago? quid proficio istis querimoniis? neque enim homines me soli infestant: tu Deus hoc fecisti, inquit. Ita Ionas semper sibi proposuit iram Dei, quia sciebat non nisi ob sua peccata sibi accidisse tale exitium. Dicit ergo Aquis se fuisse obsessum: deinde circumdatum fuisse abysso. Sed tandem addit, quod Deus adscendere fecerit vitam suam." Jonah 2:5, CO43:240.

153 "Deus autem non modo vitam illi reddidit, sed iterum ornavit officio et elogio prophetae. Hoc, quemadmodum dixi, non adeptus est Ionas nisi rara et singulari gratia Dei." Jonah 3:1, CO43:246–247.

154 "Hoc igitur modo Ionas non solum Dei sui meminit…in quibus fidem suam toto vitae cursu exercuerat…Intelligit ergo Ionas, etiamsi esset remotissimus a templo, Deum tamen sibi fuisse propinquum, quia non destitit precari Deum illum, qui se patefecerat lege data, et qui volebat coli Ierosolymae…" Jonah 2:7, CO43:243.

155 "Sed quia rursus donorum omnium plenitudinem coelestis pater in filium suum contulit, ut ex hoc fonte hauriamus omnes…" Ps(s) 8:5, CO31:93. Cf. "…ut sciamus non temere nos in spem aeternae salutis fuisse adscitos: sed quia iam coelestis pater nos filio suo destinaverat…" Ps(s) 72:11, CO31:669.

156 "…hinc etiam colligimus, in ecclesia et grege Christi esse regibus locum…" Ibid.

157 "Hac ergo circumstantia David coelestem suum iudicem ad misericordiam flectit…" Ps(s) 38:6, CO31:389.

158 "…nec Dei iudicium anticipant, sed reprobis quale merentur iudicium optantes, patienter exspectant dum reprobos ab electis discernat coelestis iudex." Ps(s) 79:6, CO31:749.

God's Church is called heavenly providence, and it will be examined in the next chapter.

Conclusion

Firstly, Calvin argues that human prayer has an active role in God's general providence, special providence, and God's providence for His Church. Secondly, he argues that there is a genuine existence of the secondary cause in *providentia Dei*. Calvin uses his exegesis of the Book of Psalms to explain these two claims.

In the *Sermons sur le livre de Job*, Calvin encourages his congregation to follow David when they face life's afflictions, as he is a virtuous sufferer. Job claims that his prayer is pure, but Calvin asserts that nobody's prayer is pure because even the faithful are sinners. However, David prays differently because he humbly admits that he is sinful, and he begs for God's pardon when he suffers. Calvin's David believes that he deserves the suffering, but Calvin's Job complains about his affliction.

In *Commentarius in librum Psalmorum*, Calvin illustrates how David deals with life's difficulties through prayer in relation to three kinds of providence: God's general providence, special providence, and God's providence for His Church. Calvin continues to use the definitions of the three kinds of providence he made in 1552, and he highly praises David's prayer for its humility, and stresses that his prayer invokes God's revelation in His providence. The role of the prayer of the faithful is to invoke God's revelation, so that the faithful are influenced to act to change. God as primary cause initiates human prayer at the beginning, but there is a genuine existence of secondary causality through human prayer in *providentia Dei*.

5. Calvin's doctrines of '*providentia coelestis*' and predestination from 1554 to 1559

In *Sermons sur le livre de Job* 1554–1555, Calvin allocates the majority of his sermons to the discussion of God's general and special providence. In these two kinds of providence, God, for the governance of the world and the benefit of humankind, shows Himself in His actions in goodness, power, justice, and wisdom through the order of nature and human history. Moreover, God has special care for the Elect, and this is called '*providence celeste*', but Calvin only discusses this topic twice in his sermons on Job. However, the elaboration of this exclusive '*providence celeste*' can be found in *De occulta providentia Dei* 1558 and the 1559 *Institutes*.

This chapter offers four arguments. First, in the *Sermons sur le livre de Job*, Calvin argues that by '*providence celeste*', God endows His children with fatherly goodness and governs the world with His justice. While heavenly providence is related to special providence, it also relates to the salvation of the Elect. Secondly, in *De occulta providentia Dei* 1558, Calvin argues that God's secret providence is the explanation of predestination. In God's secret providence, He, as the '*coelestis pater*' and the '*coelestis iudex*', decrees some people to be the Elect and the remainder to be the Reprobate. Thirdly, in the 1559 *Institutes*, Calvin argues that '*providentia coelestis*' is providence only for His children and this providence is a comfort for them as they can long for eternal life. Finally, Calvin's interpretation of the doctrine of *providentia Dei* is consistent and is related to soteriological matters regardless of the separation in the text of the doctrines of providence and predestination, in the 1559 *Institutes*. *Sermons sur le livre de Job* 1554–1555, *De occulta providentia Dei* 1558 and the 1559 *Institutes* need to be read together, to understand this claim and to grasp the meaning of heavenly providence, which also acts as a support to this claim.

Sermons sur le livre de Job 1554–1555

When Calvin preached his sermons on Job, he categorized God's providential actions into goodness, power, justice, and wisdom, and these actions are exemplified in the order of nature and human history. Not everyone can understand God's goodness, power, justice, and wisdom, but a group of special people, the godly can, for only the godly can taste God's general providence and special providence regardless of the partial understanding. However, what about '*providence celeste*'?

The term 'providence celeste' is used by Calvin twice in his sermons on Job.[1] The first was when he preached on Job 23:13–17, where heavenly providence describes two situations: everyday, God's children are sustained and protected, but the entire world is also governed so that evil deeds can be stopped.[2] Hence, the ungodly are subject to God's governance.[3] Yet, what does 'providence celeste' mean to Job? When Calvin preached this sermon, he posed Job's inquiry as "I know that God punishes me not for my sin. He is righteous in all His doing but why did God use an absolute power against me?"[4] Calvin explains Job's situation using 'providence celeste': when God sends people into the world, He has ordained who will attain life and who will be condemned to death.[5] This is to demonstrate God's justice.[6]

There are two parts in 'providence celeste'. Firstly, 'providence celeste' is not for everyone, but for the children of God. In 'providence celeste', God manifests Himself to the faithful, calls them as His children to inherit His kingdom, and shows His heart to them.[7] In this way, He deliberately gathers the faithful. Therefore, while the

---

1 Jean Calvin, *Sermons sur le livre de Job*, Sermon 90 Job 23:13–17, CO34:364 and Sermon 108 Job 30:1–10, CO34:585.

2 "Notons donc que non seulement Dieu tient ses enfans en sa charge pour les maintenir: mais qu'il gouverne tellement tout le monde, que le diable (quoy qu'il attente) ne pourra venir à bout de ses entreprinses, que tousiours ceste providence celeste ne soit par dessus." Sermon 90 Job 23:13–17, CO34:364.

3 "De nostre costé quand chacun aura cognu qu'il est sous la main et conduite de son Dieu: qu'il pense que tout le monde y est pareillement. Car si le diable n'estoit suiet à Dieu, que seroit-ce?" Ibid.

4 John Calvin, *Sermons of Maister Iohn Caluin, vpon the booke of Iob*, translated by Arthur Golding (Londini, Impensis Georgij Bishop, 1574), 421. Cf. "Maintenant venons à ce que Iob adiouste. Il dit, Quand Dieu sera en un propos, que nul ne l'en pourra destourner. C'est tousiours en poursuivant ce qu'il avoit dit, que Dieu usoit d'une puissance absolue contre luy, tellement qu'il n'estoit pas question de venir en procez, pour obtenir son droit. Or nous avons declaré que cela est excessif: car combien que Iob seust que Dieu ne le punissoit point pour ses pechez qu'il eust commis: si est-ce qu'il devoit estre resolu, que Dieu estoit iuste, et equitable en tout ce qu'il fait. Or il imagine une puissance exorbitante, et qui n'a ne regle ne mesure: en cela il fait iniure à Dieu." Sermon 90 Job 23:13–17, CO34:357.

5 "…mais il a establi de nostre vie et de nostre mort ce qui en sera…que quand Dieu nous a mis en ce monde, il a quant et quant ordonné ce qu'il veut qu'il soit fait de nous: et qu'il conduit nos pas tellement que nostre vie n'est pas en nostre main non plus que nostre mort…" Ibid., CO34:361. Cf. Richard A. Muller, *Divine Will and Human Choice* (Grand Rapids, MI: Baker Academic, 2017), 144–147.

6 David C. Steinmetz, *Calvin in Context* (New York, 1995), 49–50. Also quoted in Francis Oakley, 'The Absolute and Ordained Power of God in Sixteenth- and Seventeenth-Century', *Journal of the History of Ideas*, vol. 59, no. 3 (July 1998): 457.

7 "Car ie ne parle point maintenant de tous hommes en general, mais ie parle de la consolation que peuvent recueillir les fideles quand Dieu s'est une fois manifesté à eux, et les a appellez speciale-ment pour estre ses enfans, et qu'il leur a desployé son coeur, comme nous avons dit." Sermon 90 Job 23:13–17, CO34:360. Cf. Voila donc comme il faut que nous glorifions Dieu en ce decret, quand il lui a pleu nous choisir et nous appeller à salut, et nous constituer heritiers de son royaume." Ibid., CO34:363.

faithful should not question their salvation,[8] they also should not brag about their salvation, as the Elect are eternally chosen by God.[9] For God not only cares for the faithful's eternal life, but also their present life by leading them step by step.[10] Consequently, to the godly, God acts as a saviour and a father.[11] However, instead of being comforted by this providence, Job misapplies God's ordination and complains that God uses His lawless power and requires Job to submit to His caprices.[12]

To answer Job's inquiry completely and avoid saying that God is a tyrant, Calvin tries to use the second aspect of '*providence celeste*' to offer an explanation, but this explanation is not as detailed as the first aspect. The second aspect of heavenly providence considers the justice of God but this justice is not the same justice Calvin discussed in general providence.[13] This justice is special, and it relates to the salvation of His children: i. e., predestination and preservation.[14] Calvin confirms that God's salvation and His justice are inseparable,[15] and that God's action is upon every godly person: He ordains the faithful's eternal lives, and He also guides and preserves them on earth and governs the wicked.[16] Therefore, in '*providence celeste*', God shows that He is merciful and righteous,[17] and the faithful are assured to be kept safe both on earth and in heaven.

---

8 "Il ne faut point donc que les fideles soyent en suspens, ou qu'ils pensent que leur salut soit en branle." Ibid., *CO*34:360.

9 Ibid., *CO*34:362.

10 "...notons que Dieu a decreté de nous ce qu'il en veut faire quant au salut eternel de nos ames, et puis il l'a decreté aussi quant à la vie presente." Ibid., *CO*34:363. Cf. Voila donc comme il nous faut reposer, sachans que nostre salut n'est point variable, puis qu'ainsi est que Dieu en a fait son decret qui ne se pourra changer. Or cependant quant est du decret de ceste vie presente, cognoissons que Dieu conduit tous nos pas..." Ibid.

11 "...Ie say que Dieu qui est mon Sauveur et mon Pere..." Ibid., *CO*34:364.

12 "Or il est vrai que Iob a appliqué mal ceste sentence: car en ses premiers bouillons (comme on dit) il a ici parlé à la desesperee. Voila (dit-il) ie say que c'en est fait. Et pourquoy? Dieu a decreté de moy ce que bon lui a semblé, et il sera accompli, ie ne profiterai rien en me rebecquant à l'encontre." Ibid., *CO*34:361–362.

13 In Sermon 46, Calvin defines justice differently: "Voila donc la bonté de Dieu qui se monstre et declare: nous voyons sa iustice, comme il veille sur ses creatures, qu'il a le soin de nous: et cependant nous voyons aussi d'autre costé ses iugemens, nous voyons qu'il gouverne le monde d'une façon si admirable, qu'encores que les meschans ne cerchent qu'à y mordre, si faut-il qu'ils demeurent là confus." Sermon 46 Job 12:7–16, *CO*33:572.

14 "Au reste quand nous aurons cognu en general ceste iustice et droiture: cognoissons aussi que Dieu nous fait ce bien de conioindre et unir sa iustice à nostre salut: comme aussi il y conioint sa puissance." Sermon 90 Job 23:13–17, *CO*34:362.

15 "Puis qu'ainsi est donc qu'il y a comme un lien inseparable entre la iustice de Dieu et nostre salut..." Ibid.

16 Ibid., *CO*34:364.

17 "...mais il est passionné en sorte qu'il ne recognoist pas Dieu iuste et equitable ainsi qu'il doit." Ibid.

The second time Calvin used the term *'providence celeste'* was when he preached Job 30:1–10, and he illustrates this doctrine with two contrasting Biblical examples. God has blessed Job with extra material goods and wisdom above other godly people, to make Job a model for the godly to follow. However, Job is now suffering, and thus he complains that he is mocked by people who he once helped. Job does not have respect from these people anymore and he pathetically declares that he wishes he had not been 'elevated' by God[18] or given extra blessings.[19]

Calvin reinforces the belief that God never afflicts people without a reason,[20] and that afflictions are chastisements to train their patience. While these chastisements are judgments from God for the godly, the reason of the chastisements are incomprehensible to the godly.[21] Yet, Calvin's Job is desperate, impatient, and he refuses to submit to God's incomprehensible judgment and accept His chastisements, as God's actions are now strange to him.[22] However, Calvin has a different, more positive evaluation of David because David patiently waits for God, and shows that God's extreme training is not strange to David.[23] Calvin suggests that David is a positive

---

18 "C'est ce que Iob declare icy: car comme il a recité la reverence qu'on luy portoit, qu'il estoit ouy par tout, et non seulement en titre et qualité d'homme riche, mais pource que Dieu luy avoit donné esprit et prudence par dessus les autres, et qu'on se pouvoit reposer sur luy, qu'il estoit comme un miroir et patron de toute vertu en toute sa vie pour y prendre exemple: maintenant qu'il se voit ainsi mocqué, que chacun le monstre au doigt, ce luy est une croix beaucoup plus dure et amere à porter, que si iamais il n'eust esté ainsi eslevé." Sermon 108 Job 30:1–10, CO34:585.

19 "Voila donc ce que regarde icy Iob en disant, que ceux qui estoyent ainsi reiettez se sont eslevez contre luy. Et notons bien que Iob par cy devant a declaré, qu'il n'estoit point honoré comme un homme riche, ou d'estat, ou noble: ce n'est point là où il s'est fondé, mais qu'il avoit cheminé en si grande integrité et perfection, qu'en contemplant les vertus que Dieu avoit mises en luy, on estoit contraint de luy porter reverence, et qu'il n'avoit point abusé de telles graces. Voila donc maintenant pourquoy il trouve la chose plus dure et plus fascheuse, quand il est ainsi mesprisé par ceux ausquels il n'y a rien digne de louange." Ibid., CO34:594.

20 "Nous voyons ce qui est advenu à Iob…Pourrons-nous icy accuser Dieu et nous tempester à l'encontre de luy? Plustost nous devons-nous humilier, quand nous voyons telles afflictions estre advenues à un homme si vertueux: et encores que la raison ne nous soit point apparente pourquoy Dieu en a ainsi fait, cognoissons neantmoins que ce n'est point sans cause, et que nous le devons glorifier en tous ses iugemens, combien qu'ils nous soyent incomprehensibles." Ibid., CO34:591.

21 "Or cependant advisons de faire nostre profit de tous les chastimens que nous voyons de iour en iour…Car tout ainsi que chacun de nous en ce qu'il endure doit estre patient, et en sa patience louer Dieu: ainsi il ne faut point que nous l'accusions en voyant qu'il permettra que les bons soyent diffamez." Ibid.

22 "Il ne nous faut point trouver estrange, si des hommes vilains, et qui n'ont nulle honnesteté en eux, nulle vertu, nulle humanité…" Ibid., CO34:594.

23 "Ainsi, cognoissons que quand ils usent de mesdisances et contradictions envers nous, Dieu nous prepare par ce moyen-la, afin qu'il ne nous soit point trop nouveau quand quelquefois il nous voudra accabler. Nostre Seigneur donc nous prepare (quand telles extremitez nous viendront) à estre patiens." Ibid., CO34:587.

example to follow[24] because David knows and enjoys heavenly providence, and therefore shows a different attitude when he faces a similar situations to those faced by Job.

Calvin explains that David became king not because of his merit or for other worldly reasons but through God's ordination. However, David lost his throne to his son and was forced to flee. When he approached Bahurim, Shimei came out to curse David, and also threw stones at him in the presence of David's guards, however, David cried out to God and did not allow his army to take revenge. This behaviour earns Calvin's praise, and he depicts David as thankful to God because He 'elevates' David to the throne and endows him with a special virtue, which is not an honour for everyone.[25] Although later he has to face hostility from both his family and insults from his enemies, David does not retaliate, for he acknowledges that his suffering is God's act of *'providence celeste'*[26] – God's heavenly providence, His predestination and preservation for the Elect. Calvin affirms that human suffering is God's life lesson for His people, and that he encourages the congregation by providing two solutions in times of difficulties. If the suffering is due to a mistake they made, they should acknowledge their fault.[27] If they are not sure about the cause, they should be patient and trust in God's special grace.[28]

Calvin's David is likely one of those faithful ones who deals with his suffering with both solutions:[29] acknowledging his mistakes and trusting God's special grace.

---

24 "Et là dessus notons l'exemple de David, qui estoit homme suiet à passions comme nous: mais tant y a qu'il s'est assuietti volontairement, quand il a cognu que la volonté de Dieu estoit telle qu'il fust là comme desciré par pieces, voire combien que ce fust à tort." Ibid.

25 "Voila David (pour prendre un homme memorable entre les autres) apres avoir esté roy, et avoir prosperé en sorte qu'on voyoit à l'oeil la main de Dieu qui le guidoit, et qu'il n'estoit point eslevé par moyen des hommes, ne par son industrie seulement, mais que Dieu avoit voulu declarer en luy une vertu especiale." Ibid., CO34:586.

26 "Or il se reduit en memoire premierement que Dieu l'a exalté, voire et que cela s'est fait de sa pure grace: et que maintenant puis qu'il est ainsi abbatu, cela n'est point venu de cas de fortune, mais que Dieu veut qu'il soit ainsi mastiné par les hommes. C'est Dieu, dit-il, qui luy a ordonné de faire ainsi: non point que l'outrage et l'orgueil de Semei fust approuvé de Dieu, mais David cognoist que cela ne vient point sans une providence celeste." Ibid.

27 "Nous savons que nostre Seigneur nous recommande sur tout quand nous serons blasmez en nos personnes, d'estre patiens, et de recognoistre nos vices..." Ibid., CO34:585.

28 "...mais si nostre Seigneur permet qu'on mesdise de nous, et qu'on s'en mocque, quand nous aurons toutes fois bien vescu, et n'aurons point donné occasion aux meschans, et aux detracteurs pour nous iniurier: cognoissons que nostre Seigneur nous a fait une grace singuliere de nous exempter de la malice des hommes, tellement que c'est à tort qu'ils nous en veulent. Et au reste, puis qu'il veut que nous souffrions iniustement, que nous passions par là, et qu'il ne nous soit point trop estrange." Ibid., CO34:587.

29 "Et là dessus notons l'exemple de David...Il est vray que si nous sommes en opprobre à cause de nos pechez, cela nous doit tant plus renger à patience: mais si nostre Seigneur permet qu'on mesdise

While material gifts from God can be a comfort, they can lose their comforting function when extremities come to people's lives. Therefore, the godly should be patient, and acknowledge that God's special care is with them in their good and bad days, and realise that they can still live with the same hope they had before their suffering came.[30] This hope leads the godly to long for heavenly life, which is an everlasting rest, in contrast to the present life, which is fragile and gloomy.[31]

Calvin examines the different attitudes Job and David have when they deal with similar adversity, and from there he delivers the meaning of heavenly providence. '*Providence celeste*' shows to the faithful God's special blessings in the present life and His special grace of eternal life. While heavenly providence maintains the faithful and grants them salvation, it also acts as a shield for God's people to protect them from wicked deeds, which is part of preservation. Hence in Sermon 108, Calvin endeavours to explains the aspect about God's maintenance of the faithful in His special earthly blessings, but he aims to remind the faithful to focus on the eternal blessing of God. Calvin's Job stops at God's earthly special blessings, but Calvin's David enjoys both.

What is heavenly providence? It is probably special providence as it describes God's actions acting upon all of humanity, including the chosen and the unchosen. Yet, Calvin also stresses that in heavenly providence, God shows that He is a father and a saviour, so a soteriological dimension is also involved with this doctrine. In addition, heavenly providence describes the eternal decree of the godly and the ungodly. Thus, heavenly providence is also predestination. It seems to echo Partees's assertion that: "providence is the doctrine of predestination applied universally to the world, and predestination is the doctrine of special (particular) providence applied directly to individuals."[32]

---

de nous, et qu'on s'en mocque, quand nous aurons toutes fois bien vescu, et n'aurons point donné occasion aux meschans, et aux detracteurs pour nous iniurier: cognoissons que nostre Seigneur nous a fait une grace singuliere de nous exempter de la malice des hommes..." Ibid.

30 "Or maintenant il nous faut noter, que combine que les graces et benefices que nous avons receus de Dieu nous doivent alleger en nos afflictions: toutes fois si nous avons esté honorez, il ne se peut faire que cela ne nous contriste, et que ce ne nous soit double tourment de nous voir puis apres en opprobre: mais tant y a, qu'il nous faut resister à telles tentations. Nostre patience ne sera pas de ne rien sentir, mais c'est quand nous sentirons ce qui nous est icy declaré par Iob. Toutes fois que nous prenions courage de cheminer tousiours comme devant Dieu..." Ibid.

31 "...aspirans à la vie celeste où nous aurons une fermeté permanente: apprenons aussi de cognoistre qu'en la vie presente il n'y a que fragilité et misere, et que nous y serons tousiours suiets, iusques à ce qu'il nous en ait retirez, pour nous faire participans de ce repos eternel qu'il nous a preparé aux cieux." Ibid., *CO*34:596.

32 Charles Partee, *The Theology of John Calvin* (Louisville, KY: Westminster John Knox Press, 2008), 116.

Calvin intends to object to Job's assertion of God's lawless power using the reprobation condition of the doctrine of heavenly providence as God's actions in His goodness and justice are inseparable, but the explanation is not as detailed as the discussion concerning election. This is Calvin's general practice as he rarely talked about reprobation in detail when preaching. However, in the treatise, *De occulta providentia Dei*, Calvin provides a discussion on the relationships between secret providence, the providence provided by God when He acts as father and judge, and predestination. This discussion concerning God judging the wicked can be elaborated in greater detail.

De occulta providentia Dei 1558

In 1558, Calvin responded to fourteen objections Sebastian Castellio[33] made against fourteen of Calvin's articles, from Calvin's Latin and French works, on the subject of predestination. Castellio and Calvin had known each other long before 1558 as they had met in Strasbourg while Calvin was on exile in that city, between 1538–1541 and in 1542, Calvin invited Castellio to work at the College of Geneva. After the execution of Michael Servetus in 1553, a work was published to criticise this cruel decision, and highlighted Calvin in the decision-making process to execute. This work, titled *Historia de morte Serveti* was believed to be written by Castellio.[34]

While Stefan Zweig argues that Calvin was the sole decision maker who decided Servetus's execution,[35] Bruce Gordon argues against this assertion claiming that "it was a decision of a council not well disposed towards the Frenchman and with which he was locked in battle over excommunication".[36] Frans P.Van Stam however,

---

33 Secret Providence is written by Calvin to defend Sebastian Castellio's criticism concerning his doctrine of predestination and providence. In 1546, Michael Servetus challenged Calvin regarding his teaching on the Trinity. Eventually, Servetus was condemned as a heretic and was sentenced to burn in 1553. Servetus's execution aroused successive complaints which came mainly from Sebastian Castellio. In early 1557, Castellio refuted Calvin's view of predestination. Calvin responded in the same year and in 1558, Calvin published *Calumniae nebulonis cuiusdam calumnias, quibus odio et Invidia gravare conatus est doctrinam Ioh. Calvini de occulta Dei Providentia. Ioannis Calvini ad easdem responsio.*

34 In February 1554, *Defensio orthodoxae fidei de sacra Trinitate, contra prodigiosos errores Michaelis Serveti Hispani, ubi ostenditur haeretico iure gladii coercendos esse, et nominatim de homine hoc tam impio iuste et merito sumptum Genevae fuisse supplicium* was published to refute Castellio's charges. In March 1554, Castellio, using a pseudonym, responded by publishing *De haereticis an sint persequendi*, stating his opposition to the execution of heretics and appealing his position to the Church Fathers, and the reformers including Calvin.

35 Stefan Zweig, *Erasmus and the Right to Heresy*, chapter 5 the Murder of Servetus, translated by Eden and Cedar Paul (London: Condor Book Souvenir Press E&A Ltd., 1979), 273–292.

36 Bruce Gordon, *Calvin* (New Haven: Yale University Press, 2009), 224.

suggests that the reason Servetus lost his life is mainly because of Servetus's decision to join 'Enfants of Geneva', which ultimately influenced the decision of the council.[37] While Calvin's role in the execution might be misunderstood,[38] he was certainly not the one who executed Servetus. However, after this incident the relationship between Calvin and Castellio markedly deteriorated. Sadly, while Calvin and Castellio had been initially colleagues, they now became bitter opponents, and *De occulta Dei providentia* was Calvin's last direct interaction with Castellio.[39] Ferdinand Buisson argues that "Castellio fights for a change from liberal Protestantism to secularism and free thought".[40] The arguments raised by Castellio against Calvin in *De occulta Dei providentia* show some traces of Castellio's change, however, Calvin's replies also show that intolerance could be defended.[41]

In *De occulta Dei providentia*, Calvin largely argues that God is simultaneously merciful and just. Calvin mentions the terms '*coelestis pater*' and '*coelestis iudex*' in the Preface to this work.[42] He states that God, as the heavenly father, decrees that

---

37 Some prominent and young citizens in Geneva felt annoyed by the church because the ministers exerted power over them, and controlled their life and future development. Frans P.Van Stam, The Servetus Case An appeal for a new assessment (Genéve: Librairie Droz, 2017), 59–62, 314–317. Cf. "Calvin's Geneva is frequently criticized for producing a cramped social order with an imposed uniformity, an invasion of privacy and an overbearing moral censoriousness." David Fergusson, "Reformed Tradition and Tolerance", in *Public Theology for the 21st Century*, edited by William F. Storrar and Andrew R. Morton (London: T&T Clark, 2004), 111–112.

38 "Zweig n'écrivait point un livre sur Calvin. Il écrivait un livre sur Hitler." Valentine Zuber, "Les conflits de la tolérance (XIXe–XXe siècles). Michel Servet entre mémoire et histoire" (PhD diss., 1997), 630. Also quoted in Frank Lestringant, "Stefan Zweig contre Calvin (1936)", *Revue de l'histoire des religions*, 1, (2006), 74.

39 De Greef, *The writings of John Calvin, an introductory guide*, 176, 177.

40 Ferdinand Buisson, *Sébastien Castellion, sa vie et son œuvre (1515–1563). Étude sur les origines du protestantisme libéral français* (Paris: Hachette, 1892). Also quoted in Lestringant, "Stefan Zweig contre Calvin (1936)", 90.

41 Cf. Fergusson, "Reformed Tradition and Tolerance", 112.

42 "Sed quia ab initio earn video fuisse obnoxiam multis improborum calumniis, et Christum, quia ita decrevit coelestis pater, scopum contradictionis esse oportet, hoc quoque patienter ferendum est. Nulli tamen improborum virulenti morsus unquam efficient ut eius me doctrinae poeniteat, quam a Deo autore profectam esse certo mihi constat. Nec tam male in tot, quibus me Deus ipse exercuit certaminibus, profeci, ut ad futiles vestros crepitus adhuc expavescam. Imo quod ad te privatim attinet, larvate monitor, haec me ratio nonnihil solatur, quod in hominem melius quam dignus eras de te meritum ingratus esse non potuisti, quin foedam simul impietatem in Deum proderes. Scio quidem vobis Academicis nullum suaviorem esse ludum, quam sub dubitationis specie convellere quidquid est fidei in cordibus hominum: et quam lepida esse, quae in arcanam Dei providentiam iacis, dicteria tibi persuaseris, quamvis ipse dissimules, ex stylo tuo non obscure apparet. Sed te ac tuos sodales ad tribunal illud cito, unde olim coelestis iudex solo oris flatusque sui fulmine vestram protervicam satis valide prosternet: ut autem brevi tua dicacitas probis et cordatis lectoribus non minus foeteat quam tibi intus placet, facturum me confido." Iohannis Calvini Responsio, *CO*9:285.

Christ works against the wicked, and that God, as the heavenly judge, condemns those who object to the doctrine of secret providence. Before Calvin explains the role of 'coelestis pater' and 'coelestis iudex' in God's providence, he first warns Castellio, that God must condemn the wicked (Castellio) because He saves *and* judges. In *De occulta Dei providentia*, Calvin explains both roles of God but the discussion concerning God as 'coelestis iudex' is in greater detail.

Calvin defines predestination as "the free counsel of God by which he regulates the human race, and all the single parts of the universe according to His own immense wisdom and incomprehensible justice".[43] This definition shows that for Calvin, there is a close relationship between predestination and providence, and this could be the reason why Calvin answers the objections to the doctrine of pre-destination, under the heading of 'Secret providence of God' rather than under the heading of 'Predestination'. It seems that Calvin uses the doctrine of secret provi-dence of God in this work to explain the condemnation aspect of predestination,[44] yet could secret providence mean predestination to Calvin? Castellio cited fourteen articles to attack Calvin's doctrine of predestination, the following discusses ten of these.

Calvin's reply to Article 1

The first Article suggests that God created the world for destruction. Castellio has challenged Calvin and claims that if God is merciful and truthful, He would not have created a world only to later destroy His creation in judgement. The objection from Castellio is primarily against Calvin's advocacy that some people are predestined to be Reprobates. Castellio argues that "God by His simple and pure act of will, created the greatest part of the world for destruction".[45] Calvin refuses to accept these vague descriptions of 'greatest part' and 'God's will',[46] believing God shows His gracious act in a different way.[47] It seems that Castellio refers 'the greatest part

---

43 John Calvin, *The Secret Providence of God*, ed. Paul Helm, First edition (Wheaton, IL: Crossway, 2010), 61. "Praedestinationem, ut sacrae scripturae docent, definio liberum esse Dei consilium, quo et humanum genus et singulas mundi partes pro immensa sua sapientia et iustitia incomprehensibili moderatur." CO9:287.

44 "Etsi enim se et suos perdidit Adam, corruptionem tamen et reatum arcano Dei iudicio adscribere necesse est: quia nihil ad nos unius hominis culpa, nisi nos coelestis iudex aeterno exitio addiceret." Article 1 CO9:289.

45 "Primum articulum arripis : Quod Deus nudo puroque voluntatis suae arbitrio maximam mundi partem creaverit ad perditionem." Ibid., CO9:288.

46 "Atqui totum illud de maxima parte mundi, et de nudo puroque Dei arbitrio fictitium est, atque ex malitiae tuae officina productum." Ibid.

47 "Atqui longe aliter gratiam suam nobis commendat, nempe dum tot tamque variis peccatis ignoscens, certat cum obstinata hominum malitia, usque dum ad cumulum perveniat." Ibid., CO9:293.

of the world' and 'God's will' to humankind and double predestination respectively. For if humankind were God's greatest creation, why would He destroy them in His predestination? Calvin stresses that these two issues are not contradictory[48] because they need to be set on the foundation of the secret decree of God.[49] Additionally, Castellio's argument is not tenable because God is not only merciful and truthful, but is also good, powerful, and just. Calvin tries to give an explanation to both situations of the godly and ungodly using secret providence and the inseparability of God's actions in power, goodness, justice, and wisdom.

Firstly, considering God's children, Calvin suggests that everyone should honour the sovereign God as the highest power, as He exercises this power over all creation. While acknowledging that God is indeed merciful, Calvin also emphasises God's justice in His secret providence, to manifest that His care is wise and just.[50] God's goodness, power, and justice are exemplified by God's activities on earth, but these activities are not considered to be 'good' to people, especially for those who suffer. For example, God loves His children and He is supposed to show His fatherly love all the time. However, as a Father, He acts in ways that some think are unwise and unjust.[51] For example, God's activities also include afflicting His offspring, but He is not unjust because He does this according to His secret counsel.[52] Contrary to Castellio's allegation, Calvin holds that God will not create a good thing for destruction as this is unjust, and that God also executes His saving activity by the grace of adoption.[53]

This grace is special and is graciously given to the people who lost their eternal lives when they inherited sin from Adam.[54] However, God initiates salvation by first adopting the Elect who are then reconciled to God in Jesus Christ through the Holy Spirit who draws them to God in secret counsel.[55] While people might be frightened in the abyss of secret providence, instead of being fearful, they should

---

48 "Itaque, instar porci, boni odoris doctrinam rostro tuo evertis, ut aliquid foetoris reperias." Ibid., CO9:288.

49 "Non solo Dei permissu, sed arcano etiam consilio lapsum fuisse Adam, omnesque posteros suo lapsu in aeternum interitum traxisse." Ibid.

50 "Deinde, quanquam mihi Dei voluntas summa est causa, ubique tamen doceo, ubi in eius consiliis et operibus causa non apparet, apud eum tamen esse absconditam, ut nihil nisi iuste et sapienter decreverit. Itaque quod de absoluta potestate nugantur Scholastici non solum repudio, sed etiam detestor, quia iustitiam eius ab imperio separant." Ibid.

51 Ibid., CO9:289.

52 Ibid., CO9:290.

53 Ibid., CO9:289, 290.

54 "Atqui omnes constat in Adam abdicatos esse vita aeterna: adoptionis vero specialem esse gratiam." Ibid., CO9:290.

55 "Imo nisi idem Deus, qui ad poenitentiam omnes voce hortatur, arcano spiritus motu electos adduceret, non diceret Ieremias (31:18)...Deinde cur non omnium oculos peraeque aperuerit,

reconcile to God in His only begotten son, and then peacefully experience God's paternal love, inherit His kingdom, and hope for eternal salvation.[56]

Secondly, considering judgement, Calvin asserts that God acts by choosing some for condemnation, but He also promises He will be merciful, patient, and slow to anger in order to display His goodness.[57] Furthermore, God will give people a lifetime before He judges them. However, while God acts with ordained power, He executes His authority together with His justice, and His authority and justice are inseparable.[58] God has the authority to will the destruction of some people in His secret providence[59] but the reason is incomprehensible to human beings. However, the faithful should not worry because God is just, and He will not create a good being for destruction.[60]

It is also because God's actions manifest together in His goodness, power, wisdom, and justice,[61] not everyone is destined for eternal life.[62] Calvin constantly stresses the significance of God's actions as a whole to explain the two situations in double predestination: God cannot simply be powerful by saving people,[63] but He is also

---

quando interior spiritus illuminatio, qua non nisi paucos dignatur, ad fidem necessaria est?" Ibid., CO9:292–293.

56 "Iam Christus non humanum genus, ac ne Iudaeos quidem passim, sed pusillum gregem compellans, non frustra dicit: Nolite timere, quia complacuit patri vestro in vobis. Nempe quia paternum eius favorem in spem aeternae salutis non experiuntur alii, nisi quos sibi gratos reddit in filio unigenito." Luke 12:32, Article 1 CO9:289

57 "Iam quamvis in multis irae suae documenta exserat Deus, verum tamen illud manet, propensum esse ad bonitatem, tardum ad iram, quando in tolerantia qua. sustinet reprobos, non obscura refulget eius bonitas." Ibid., CO9:293.

58 "Itaque quod de absoluta potestate nugantur Scholastici non solum repudio, sed etiam detestor, quia iustitiam eius ab imperio separant." Ibid., CO9:288.

59 "Etsi enim se et suos perdidit Adam, corruptionem tamen et reatum arcano Dei iudicio adscribere necesse est..." Ibid., CO9:289.

60 Ibid., CO9:290.

61 "Calvin also shows that in God's predestination, He shows His actions in goodness, power, justice and wisdom. "Deinde, quanquam mihi Dei voluntas summa est causa, ubique tamen doceo, ubi in eius consiliis et operibus causa non apparet, apud eum tamen esse absconditam, ut nihil nisi iuste et sapienter decreverit." Ibid., CO9:288. Cf. Iam quam vis in multis irae suae documenta exserat Deus, verum tamen illud manet, propensum esse ad bonitatem, tardum ad iram, quando in tolerantia qua. sustinet reprobos, non obscura refulget eius bonitas." Ibid., CO9:293.

62 "Nam ut fatear nihil in homine fuisse saluti contrarium, proba omnibus salutem occulto Dei consilio fuisse praedestinatam. Breviter idem repetam aliis verbis: Si naturae spectetur integritas qua donatus in prima creatione fuit Adam, ad salutem creatum fuisse, quia nulla illic reperietur mortis causa: si de occulta praedestinatione quaeritur, occurrere profundam illam abyssum, quae in admirationem rapere nos debet." Ibid., CO9:291.

63 "Si quis occurrat morio, eius conspectu admoneor qualem me creare Deus potuerit: quotquot sunt stupidi et hebetes in mundo, totidem mihi specula proponit Deus, in quibus potentia sua non minus formidabilis quam mirifica mihi appareat. Ibid., CO9:290. Cf. Ad quoscunque circuitus te vertas,

powerful because He condemns sinners to show His justice,[64] to refute Castellio's argument about God's destruction of His own creation.

In double predestination, God shows His justice to the Reprobate but He shows His justice, power, and mercy to the Elect.[65] God as a 'coelestis iudex', could have condemned the Elect by His justice because of their corruption inherited from Adam, but as a 'coelestis pater', He wills to save them through His power. Calvin explains the two situations of double predestination: salvation and condemnation, using the actions of God in His goodness, justice, and power in *providentia Dei*. In the situation of salvation, the Elect participate in God's goodness and then hope for eternal life in the future.[66]

Through predestination God also displays His justice and wisdom. While acknowledging that God is merciful, Calvin also emphasises God's justice in His secret providence to manifest that His care is just and wise.[67] That means secret providence is revealed to the faithful. God's justice and wisdom cannot be fully understood but the faithful can be assured that God as the heavenly father, through Christ, bestows the kingdom upon those whom He desires to do so, and He lets them experience His paternal love and the hope for eternal life. God as the heavenly judge, rejects the remainder of humankind and because of their sins, He lets them experience eternal ruin.[68] Combined with the previous analysis, God's goodness,

---

hoc principium tenebo: Quamvis infirmus, et ad defectionem flexibilis creatus fuerit homo, hanc debilitatem fuisse valde bonam, quia paulo post docuit eius ruina, extra Deum nihil firmum esse, vel stabile. Unde etiam conficitur, quod de hominibus ad salutem creatis garris, mutilum esse et inconsiderate positum." Ibid., *CO9*:291.

64 "Deinde hoc non obstat quo minus reiiciat tanquam iustus iudex, quos amore et indulgentia, ut optimus pater, prosequitur." Ibid., *CO9*:289.

65 "Etsi enim se et suos perdidit Adam, corruptionem tamen et reatum arcano Dei iudicio adscribere necesse est: quia nihil ad nos unius hominis culpa, nisi nos coelestis iudex aeterno exitio addiceret." Ibid.

66 "Nempe quia paternum eius favorem in spem aeternae salutis non experiuntur alii, nisi quos sibi gratos reddit in filio unigenito." Ibid.

67 "Deinde, quanquam mihi Dei voluntas summa est causa, ubique tamen doceo, ubi in eius consiliis et operibus causa non apparet, apud eum tamen esse absconditam, ut nihil nisi iuste et sapienter decreverit." Ibid., *CO9*:288.

68 "Quod etiam repudiato Esau, Iacob natu minorem praetulit, in, eo delectu clarum documentum praebuit liberi sui amoris, quo non alios prosequitur nisi quos vult…Iam Christus non humanum genus, ac ne Iudaeos quidem passim, sed pusillum gregem compellans, non frustra dicit: Nolite timere, quia complacuit patri vestro in vobis. Nempe quia paternum eius favorem in spem aeternae salutis non experiuntur alii, nisi quos sibi gratos reddit in filio unigenito…Etsi enim se et suos perdidit Adam, corruptionem tamen et reatum arcano Dei iudicio adscribere necesse est: quia nihil ad nos unius hominis culpa, nisi nos coelestis iudex aeterno exitio addiceret." Article 1 *CO9*:289. Cf. Deinde hoc non obstat quo minus reiiciat tanquam iustus iudex, quos amore et indulgentia, ut optimus pater, prosequitur." Ibid., *CO9*:289

power, wisdom, and justice work together to manifest His predestination. No matter whether God is playing the roles of heavenly father or heavenly judge, He does everything for the benefit of the faithful.

Calvin's reply to Article 2

In responding to Castellio's Article 2, Calvin also uses God's providence, to explain predestination. He does so by emphasising that God's foreknowledge and power are inseparable.[69] That is, God not only permits, He also acts over the two conditions of predestination. The Elect will strive for eternity because God endows them with invincible fortitude.[70] God foresees that the Elect can attain eternal life; similarly, He also foresees that the Reprobate will fall, but the reason for this judgement is hidden in God's secret providence.[71] God's predestination shows His foreknowledge and power working together.

Calvin's reply to Articles 3, 7, 11

In refuting Castellio's Articles 3, 7 and 11, Calvin argues that God's justice is closely related to His wisdom. In God's secret counsel, God judges the condemned, as well as the Elect. Calvin emphasises, that God permits and wills David's adulterous sin, and Job's suffering, and yet God judges their situations with His wisdom.[72] Yet, how can God permit and will everything, including sinful acts? Calvin claims no answer for this, but he encourages believers not only to be content with God's mysteries, without being miserable, but also to renounce their own wisdom.[73] Calvin's responses to Castellio's Articles 3, 7, 11 show that God's will, wisdom, and justice work together, and Calvin argues that God's actions in His providence are inseparable.

Calvin's reply to Articles 3, 4, 5, 8 & 9

Although the reasons God condemns the ungodly are in God's secret, Calvin does explain the result of this secret. By God's eternal decree, He condemns the ungodly, resulting in the execution of His judgement. In the incidents such as the Assyrian

---

69 "Praescientiam Deo affingitis, qua otiosus e coelo speculetur hominum vitam: Deus ipse gubernacula totius mundi sibi vendicans, potentiam suam a praescientia separari non patitur." Article 2 *CO*9:294.

70 "Deus quos elegit, invicta fortitudine fulcit ad perseverantiam." Ibid.

71 Ibid.

72 2 Sam 12:11–12; Job 1:21, Article 3 *CO*9:296

73 Article 3 *CO*9:299.

conquest,[74] Job's afflictions,[75] and the hardening of Pharaoh's heart,[76] the Assyrians, the robbers, and Pharaoh are the axe, rod, or instrument of the heavenly judge to execute His judgements. Sometimes he uses tools, for example Satan, and Pharaoh to carry out this execution even as they are condemned because of their own sins.[77] God guides human actions in His secret providence but human beings, as the second cause, are responsible for their own eternal death.

To summarise, Calvin argues that God as the heavenly father and the heavenly judge, ordains His decree, and carries out His governance and executions using many instruments in His secret providence. Calvin's idea of decree and execution is continued in the work of his student, Theodore Beza in explaining the doctrine of 'singularissima providentiam'. Beza formulates a decree and execution framework, in *Tabula Praedestinationis* 1555, which shows traces of Calvin's ideas in explaining secondary causality in the execution of God's judgement.[78]

In *De occulta providentia Dei*, Calvin's doctrine of predestination is related to God's special providence. This special providence is especially for humankind (singular providence for the singular divine creation), in which God shows them His actions in goodness, power, justice, and wisdom. These four actions together with God's foreknowledge and mercy work inseparably in the world, where God as the heavenly father and the heavenly judge, governs by choosing some people to be the Elect and the rest of humanity to be condemned. The reason for the election and the reprobation is explained by secret providence and the execution of the judgement is carried out by instruments appointed by God. Calvin's interpretation of predestination starts from special providence, suggesting a significant providential sense. It

---

74 "...Assyrios esse conductitios eius milites: Nabucadnezer in expilanda Aegypto esse eius servum: item Assyrios in excidenda Iudaea securim esse in eius manu, et virgam furoris eius." Ibid., *CO*9:297.

75 "Atque ut intelligas non: mecum tibi negotium esse vel certamen, sed cum iudice coelesti, cuius tribunal non, effugies: certe non alio quam spiritus instinctu pronunciat Iob, Dei esse opus, quod et Satanae et latronum erat (Iob 1:21)..." Ibid., *CO*9:300. Cf. "Si in spoliatione Iob commune est Dei, Satanae et latronum opus, quomodo a culpa eximetur Deus, cuius Satan cum suis organis reus erit?" Articles 4&5, *CO*9:301.

76 "...Deus cor Pharaonis induravit? Atqui non aliunde petenda est mihi solutio, quam ex verbis noni articuli, quae tu recitans vel depravas vel non assequeris: quia si Dei voluntas summa est, vel remota indurationis causa, homo ipse cor suum indurans sibi propior causa est." Articles 8&9, *CO*9:306.

77 "Clamat Moses sua Deo arcana esse: in lege vero patefactum esse hominibus quod utile cognitu est. (Deut 29:29)...Iam aut plus quam caecus es, aut vides, quum te ab adulterio prohibet voce sua Deus, nolle te esse adulterum: et tamen in adulteriis quae damnat, iusta iudicia exercere...quam aliis maleficiis utitur ad exsequendas suas vindictas..." Article 7 *CO*9:303. Cf. "Primam causam vel remotam a mediis et propinquis ubique distinguo: quia dum mali affectus radicem in se reperit peccator, non est cur in Deum culpam derivet." Articles 8&9, *CO*9:306.

78 This is discussed in chapter 6.

also resembles the doctrine of heavenly providence, as suggested in his sermons on Job, but the term *'providentia coelestis'* is not used in *De occulta providentia Dei*.

The 1559 *Institutes* – *'providentia coelestis'*

In Book 1 of the 1559 *Institutes*, Calvin seems to convey the same message as in his *Sermons sur le livre de Job* regarding *'providentia coelestis'*. This message is that *'providentia coelestis'* is not like general providence which bestows benefits and shows kindness to all human beings.[79] Rather, in *'providentia coelestis'*, God endows the godly with clemency and blessings, but in His judgement, He punishes the wicked because of His vengeance.[80] *'Providentia coelestis'* is God's governance and judgement acted upon human beings, but it especially shows God's fatherly kindness.[81] This explanation is similar to the example in the sermons on Job and to the discussion in *De occulta providentia Dei* as they all stress God's actions as a whole,[82] but in the 1559 *Institutes*, Calvin adds that *'providentia coelestis'* is part of the knowledge of God which the faithful should trust. This kind of knowledge encourages the godly to worship God and to hope for eternal life as God's clemency and His judgement are not yet fulfilled in the present life.[83]

---

79 "In secundo quoque genere operum eius, quae scilicet praeter ordinarium naturae cursum eveniunt, nihilo obscuriora se proferunt virtutum eius argumenta. Nam in administranda hominum societate ita providentiam suam temperat, ut quum sit erga omnes innumeris modis benignus ac beneficus, apertis tamen ac quotidianis indiciis, suam piis clementiam, improbis ac sceleratis severitatem declaret." 1559 *Institutes* 1.5.7, CO2:46. Cf. "…sive attollat contemptissimos e vulgo, sive proceres deiiciat ex alto dignitatis gradu: propositis eiusmodi exemplis colligit, qui censentur esse fortuiti casus, totidem esse providentiae coelestis testimonia, praesertim vero paternae clementiae; atque hinc piis dari materiam laetitiae, impiis vero et reprobis ora obstrui." Ps(s) 107, Ibid., 1.5.8, CO2:47.

80 "Non enim dubiae sunt quas de flagitiis sumit ultiones; quemadmodum non obscure tutorem, ac etiam vindicem se innocentiae esse demonstrat, dum bonorum vitam sua benedictione prosperat, necessitati opitulatur, dolores lenit ac solatur, calamitates sublevat, saluti per omnia consulit." Ibid., 1.5.7, CO2:46.

81 "…totidem esse providentiae coelestis testimonia, praesertim vero paternae clementiae; atque hinc piis dari materiam laetitiae, impiis vero et reprobis ora obstrui." Ibid., 1.5.8, CO2:47.

82 "…si nullum peccatum nunc aperte Deus puniret, nulla esse divina providentia crederetur. Fatendum est igitur, in singulis Dei operibus, praesertim autem in ipsorum universitate…Porro lucidissimae quum illic appareant: quorsum tamen potissimum spectent, quid valeant, quem in finem a nobis sint reputandae, tum demum assequimur dum in nos ipsos descendimus, ac consideramus quibus modis suam in nobis vitam, sapientiam, virtutem Dominus exserat, suam iustitiam, bonitatem, clementiam erga nos exerceat. Ibid., 1.5.10, CO2:48.

83 "Deinde eiusmodi notitia non modo ad Dei cultum excitare nos debet, sed ad spem quoque futurae vitae expergefacere, et erigere. Quum enim animadvertamus quae Dominus tum clementiae, tum severitatis suae specimina edit, inchoata duntaxat et semiplena esse, haud dubie ad maiora sic ipsum

Calvin's discussion of the doctrine of '*providentia coelestis*' is not frequent but Book 2 of the 1559 *Institutes* may provide some resonances. Book 2 is about human knowledge, humanity's corrupt mind, and the restoration of human relationship with God through Jesus Christ. When Calvin explains the condition of human will, he distinguishes two kinds of '*res*' which the possessors of corrupt human will can understand when God grants them His grace.[84] They are earthly things (*res terrenas*) and heavenly things (*res coelestes*). Earthly things do not contribute to 'God's kingdom, true justice, or to the blessedness of the future life'.[85] They are, rather, things which facilitate humankind to live on earth, for example, policy, the economy, mechanical skills, and liberal studies.[86] The heavenly things are 'the pure knowledge of God, the nature of true righteousness, and the mysteries of the heavenly kingdom'.[87] They are 'knowledge of God and of His will, and the rule to which His people conform their lives'.[88] Earthly things are valued in the present life and they are not comparable to eternal happiness.[89] However, enjoying earthly benefits can lead to an understanding of heavenly bliss.[90] Calvin argues that God's people are encouraged to aspire to a heavenly heritage but in the present life they are able to see, speak about and taste only earthly benefits.[91] In '*providentia coelestis*', God as a merciful father endows the godly with benevolence and eternal life. Through distinguishing the meaning of the earthly things and heavenly things, the Elect come to appreciate and enjoy this providence, and they are assured of God's protection and salvation. The explanation of '*providentia coelestis*' in the 1559 *Institutes* is similar to the explanation of '*providence celeste*' in the *Sermons sur le*

---

praeludere reputemus oportet, quorum manifestatio plenaque exhibitio in aliam vitam differtur." Ibid.

84 "Ac illa quidem vulgaris sententia, quam sumpserunt ex Augustino, mihi placet, naturalia dona fuisse corrupta in homine per peccatum, supernaturalibus autem exinanitum fuisse…Unde sequitur, ita exsulare a regno Dei, ut quaecunque ad beatam animae vitam spectant, in eo exstincta sint, donec per regenerationis gratiam ipsa recuperet." Ibid., 2.2.12, *CO*2:195.

85 "Res terrenas voco, quae ad Deum regnumque eius, ad veram iustitiam, ad futurae vitae beatitudinem non pertingunt, sed cum vita praesenti rationem relationemque habent, et quodammodo intra eius fines continentur." Ibid., 2.2.13, *CO*2:197.

86 Ibid.

87 "Res coelestes, puram Dei notitiam, verae iustitiae rationem, ac regni coelestis mysteria." Ibid.

88 Ibid.

89 Calvin has discussed this aspect in *Sermons sur le livre de Iob* 1554–1555. In the sermons, Calvin exhorts his congregation to think about the eternal bliss and not just the present goodness God endowed onto His people in the present life.

90 1559 *Institutes* 2.11.1, *CO*2:329.

91 "Porro prima est, quod tametsi olim quoque Dominus populi sui mentes in coelestem haereditatem volebat collimare arrectosque esse animos, quo tamen in spe illius melius alerentur, contemplandam sub beneficiis terrenis ac quodammodo degustandam exhibebat…" Ibid.

livre de Job, but here Calvin elaborates more about earthly things (*res terrenas*) and heavenly things (*res coelestes*).

Relationship between 'providentia coelestis' and 'aeterna Dei providentia'

In 1548, Calvin discussed '*providentiae coelestis*' when he wrote *Commentarius in epistolam ad Galatas*, six years earlier than when he discussed the same doctrine in his *Sermons sur le livre de Job*, in 1554. Calvin dedicated the commentary to Christoph of Württemberg, Duke of Württemberg (1515–1568), who had converted to Protestantism by 1540 and succeeded his father's political leadership in German reformation. Calvin reminds Christoph that the commentary on Galatians is a profitable and religious book which offers instructions and consolations in the midst of the stressful situation at Church.[92] Another reason Calvin presents the commentary to Christoph is because Christoph is a good example for the Church people to follow.[93] Calvin's argument in this commentary highlights that during the time when Paul left Asia, where the Galatians lived, the false Gospel influenced the faith of the Galatian Christians and the false apostles taught that people are saved by external rites.[94] Calvin strongly recommended readers to carefully learn from Paul's correct teaching,[95] and regard Paul as a true apostle, as opposed to the false apostles who promote the teaching of justification by observing ceremonies.[96]

---

92 "Quod si ullum fuit unquam tempus quo necessariae essent ex pia doctrina consolationes, quid aliud vel maxime heroicis pectoribus reliqui facit praesens ecclesiae calamitas, imo plures ac indigniores quae instare etiamnum videntur? Itaque ut quisque ad extremum invictus stare cupit, in hanc fulturam totus recumbat. Ut quisque firmum praesidium appetit, conferre se discat in hoc veluti asylum. Porro in his quatuor epistolis, quas meo labore explicatas tibi offero, eximie Princeps, multa consolationis argumenta reperies his temporibus valde apta, quibus recensendis ideo nunc supersedeo quod ultro suis locis, et quidem melius, patefient." *Calvinus Christophoro Duci* CO12:659.

93 "Nam quum in hac rerum perturbatione, quae alios concutit alios deiicit prorsus, mira tibi constet animi aequabilitas et moderatio, et simul adversus quasvis procellas singularis constantia, totius ecclesiae magnopere referre existimo, in te, quasi in illustri speculo, propositum omnibus esse exemplum quod imitentur." Ibid.

94 "Tempore Pauli sub Romanorum ditione erant. Porro quum pure ac fideliter eos instituisset in evangelio: supervenerant eo absente pseudoapostoli, qui verum semen falsis et vitiosis dogmatibus corruperant. Docebant enim necessariam esse adhuc observationem caeremoniarum. Videri poterat res levis momenti in speciem. At Paulus tanquam de primario christianae fidei capite dimicat: neque immerito…" *Commentarius in epistolam ad Galatas* Argumentum, CO50:161–162.

95 "Nos quoque admoniti quam gravis et seria disputatio hic tractetur, eo plus attentionis afferamus ad legendum." Argumentum, CO50:162.

96 "Quamquam semper admista est ambitio: imo semper nimia morositas est ambitiosa. Ut redeam ad istos pseudoapostolos: si tantummodo prava aemulatione ubique usum caeremoniarum ingerere tentassent, quas Ierosolymis viderant servari: iam in eo non leviter peccassent. Est enim iniquum,

Commentarius in epistolam ad Galatas is not a work composed for the sake of a discussion of the doctrine of *providentia Dei*, but Calvin endeavours to make a distinction between the false and true Gospel, and the false and true apostles. This distinction leads him to discuss the result of those false Christians. When Calvin comments on 4:30, he stresses that believers inherit a place in the Church, while hypocrites (false Christians), will be cast out like strangers. This is governed by '*providentia coelestis*'.[97] Calvin uses this term, heavenly providence, to assure true Christians that they are members of the Church. The meaning of '*providentia coelestis*' is the same as '*praesentissima Dei*', the third kind of providence Calvin suggested in 1552. The period from 1548 when he wrote *Commentarius in epistolam ad Galatas*, to 1552 when he authored *De aeterna Dei praedestinatione*, to 1554 when he preached *Sermons sur le livre de Iob*, and to 1558 when he composed *De occulta providentia Dei*, was the time when Calvin was formulating the doctrine of '*providentia coelestis*'.

The idea of inheriting a place in the Church, is further elaborated in Book 3 of the 1559 *Institutes*, when Calvin discusses the topic of predestination. God wills to predestine some to be His children, and wills to exclude the remainder from the inheritance of salvation.[98] The one who has not become part of Christ, will not inherit God's kingdom,[99] and by '*aeterna Dei providentia*', these people are

---

ex consuetudine protinus facere regulam. Sed plus erat mali in doctrina impia et perniciosa, quod religione volebant obstrictas tenere conscientias: quod iustitiam in observatione collocabant. Nunc tenemus cur in asserendo suo apostolatu tam animosus sit Paulus, et cur reliquis apostolis se opponat." Ibid., *CO*50:164.

97 "…sed haec aliquanto efficacior, dum addit, hypocritas cum sua iactantia nihil aliud profecturos, quam ut eiiciantur ex spirituali Abrahae familia: nobis vero nihil ominus salvam fore haereditatem, utcunque insolenter nos ad tempus lacessant…Locus pulcherrimus, ne turbemur hypocritarum fastu: aut illorum sorti invideamus, quum temporariam cum dignitate mansionem habent in ecclesia: sed patienter exitum, qui eos manet, exspectemus. Multi enim vel spurii, vel alieni locum usurpant in ecclesia: sed fidem perpetuo fixam non habent. Quemadmodum instar alienigenae, eiectus fuit cum posteris suis Ismael, qui tamen primogenitura inflatus initio regnabat. Rident hic nasuti quidam homines Pauli simplicitatem, quod bilem foeminae ex futili rixa natam comparet Dei iudicio: sed non animadvertunt, interpositum fuisse Dei decretum, quo palam fieret totum id coelesti providentia gubernari." Gal 4:30, *CO*50:242.

98 "Dicitur segregare Deus quos adoptat in salutem…Quos ergo Deus praeterit, reprobat; neque alia de causa nisi quod ab haereditate, quam filiis suis praedestinat, illos vult excludere." 1559 *Institutes* 3.23.1, *CO*2:698.

99 "Si salutem, vitam et regni coelestis immortalitatem, non alio tum quoque confugiendum est, quando ipse unus et vitae fons est, et salutis anchora, et regni coelorum haeres. Iam quorsum electio pertinet, nisi ut in filiorum locum a coelesti patre cooptati eius favore salutem et immortalitatem obtineamus ? Quantumlibet revolvas et excutias, ultimum tamen eius scopum non ultra tendere intelliges. Proinde quos Deus sibi filios assumpsit, non in ipsis eos dicitur elegisse, sed in Christo suo; quia non nisi in eo amare illos poterat (Eph. 1, 4), nec regni sui haereditate honorare, nisi eius consortes ante factos." Ibid., 3.24.5, *CO*2:715–716.

condemned to eternal death.[100] Calvin further discusses the doctrine of eternal providence in Book 4 when he confirms that the salvation of church members rests upon the unshakable nature of the Church, as the Church stands firmly because God's election is in His eternal providence.[101]

In the 1559 *Institutes*, Calvin shows his meaning of the doctrine of '*providentia coelestis*' by walking his readers from the introduction of the doctrine in Book 1 to heavenly heritage in Book 2 to eternal providence in Book 3, and finally to the assurance of salvation in Book 4. It is only in the 1559 *Institutes* a full picture of the doctrine of '*providentia coelestis*' can be discerned. Furthermore, starting from the 1536 *Institutes*, Calvin used the doctrine of eternal providence to describe the condition that God's election gathers the faithful as members of the Church.[102] It is confirmed that both '*providentia coelestis*' and '*aeterna Dei providentia*' are similar doctrine relating to predestination, and that both doctrines assure the certitude of salvation for the Elect, which is the concern of most Reformers.[103] The third kind of God's providence Calvin defined in *De aeterna Dei praedestinatione* 1552 for His Church, is '*providentia coelestis*'.

'*Providentia coelestis*' as employed in Book 1 of the 1559 *Institutes* is '*providentia specialissima*', which also means predestination as decreed in God's secret providence. Although the doctrine of providence is placed in Book 1 in the 1559 *Institutes*, Calvin uses the term heavenly providence to bridge the gap between providence and predestination. Precisely, Calvin links divine providence and eternal predestination with the doctrine of heavenly providence. Richard Muller asserts that the placement of the doctrine of predestination in the Reformed theologies of the sixteenth and seventeenth centuries is primarily 'a matter of genre', and although various placements of the doctrine are found, there is no shift in doctrinal implication in

---

100 "Hanc autem imputare ne Deo possint, obstat quod suae creationi testimonium reddat. Tametsi enim aeterna Dei providentia in eam cui subiacet calamitatem conditus est homo, a se ipso tamen eius materiam, non a Deo sumpsit; quando nulla alia ratione sic perditus est, nisi quia a pura Dei creatione in vitiosam et impuram perversitatem degeneravit." Ibid., 3.23.9, *CO*2:706.

101 "Hac enim lege credimus ecclesiam, ut certo persuasi simus nos esse eius membra. Hoc enim modo nititur salus nostra certis solidisque fulcris, ut etiamsi tota orbis machina labefactetur, corruere ipsa et concidere nequeat. Primum stat cum Dei electione, nec nisi cum aeterna illius providentia variare aut deficere potest. Deinde quodammodo coniuncta est cum firmitudine Christi; qui non magis patietur a se divelli suos fideles, quam membra sua discerpi ac dilaniari. Accedit quod veritatem, dum in ecclesiae sinu continemur, semper nobis constaturam securi sumus. Postremo quod promissiones istas sentimus ad nos pertinere: salus erit in Sion…" Ibid., 4.1.3, *CO*2:748.

102 "It is also holy, because as many as have been chosen by God's eternal providence to be adopted as members of the church – all these are made holy by the Lord. "Sancta etiam est, quia quotquot aeterna Dei providentia electi sunt, ut in ecclesiae membra cooptarentur, a Domino omnes sanctificantur (Ioan 17; Eph 5)." 1536 *Institutes* Book 2; *CO*1:73.

103 Susan Elizabeth Schreiner, *Are You Alone Wise? The Search for Certainty in the Early Modern Era*, Oxford Studies in Historical Theology (New York: Oxford University Press, 2012), 58.

the generations after Calvin.[104] This work agrees with Muller's claim but the role of 'providentia coelestis' is missing in this claim. However, the argument of this work proves that Calvin's doctrine of 'providentia coelestis', discussed in Book 1 of the 1559 *Institutes*, supports an inseparable relationship between the doctrines of providence and predestination for the children of God. The doctrine of heavenly providence makes the 'placement' of the doctrine of predestination less important, and therefore the role of this doctrine strengthens Muller's claim.

Predestination is governed in God's special providence. The reason for the affliction of the Elect and the condemnation of the Reprobate are explained by God's secret providence but it is being taken care of by 'providentia coelestis'. The purpose of 'providentia coelestis' is to separate the true Christians from the false ones in the Church. Some scholars of Calvin studies of post-Calvin Reformed theology call this kind of providence for the Church as 'providentia specialissima'.[105] However, to Calvin, this kind of providence is not simply 'providentia specialissma' but is also 'providentia coelestis', which consists of general providence, special providence, secret providence, providence for the Church and eternal providence from the faithful's point of view. This is the full meaning of his doctrine of 'providentia Dei'.

Conclusion

In *Sermons sur le livre de Job*, Calvin argues that in 'providence celeste', God endows His children with fatherly goodness and governs the world with His justice. Heavenly providence is a special type of special providence, and it also has a sense of predestination. In *De occulta providentia Dei*, Calvin argues that God's secret providence is the explanation of the cause of the faithful's suffering and predestination. He especially offers a comprehensive account of the doctrine of predestination by precisely asserting that God, as the 'coelestis pater' and the 'coelestis iudex', decrees some people to be the Elect and the remainder to be the Reprobate in His decree. In the 1559 *Institutes*, Calvin argues that in 'providentia coelestis', God as the heavenly father bestows genuine Christians with goodness and predestines them to have salvation and to inherit the Church. God as the heavenly judge, predestines false

---

104 Richard A. Muller, "The place of predestination in Reformed theology: issue or non-issue?" *Calvin Theological Journal*, 40 no. 2 Nov 2005, 195, 209–210.

105 Gulielmus Bucanus could be the first Reformed theologian who used 'specialissima' to describe this non-universal providence. Gulielmus Bucanus, *Institio theologica* (Lausanne, 1605), 151. Also quoted in Mark W. Elliott, *Providence Perceived: Divine Action from a Human Point of View* (Berlin/Boston: De Gruyter, 2015), 154. Cf. Werner Krusche, Das Wirken des Heiligen Geistes nach Calvin. (Göttingen: Vandenhoech & Ruprecht, 1957), 14. Also in Charles Partee, *Calvin and Classical Philosophy* (Leiden: E. J. Brill, 1977), 135.

Christians, to be cast away from the Church. The purpose of '*providentia coelestis*' is for the protection and salvation of the faithful, and in this special care, the godly can long for life in eternity. Furthermore, they can see part of divine mercy and divine justice, so they can honour and glorify God on earth.

From examining Calvin's works from 1554–1559 concerning *providentia Dei* and predestination, it is noticeable that Calvin's interpretation of God's providence is deeply intertwined with both soteriological matters and the doctrine of predestination. In the 1559 *Institutes*, Calvin's interpretation of God's providence relates to soteriological matters, regardless of the placement of the doctrines of providence, and predestination. *Sermons sur le livre de Job* 1554–1555, *De occulta providentia Dei* 1558, and the 1559 *Institutes* need to be read together to understand this claim and to grasp the meaning of heavenly providence, which acts as a support to this claim.

From 1536 to 1559, Calvin consolidated his doctrine of the very special providence, and these terms show the continuation, development, and confirmation of his thoughts: from '*aeterna Dei providentia*' in 1536, to '*providentia coelestis*' in 1548, to '*praesentissima Dei*' in 1552, to '*providence celeste*' in 1554, to '*coelestis pater* and *coelestis iudex*' in 1558, and finally back to '*providentia coelestis*' and '*aeterna Dei providentia*' in 1559. Calvin's doctrine of *providentia Dei* is truly the doctrine of '*providentiae coelestis*' from the faithful point of view. The term heavenly providence implies that God's providence spans from earth to eternity, and that faithful should hope for eternal happiness.

6. Beza's interpretation of the doctrine of *providentia Dei* from 1555 to 1589

Théodore de Bèza (1519–1605) was Calvin's student and he succeeded Calvin in leadership of the Genevan churches after Calvin's death. Calvin showed tremendous respect to his successor by delegating to him important tasks such as revising Bible translations and responding to Sebastian Castellio.[1] Similarly, Beza showed his appreciation of his teacher by writing a biography of Calvin, and honouring him as one of the most beautiful examples of the pious life, describing him as a genuine man, with excellent qualities and splendid virtues.[2] Beza appreciated Calvin's faithfulness to God and his kindness towards the French refugees. Beza also wrote to defend Calvin's doctrine of predestination and to support Michael Servetus's condemnation. Apparently, Beza allied himself with Calvin's position on many doctrines.[3] However, regarding Job, Beza took a different view to Calvin.

The exegesis of the Book of Job by Beza and Calvin shares a common starting point, with both accepting God's providence as the Book's theme, but Beza moves away from Calvin's position when Beza considers Job's case in particular. However, this consideration is not established within a vacuum, for it is evident that there is a development of his doctrine of predestination in Beza's works from 1555 to 1589. This development illustrates the differences Beza and Calvin hold concerning Job. Therefore, this chapter proposes three arguments. Firstly, Beza's decree-execution framework suggested in his work, *Tabula praedestinationis* and Calvin's doctrine of heavenly providence demonstrate lines of continuity. Secondly, there is an increase in use of some scholastic terms in Beza's interpretation of the doctrine of predestination and in his apology.[4] Thirdly, Beza's doctrine of predestination starts

---

1 Scott, M. Manetsch, "The Journey towards Geneva: Theodore Beza's Conversion, 1535–1548" in *Calvin, Beza, and Later Calvinism: Calvin Society Papers 2005*, edited by David Foxgrover (Grand Rapids, MI: CRC Produce Services, 2006), 38–57. Also in Bruce Gordon, *Calvin* (New Haven: Yale University Press, 2011), 282.

2 Théodore de Bèze, "*Life of John Calvin*", in John Calvin, *Tracts and Treatises on the Reformation of the Church*, translated by Henry Beveridge (Grand Rapids, MI: WM.B. Eerdmans Publishing Company, 1958), lxi, cxxxvi–ii.

3 "...Beza was utterly loyal to Calvin's teaching on consistorial church structures and the doctrines of predestination and the sacraments." Gordon, *Calvin*, 283.

4 In 1555, Beza started to adopt some content from the Aristotelian fourfold causality to explain the execution aspect of his framework for the doctrine of predestination. In 1589, he adopted another scholastic explanation: '*intrinsic motus*' to explain human will. Beza said, "Sunt autem haec instrumenta in triplici differentia. Quaedam enim sunt mere παθητικα...Quaedam sic extrinsecus mouentur, ut simul sese etiam ipsa moueant naturali quodam appetitu, sed citra intelligentiae &

to discuss causality, as a defence against God as the author of sin and gradually moves to the discussion of human righteousness, to assure salvation for the Elect.

Tabula praedestinationis 1555

Jérôme-Hermès Bolsec was a French medical doctor and Catholic, yet after preaching an evangelical sermon, he had to flee France to a place just outside Geneva, where he lived in exile to avoid being persecuted in France.[5] When he practiced his profession in this new region, he healed the son of Calvin's friend, and through contacts with people from the Reformed tradition, he converted to the Reformed faith around 1550.[6] Bolsec appreciated Calvin's theology but he openly objected to his doctrine of predestination after a Sunday sermon in 1551, because he believed Calvin's doctrine made God the author of sin.[7] Bolsec was sentenced to prison and then banished from Geneva in December 1551. When Bolsec attacked Calvin's doctrine of predestination, Calvin was busy responding to Albert Pighius and Georgius Siculus's refutation on the same doctrine, so Calvin's student Beza helped him to respond to the controversy created by Bolsec.[8] The *Tabula praedestinationis* was published in 1555, yet it was believed to have been composed as early as 1551, the same year when Beza answered Bolsec's attack on Calvin's doctrine of predestination. Beza puts the table of predestination on the first page of his *Summa totius Christianismi sive descriptio et distributio causarum salutis electorum, & exitii reproborum, ex sacris literis collecta et explicate,*[9] and he uses eight chapters to explain this table.

---

rationis vsum praeeuntem: cuiusmodi sunt bestiae omnes, quarum diuersos gradus nihil opus est nunc attingere, & quae propterea proprie nec bene agere nec peccare dicuntur. Quaedam denique sic mouentur, extra se ut quum, intelligentia & ratione praedita sint, sint etiam ipsorum aliquae agendi partes unde proprium ipsorum opus nascitur…Lapsus iste nec Angelos illos nec homines aboleuit, sed naturam duntaxat eorum deprauauit: usque adeo tamen ut intrinsecus omnis illorum motus, manens quails nunc est, nunquam nisi male sese moueat, ac proinde nunquam vere bonum, sed vitiosum semper opus edat." Théodore de Bèze, *Jobus Theodori Bezae Partim Commentariis Partim Paraphrasi Illustratus* (Genève: Bibliothèque de Genève, 1589), Job 1:21, 52. Cf. Théodore de Bèze, *Iob Expounded by Theodore Beza: Partly in Manner of a Commentary, Partly in Manner of a Paraphrase* (London: Iohn Legatt, Vniversitie of Cambridge, 1589), Job 1:21.

5 Shawn D. Wright, *Theodore Beza: The Man and the Myth* (Fearn, Ross-shire: Christian Focus, 2015), 119.

6 Gordon, *Calvin*, 205.

7 Wright, *Theodore Beza*, 119.

8 Ibid., 122.

9 Théodore Bèze, *Summa totius Christianismi sive descriptio et distributio causarum salutis electorum, & exitii reproborum, ex sacris literis collecta* (Geneva: Ioannis Crispini, 1570).

In *Tabula praedestinationis*, Beza puts the two aspects of predestination in 'order', and later in the seventeenth century these became regarded as supralapsarianism. Donald Sinnema believes that Beza was the first theologian to adopt a supralapsarian position. [10] However, Beza's original aim of formulating *Tabula praedestinationis* was to present the doctrine of predestination as a biblical doctrine, and orderly to prevent speculation about it. The title, *Summa totius Christianismi sive descriptio et distributio causarum salutis electorum, & exitii reproborum, ex sacris literis collecta et explicate* states that this is a biblical exploration of causes of election and reprobation, and the vast amount of Scripture used in the context serves the same purpose. This order of *Tabula praedestinationis* describes that God's eternal decree is incomprehensible,[11] and is the first cause of the salvation of the Elect, and that similarly, He ordains the Reprobate's damnation in His eternal decree.[12] The purpose of God's eternal decree is neither the salvation of the Elect, nor the eternal death of the Reprobate but the glorification of God in His mercy and justice.[13]

To explain the situation of the Elect, Beza asserts that God, on the one hand, has determined who He will choose. On the other hand, he considers that God

---

10 Donald Sinnema, "Beza's view of predestination in historical perspective", in *Théodore de Bèze, 1519-1605: actes du colloque de Genève*, septembre 2005, Travaux d'humanisme et Renaissance, Irena Backus and Institut d'histoire de la Réformation, eds., no. 424 (Genève: Droz, 2007). 219-239.

11 "Idem ille Deus ab aeterno proposuit & decreuit in semetipso omnia suis temporibus ad gloriam suam creare, ac nominatim quidem homines, idque duobus modis penitus diuersis: ita nempe, ut alios quos sibi visum fuerit pro arcana sua voluntate faciat per misericordiam gloriae suae participes, quos vasa honoris, electos, filios promissionis, & praedestinatos ad salutem ex Dei verbo appellamus: in alteris vero, quos item placuerit in eum vsum suscitare, iram ac potentiam suam ostendat, ut in ipsis quoque glorificetur, quos vasa contumeliae & ira, & ad omne bonum opus reprobos vocamus." Theodori Bezae Vezelii, *Tractationum Theologicarum, in quibus pleraque Christianae Religionis dogmata adversus haereses nostris temporibus renovatas solide ex verbo Dei defenduntur* (Genevae, 1582), Chapter 2, 173.

12 "Haec electio seu praedestinatio ad salutem in ipso proposito Dei considerata, id est, decretum ipsum & propositum eligendi…Itaque Scriptura quoties filios Dei vult spe certa confirmare, non haeret vel in secundarum causarum testimoniis, id est, fidei fructibus, neque in ipsis secundis & proximis causis, fide videlicet & vocatione…Item quum de reproborum interitu agitur, quanuis tota culpa intra ipsos maneat, interdum tamen, quoties ita opus est, Spiritus Dei ut melius ex comparatione notas faciat diuitias gloriae erga misericordiae vasa, insignemque suam potentiam atque adeo lenitatem, usque in altum illud mysterium nos subuehit, quod omnes damnationis illorum causas ordine antecedit." Ibid., Chapter 3, 174–176.

13 "Dominus ut aeternum illud consilium ad gloriam suam exequeretur, viam quandam sibi muniit pro sua infinita sapientia, utrisque tum eligendis, tum reprobandis communem. Quum enim in electorum salute constituisset insigne misericordiae suae specimen edere: itemque in reprobis condemnandis iustum suum iudicium ostendere, necesse fuit ut utrosque sub contumacia & peccato includeret, ut omnium credentium, id est, electorum (est enim fides donum Dei electis peculiare) misereatur: & e contrario ut iustae damnationis argumentum in iis inueniat, quibus neque credere, neque mysteria Dei nosse datum est." Ibid., Chapter 3, 177.

displays His nature of justice and mercy.[14] The Elect are sinful, so in God's justice, they are deemed to be condemned to death, however, in God's infinite mercy, He appoints His only son to die for the Elect to display His justice and appease God's wrath. Sinful humans are justified and sanctified through Jesus's death, burial, and resurrection. Yet, how can the Elect benefit from these? It is through listening to the preaching of the Gospel, that the Elect, as distinct from other people, are drawn to God's revelation which is especially for them.

This message, which is originally mysterious, is no longer a secret after God's revelation of it to them. The Elect attain this inspiration partly by the inward testimony of their conscience, as enabled by the Holy Spirit and partly by the deliverance of sin through the same Spirit. The Elect are granted the gift of faith, adopted as God's children, and are entitled to inherit God's kingdom in eternity. This faith is weak, but their adoption is revealed to them through the Sacrament of Baptism and confirmed by the Sacrament of the Lord's Supper.[15]

In the explanation of God's eternal election, Beza's proposition of the decree and execution framework is apparent: in God's secret decree, He chooses some to be saved and through a manifest of orderly causes – for example father God, Jesus Christ, the Holy Spirit, human conscience, preaching of the Gospel, and sacraments – God executes salvation. God as a judge, shows Himself as most just and could condemn the sinful Elect. However, God as a saviour, shows Himself as merciful and saves the Elect. He eternally decrees who is to be saved, while humanity has a voluntary participation in the execution process. However, Beza emphasises that God's purpose of election is ordained in God and appointed in Christ, and this precedes the secondary causes which can affect the execution process.[16] The order of the decree and execution is stressed and explicit.

---

14 "Hac igitur duplici ratione, ea que plane diuersa, vltimus ille iudiciorum Dei exitus gloriam ipsius omnibus pate faciet, ut qui in electis suis & summe iustum & summe misericordem sese declarauerit..." Ibid., Chapter 6, 196.

15 "Quum superiora illa Dominus in sese, uti diximus, constituisset, deinde serie causarum proxima, & tamen aeterna, ut sunt illi omnia praesentia, eos omnes gradus sigillatim ordinauit quibus eligendos suos in regnum suum subueheret." Ibid., Chapter 4, 180. Cf. "Altera, quae electis propria est atque peculiaris, in eo posita est, ut Christum universaliter & promiscue oblatum, nobis ipsis tanquam nostrum applicemus, & singuli nostrae electionis certiores reddamur, olim quidem ab aeterno in arcano Dei absconditae, postea vero nobis declaratae, partim intrinseco conscientiae testimonio per Spiritum Dei externae praedicationi adiunctum..." Ibid., Chapter 4, 186. Cf. "...idcirco primum omnium, Sacramento Baptismi initiamur: deinde praeter auditum verbi, ea fides in nobis rursus obsignatur Sacramento Coenae Domini: quorum quidem Sacramentorum hic est praecipuus finis, ut certa sint & efficacia signa..." Ibid., Chapter 4, 187.

16 "Sic quum de causis salutis in gradus & certa serie describendis agitur, in electorum salute propositum eligendi, quod Deus in semetipso decreuit, ab electione ipsa distinguimus, quae est in Christo constituta, ita ut illud ista & caetera omnia quae consequuntur, in causarum serie ante grediatur." Ibid., Chapter 2, 177.

For the explanation of the situation of the Reprobate, Beza stresses that it is necessary to separate the ordinance of reprobation and reprobation itself,[17] the same way as he specifies the aspect of election: for God's decree in election and the election itself are separated. The separation in the aspect of reprobation describes two situations where in God's secret decree, He ordains the condemnation of some people, and in God's will, these people voluntarily sin against God because of human corrupted will and lack of faith, thus God moves all the causes towards the end so that He is glorified in their just condemnation. God causes them to hear the Gospel and they are moved to have some taste of the heavenly gift,[18] however, they fall away from faith because of their own vile concupiscence and corruption. They can only exhibit infidelity, ignorance, and iniquity and then should be condemned in God for the glorification of His justice.[19] To put it succinctly, the eternal decree of reprobation is caused by God and execution of the Reprobate is caused firstly by God and secondly, by some other causes, such as human sinfulness. Therefore, the ungodly are condemned through their own fault. However, God as judge, shows Himself as the most just and He is not to be blamed for their condemnation.[20] In this way, Beza defends the view that God is not the author of sin.

Sinnema stresses that for Beza, decree and execution have different causes and that the cause of the decree must be distinguished from the cause of the execution of the decree.[21] Sinnema believes that Beza,

> avoids reference to God as a cause of sin in any positive sense. Instead, he uses the decree-execution framework to provide a somewhat more moderate solution: God executes his decrees by use of secondary causes, and the human will intercede between the decree and its execution. Though moved by God, human agents as secondary causes or instruments also voluntarily move themselves, sometimes in a contrary evil direction. By moving evil instruments God is a concurrent cause of their actions, but not of the evil. Hence the cause of sin is not the decree…[22]

---

17 "…quod omnes damnationis illorum causas ordine antecedit." Ibid., Chapter 2, 176.

18 "…ut etiam aliquatenus commoueantur ad donum caeleste degustandum…" Ibid., Chapter 5, 192.

19 "Utiturque ad eam rem persiciendam partim sceleratis illorum cupiditatibus, quibus ipsos regendos tradit…perpetuus infidelitatis, ignorantiae, & iniquitatis riuus manat…" Ibid., Chapter 5, 193.

20 "Quum enim Dominus, iis causis adductus quas ipse solus nouit, proposuisset eos in hunc finem creare, ut in ipsis iram & potentiam suam ostenderet, simul eas causas gradatim ordinauit quibus fieret ut tota ipsorum exitis culpa in ipsis haereret, quem admodum a nobis est antea demonstratum." Ibid., Chapter 5, 190.

21 Donald Sinnema, "Calvin and Beza: The Role of the Decree-Execution Distinction in Their Theologies," in *Calvinus Evangelii Propugnator; Calvin, Champion of the Gospel,* Anthony Lane, Jon Balserak, eds., (Grand Rapids, MI: Calvin Studies Society, 2006), 205–6.

22 Sinnema, "Calvin and Beza: The Role of the Decree-Execution Distinction in Their Theologies," 206.

Sinnema therefore argues that Beza differs from Calvin in the sense that Beza denies God's decree is a cause of condemnation while for Calvin, God's decree is a remote cause of condemnation.[23] However, the theological treatment of God's decree and execution by these two Reformers is similar, and not as Sinnema described.

In *Tabula praedstinationis*, Beza is not primarily using the decree-execution framework to argue that God is not the author of sin. Instead, the framework shows the order of election and condemnation. In *Tabula praedestinationis*, Beza shows the order of salvation by arranging the causes of execution as follows: God, Jesus Christ, Holy Spirit, etc. The execution is in God's eternal decree and therefore the causes of decree and execution are distinguished.[24] Where does Beza lay out his argument against God as the author of sin? It is in the Colloquy of Montbéliard and in his exegesis on the Book of Job when Beza explains the meaning of God's instruments and the way they operate their roles. This will be discussed in the later part of this chapter.

In *Tabula praedestinationis*, the interaction of different types of causality in the two aspects of election and reprobation of predestination, formulates the framework of decree and execution, and Beza believes that this interaction provides the method for correctly understanding the doctrine of predestination. Sinnema asserts that "Calvin makes use of the distinction between God's eternal decree and its execution in his discussions of providence frequently, but he seldom refers to this distinction when discussing predestination",[25] implying a different stress in the doctrines of providence and predestination by Calvin as compared to Beza. The likely cause for this is that the soteriological feature of Calvin's doctrine of double predestination is overly emphasised while the providential aspect of this doctrine is often underestimated, and therefore the relationship between double predestination and providence shown by the doctrine of '*providentia coelestis*', is not examined. Beza's decree and execution framework mirrors the image of Calvin's '*providentia coelestis*' and this is often unnoticed.

As discussed in the last chapter, Calvin's doctrine of '*providentia coelestis*', which partly means '*providentia specialissma*', is a combination of *providentia Dei* and predestination. Heavenly providence shows that God is the heavenly father and the heavenly judge. In God's secret decree, He predestines some to be the Elect and the rest to be condemned, and executes His judgement through different secondary causes. While Calvin's doctrine of heavenly providence is soteriological showing the interaction of God's decree and secondary causes, Beza's doctrine of predestination

---

23 Ibid., 206.
24 "Debemus enim inter reprobandi propositum & reprobationem ipsam distinguere." Bezae, *Tractationum Theologicarum*, 176.
25 Sinnema, "Beza's view of predestination in historical perspective", 222, 239. Cf. Sinnema, "Calvin and Beza: The Role of the Decree-Execution Distinction in Their Theologies", 194.

(decree-execution framework) is shaped by his doctrine of providence, showing the interaction of God's decree and secondary causes. Beza's decree-execution framework has an outline of Calvin's doctrine of heavenly providence and both doctrines advocate a close link between providence and predestination. Beza's understanding of predestination shows a line of continuity with Calvin's, but Beza labours in an orderly way to demonstrate the causes of the salvation of the Elect and the condemnation of the Reprobate.[26] Calvin is less explicit than Beza in his explanation about the order of causes in both aspects, but they both advocate the same elements. Essentially, they both agree that predestination is providential.[27]

Although Beza continues with Calvin's interpretation of predestination or providence, their biblical understanding of the Book of Job is different. Beza wrote a commentary on the Book of Job in 1589, thirty-four years after the 1555 publication of *Tabula praedestinationis*. However, before considering their similarities and differences, two incidents that happened between these dates need to be considered and one work that Beza composed in 1570 also needs to be examined.

The Colloquy of Poissy 1561

In 1561, Beza represented the Reformed churches to speak about the presence of Christ in the Supper. He objected to the advocation of transubstantiation and consubstantiation from Catholic and Lutheran theologians, and stressed that "the bread is the communication of the true body of Jesus Christ and the cup is the communication of the true blood shed for sinners, the blood being the same substance which he took from the womb of the virgin Mary".[28] As the terms transubstantiation

---

26 Muller suggests that Beza's *Tabula* does not argue any particular order of doctrine to be followed in a theological system but a Pauline order of teaching, moving from sin to law, grace, and only then to predestination, arguably echoes the actual order of topics in the 1539 *Institutes*, an order which remained intact in 1559. Richard Muller, "The Use and Abuse of a Document: Beza's *Tabula praedestinationis*, the Bolsec Controversy, and the Origins of Reformed Orthodoxy", in *Protestant Scholasticism: Essay in Reassessment*, edited by Carl R. Trueman and R. Scott Clark (Eugene, OR: Wipf & Stock, 2006), 60–61.

27 "For Beza, Predestination and Providence went hand in hand…" Mark W. Elliott, *Providence Perceived: Divine Action from a Human Point of View* (Berlin/Boston: De Gruyter, 2015), 148.

28 C.R., KLVI, 698: "Que le pain que nous rompons selon son ordonnance, est la communication du vray corps de Iesus Christ qui a este livre pour nous: et la coupe don't nous bouvons, est la communication du vray sang qui a este respandu pour nous: voire, en ceste mesme substance qui'il a emportee d'avec nous au ciel. Et ie vous prie, messieur, au nom de Dieu, que pouvez vous doncques chercher ni trouver enc e sainct Sacrament, que nous n'y cherchions et trouvions aussi?" See also Jill Raitt, *The Eucharistic Theology of Theodore Beza: Development of the Reformed Doctrine*, AAR Studies in Religion, no. 4 (Chambersburg: American Academy of Religion, 1972), 34.

and consubstantiation were not included, this description was rejected and finally Beza was banished.[29]

In the same year 1561, that Beza engaged in the Colloquy of Poissy, he also published *Summa Doctrinae de re Sacramentaria*. In this work, he uses the term '*causae formalis*' to explain the causality of the sacrament.[30] God's ordination is the formal cause and this cause changes the use of the elements so they are in a new form, and they become not some general bread and wine but sacramental.[31] The bread is not changed substantially, but sacramentally, so it is no longer simply bread, but 'that' bread. Christ is spiritually and mystically present in the Supper, and therefore humankind is not able to comprehend this invisible presence.[32]

Beza discusses the sacramental causality under the fourfold Aristotelian categories: final, efficient, formal and material, but the discussion on formal cause is in greater detail.[33] Although the use of causality in explaining Christ's presence in the Supper, shows traces of scholasticism, Raitt still believes that Beza and Calvin are aligned in their thoughts.[34] In the explanation of the causality of the sacrament, Beza does adopt a philosophical methodology to explain some parts of the doctrine but he also follows Calvin's arguments concerning the change of the use of the elements in the Supper.

The Colloquy of Poissy was significant because it encouraged Beza to work out a scholastic way of explaining Christ's presence in the Supper and he continued to employ the same methodology to interpret the doctrine of *providentia Dei*. The discussion is located later in this chapter.

Quaestionum et Responsionum Christianarum Libellus 1570

This work was written in the form of a catechism and a section was dedicated to the discussion of the doctrines of providence and predestination. Beza asserts

---

29 Raitt, *The Eucharistic Theology of Theodore Beza*, 35.

30 "Quae est vis huius causae formalis? Ut signa non in ipsa sui natura sive substantia, sed quod ad vsum duntaxat attinet mutentur, idque tantisper dum action viget cui subseruiunt. Neque enim simpliciter aquam ut aquam, vel panem ut panem, aut vinum ut vinum in sacris mysteriis habemus, set ut certa & vera symbola ac pignora earum rerum quas nobis Dominus alio quidem modo (ut mox dicemus) sed tamen certissime & verissime donat, nempe ipsius Christi cum omnibus eius donis." Theodore Beza, "Summa Doctrinae de re Sacramentaria", in *Theodori Bezae Vezelii volumen primum tractationum*, 207.

31 Raitt, *The Eucharistic Theology of Theodore Beza*, 36.

32 Ibid., 40–41, 69.

33 Beza, "Summa Doctrinae de re Sacramentaria", 207–208. Cf. Raitt, *The Eucharistic Theology of Theodore Beza*, 35, 45.

34 Raitt, *The Eucharistic Theology of Theodore Beza*, 69.

that the interpretation of the doctrines of providence and predestination each has two parts to be considered: God's eternal decree and the order of causes. Beza's doctrine of providence stresses that God is not moved by external means, but He moves all things in His eternal providence.[35] God moves good and evil causes using secret motion[36] to execute His decree. However, the evil work done by human beings does not originate from God but from human's corrupted will.[37] Beza asserts that the doctrine of predestination is to govern both the Elect and the Reprobate. The condemnation for the Reprobate is eternally decreed but the Reprobate are responsible for their own condemnation.[38]

Many similarities can be found comparing Calvin's doctrine of heavenly providence to Beza's doctrines of providence and predestination but in *Quaestionum et Responsionum Christianarum Libellus*, Beza highlights the issues of divine 'secret motion', which are not included in Calvin's explanation. Beza also delivers a more thorough discussion about 'secret motion' in his commentary on the Book of Job.

Compared to his work of *Tabula praedestinationis*, Beza in *Quaestionum et Responsionum Christianarum Libellus* emphasises that God's eternal decree must be distinguished from its execution and that while the execution of the decree of election depends on the faith in Christ of the Elect, the execution of the decree of reprobation originated from the sin of the Reprobate.[39] The difference between the decree and the execution is posed again in the heated debate about predestination in the Colloquy of Montbéliard.[40]

---

35 '…ita quiden ut ipse nullo modo moveatur, omnia vero secundum suan aeternam providentiam moveat. Theodoro Beza, *Quaestionum et responsionum christianarum libellus: In quo praecipua Christianae religionis capita* (Genève: Musée historique de la Rèformation, 1570), 94.

36 'Nam arcano etiam motu omnia seruiunt exequendis Dei decretis.' Ibid., 115.

37 See answer to 'An vero censeri potest Deus aliquid voluisse seu decreuisse quod non approbet, ac proinde quod malum sit?' Ibid., 109.

38 'Concedo, si de causis medius agitur, quibus vasa irae ad iram destinatam seruntur, ipso uno sibi causam esse exitii.' Ibid., 119.

39 'Sed inprimis decretum illud aeternum Dei sapientissimi simul & iustissimi, ex quo quicquid fuit, fuit: quicquid est, est & quicquid futurum est, erit, prout ipsi ab aeterno decernere libuit…Aio, & ita quidem ut execellentius quodam quam causas omnes ordinat, & sigularissima etiam illarum effecta regit, ut ad decretum finem serantur.' Ibid., 92. 'Aliud enim est decretum de seruan dis electis, quam ipsa elctorum glorificatio : aliud est decretum de damandis reprobis, quam reproborum damnatio, qumm decretum ipsum necessario sit distinguendum ab eius executione.' Ibid., 126.

40 'Quando igitur glorification electorum, & damnatio reiectorum opponuntur, diversitas haec diligenter consideranda est, in executione decreti Dei, ne causa huius damnationis Deo tribuatur, qua solius hominis malitiae adscribenda est. Non enim decretum Dei, sed malitia hominis & corruption eius causa est aeterni interitus damnatorum hominum.' *Ad acta colloquii Montisbelgardensis Tubingae edita*, Theodori Bezae responsionis, pars prior, editio secunda (Genève: Bibliothèque de Genève, 1588), 531.

The Colloquy of Montbéliard 1586

The county of Montbéliard is located in the French city of Montbéliard. In 1585, it was held by the house of Württemberg which was strictly Lutheran, but it allowed French refugees, who were strict Calvinist Huguenots, to stay there.[41] Count Frederick, who ruled the county of Montbéliard, had struggles with his own faith and was indecisive about whether to support Reformed theology or Lutheran theology, as his father was Reformed but his uncles were from the house of Württemberg. Furthermore, he had been influenced by Jacob Andreae when he was educated at the University of Tubingen. Andreae asserted that the Calvinists and Zwinglians were allies in their belief in the Supper, therefore the Calvinists should be banned.

The Huguenots asked Frederick to allow them to participate in communion under their French Reformed Confession. Frederick, however, would not allow them to receive communion unless they signed the Augsburg Confession, therefore the Huguenots called for a Colloquy, with the desire of settling this issue, in the hope of being allowed to receive communion under their own confession and to appoint ministers who could administer the Supper in a French way. Beza was assigned to represent the Huguenots to discuss the issues related to the Lord's Supper, adornment, music, baptism, and predestination, with Andreae who represented the Lutheran side. The outcome of the colloquy was favourable to the Lutherans.

This chapter explores no further details about their discussion on the Lord's Supper, but it endeavours to highlight one point. In the discussion with Andreae, instead of emphasising the formal cause which changed the bread sacramentally, Beza suggests that the union with Christ is effected by instrumental causes but through the Holy Spirit. The instrumental causes include the minister who does what Christ commanded, the words of institution, the signs themselves, the sacramental rites, and faith, but only the working of God inwardly (the working of the Holy Spirit) in the believers has intrinsic efficient power.[42] It is interesting that Beza seems to tell the Huguenots to pay attention to the significance of the efficient cause, the Holy Spirit working in their hearts rather than the instrumental causes

---

41 Jill Raitt, *The Colloquy of Montbéliard: Religion and Politics in the Sixteenth Century* (New York; Oxford: Oxford University Press, 1993), 8–9.

42 "Instrumentales vero causas, ipsius Dei respectu, constituimus, partim Pastorem, Dei nomine & mandato agentem quod agit: partim verba institutionis: partim symbola, & sacramentales ritus. Nostri vero respectu fidem, nobis ex Dei dono insitam. Istis autem suis instrumentis sic uti Deum docemus, ut tamen illis nullam vim intersecam efficientem insinuet, sed duntaxat, quod ipse vnus intus agat, nobis per ea testificetur, nempe spiritualem illam Christi nobiscum consociationem, & quaecunque inde nanciscimur." *Ad acta colloquii Montisbelgardensis Tubingae edita*, Theodori Bezae responsionis, pars prior, 71. Cf. Jakob Andreae, Beze Theodore de, and Clinton J. Armstrong, *Lutheranism vs. Calvinism: the Classic Debate at the Colloquy of Montbeliard 1586* (Concordia Publishing House, 2017), 43, 100. Also quoted in Raitt, *The Colloquy of Montbéliard*, 78.

as represented by the French liturgy, which they were focusing on. No matter what concerns Beza has about the nature of the bread, he extensively uses the concept of causation to support his advocacy and continues to use the same method to defend his position regarding the doctrines of predestination and providence. The discussion about Beza's use of the concept of causation in the explanation of these two doctrines is discussed after this section.

In response to the inquiry about double predestination in the Colloquy of Mont-béliard, Beza, firstly stresses that this doctrine is built upon the efficient cause of God's eternal decree for both salvation and reprobation.[43] He had already made similar statements about sinners as the cause of their own damnation earlier when he and Andreae debated the topic of the Lord's Supper,[44] but in the discussion of the doctrine of predestination, he adds that God also works through secondary and mediating causes to carry out His salvation and reprobation.[45] However, the causes of reprobation are from human sinfulness, therefore, God is not the author of sin. Raitt asserts that Beza's expression is sometimes scholastic and sometimes scriptural, and that he intends to express that God is the efficient cause of the eternal decree of both salvation and reprobation, but sinner's corrupt nature is their condemnation.[46] In addition, Beza emphasises that although God's eternal predestination is inscrutable, His decree works through an order before all the causes can take effect.[47]

Compared to *Tabula praedestinationis*, where Beza debated in the Colloquy of Montbéliard, whether or not the doctrine of predestination led to God as the author of sin, he adopts more scholastic terms.[48] For example: '*causam efficientem*', '*secundarias & medias causas*', and '*ordo*' are some scholastic terms Beza used frequently

---

43 "Si per reprobationem intelligitur eius decretum, inepte dicitur: propositum Dei, id est, ipsius decretum esse ipsius causam efficientem. Sin vero eo nomine accipitis eius decreti executionem: falsum esse consitemur, quod repudiatis…" *Acta colloquij Montis Belligartensis: quod habitum est, anno Christi, 1586. fauente Deo opt.max. Praeside, … Friderico, comite VVirtembergico et Mompelgartensi, &c. inter clarissimos viros, D.Iacobum Andreae, praepositum & concellarium Academiae Tubingensis: & D.Theodorum Bezam, professorem…* (Georgium Gruppenbachium, 1587), 517.

44 "Dico Christum non receptum, sed repudiatum impios damnare; ideoque, solam incredulitatem causam efficientem damnationis impiorum, non Christum esse dico." Ibid., 129.

45 "Quemadmodum autem per secundarias & medias causas agit cum electis ad salutem: ita quoque cum reprobis agit per ordinatas causas." Ibid., 529.

46 Raitt comments that Beza's response is both scholastic and scriptural. Raitt, *The Colloquy of Mont-béliard*, 150.

47 "Esti vero via DOMINI imperuestigabiles sunt, tamen ex his, quae euenerunt, colligimus, quis finis creationis hominum fuerit. Propositum enim Dei aeternum & immutabile, omnes causas ordine quoque, antegrediens fuit, quod in semetipso ab aeterno decreuit, omnes homines ad suam gloriam condere." *Acta colloquij Montis Belligartensis: quod habitum est, anno Christi, 1586*, 523.

48 Raitt comments that Beza's response is scholastic and scriptural. Raitt, *The Colloquy of Montbéliard*, 150.

in explaining the two situations in the doctrine of predestination at the colloquy.[49] Beza used the scholastic terms to explain God's role in predestination more explicitly in the Colloquy of Montbéliard than in his *Tabula praedestinationis*. However, Beza's effort did not impress Andreae. Still accusing Beza as a flawed interpreter of the doctrine of predestination, Andreae, along with the other theologians of Württemberg, rejected his doctrine and condemned it as false.

Beza's *Tabula praedestinationis* follows Calvin's doctrine of heavenly providence and there is a line of continuity in the two Reformers' interpretation of the doctrines of predestination and providence. However, Beza also employs a combination of methodologies available in the sixteenth century, such as Aristotelian fourfold causality, to help him clarify his theology, and for apologetic argumentation, as seen in his presentations at the Colloquies of Poissy and Montbéliard. Although these two Reformers focus on the same fundamentals, it must be asked whether they also interpret the Book of Job in the same way.

Jobus Theodori Bezae partim commentariis partim paraphrasi illustratus 1589

In his *Commentary and Paraphase on the Book of Job* 1589, Beza asserts that while agreeing with the main theme of God's providence entailed in the Book of Job, there are other specific situations concerning God's justice and man's righteousness that also need to be considered. Beza deliberately avoids in-depth discussion of the doctrine of God's providence, and instead focuses on 'God's justice' and 'human righteousness'.[50] This avoidance does not necessarily mean that Beza disagrees with Calvin's doctrine of God's providence, but he prefers to treat the book differently in some specific areas.[51] These specific areas include the question of whether it is unjust if the wicked prosper, while the godly suffer (i. e. is God just?) and the

---

49 "...suo paterno amore dignatus est, itaetiam rationem inuenit, qua id decretum ordine quodam causarum secundarum & mediarum exequeretur." *Acta colloquij Montis Belligartensis: quod habitum est, anno Christi.1586*, 529. Cf. "Ubi ordo causarum considerandus venit, in Adamo lapso, quem Deus saluum fecit."Ibid., 528; cf. "Dico Christum non receptum, sed repudiatum impios damnare; ideoque, solam incredulitatem causam efficientem damnationis impiorum, non Christum esse dico." Ibid., 129.

50 "...commodius mihi videntur sentire qui potius de Dei & Hominum iustitia..." Bèze, *Jobus Theodori Bezae partim commentariis partim paraphrasi Illustratus*, Preface, 3.

51 "Eum nonnulli esse statuunt providentiae divinae explicationem. Et fateor quidem ego de hac re in hoc libro copiosissime & divinissime disputaria sapientissimis hominibus, quod etiam Deus ipse sua voce definit. Sed quum latius pateat Providentiae argumentum, commodius mihi videntur sentire qui potius de Dei & Hominum iustitia, idque non vniuersaliter, neque ἀωλῶς sed κατα τι & certo respectu quaeri in hoc libro existimant: nempe, quod ad Deum attinet, An ferat Dei Iustitia ut vere

question of whether the lack of material riches is a sign of punishment to the sinners, or even to the Elect. (i. e. are God's children righteous?)

Beza discusses his decree-execution framework early in the Preface to this commentary, in order to set the foundation on which he builds his arguments regarding God's justice and human righteousness. He uses the framework to explain why justified people suffer.[52] He uses the doctrine of predestination to reinforce the doctrine of providence. Earlier, this chapter has shown the similarities between Beza's decree-execution framework and Calvin's heavenly providence. Although Beza aims to buttress his teacher's doctrine of double predestination, their opinions about Job in some specific situations are in opposition. The following discussion will compare the exegesis of Beza and Calvin on a number of chapters from the Book of Job which are related to God's providence and to show their similarities between these two reformers' positions.[53]

General providence Job 1:6

Beza agrees with Calvin that in God's providence, He created everything and continues to govern, with Angels and Satan, as part of God's creation, also being under His authority. Beza denies that God's actions depend on some kind of middle[54] and

---

bonae & integrae vitae homines durissimis & asperrimis omnis generis calamitatibus afficiantur, sive, ut breuius loquar, An Dei iustitia patiatur ut in hac vita vel Malis Bene, vel Bonis Male sit." Ibid.

52 "Eiusmodi sunt hodie illorum quoque clamores qui contendunt a nobis fieri Deum auctorem mali, quum affirmamus nihil neque temere, neque Deo vel inuito vel nesciente, immo Deo sapienter & iuste quidquid cogitatur, dicitur vel sit decernente, euenire, sive bonis, sive malis instrumentis vtatur. Itidem eorum blasphemiae qui aeternum reprobationis decretum tollunt, qui Stoicam necessitatem a nobis inuehi contendunt...Hinc apparet quam vtilis sit huius libri doctrina in explicatione tam grauis argumenti, ut neque, trium amicorum Iobi exemplo, Dei sapientiam & iustitiam ex captu nostro metiamur, neque in ipsam diuinae sapientiae abyssum nos immergamus, sed sicut audita Dei redargutione loquitur Iobus, manum oriapponamus, & arcana Domini non curiose scrutemur..." Ibid., 5.

53 Raitt's paper explores the interaction of divine will and human will in Beza's commentary but her focus is on chapter 1 of the Book of Job only. Jill Raitt, 'Lessons in Troubled Times: Beza's Lessons on Job,' in *Calvin and the State: papers and responses presented at the Seventh and Eighth Colloquia on Calvin & Calvin Studies*, sponsored by the Calvin Studies Society, edited by Peter De Klerk (Grand Rapids, Michigan: Calvin Studies Society, 1993), 21–45.

54 "Itaque, quod ad Deum ipsum & proprium eius opus attinet, bene semper vult, decernit, gerit, quicquid ipse per quemcunque, quandocumque & quomodocunque in mundo gerit, id est quicquid in mundo sit & euenit, & generaliter & sigillatim. Instrumentorum autem mediorum sese quoque mouentium respectu, quamuis bene semper quoque illa moueat..." Bèze, *Jobus Theodori Bezae Partim Commentariis*, Job 1:21, 53. Cf. the next footnote. It seems that there is no difference between the meaning of middle and secondary causes. Cf. Beza used these two terms indiscriminately at the Colloquy of Montbéliard 1586: "Quemadmodum autem per secundarias & medias causas agit

secondary causes.[55] Instead, Beza argues that God as creator, decrees and appoints everything in general (*generalis*) providence, special providence (*sigillatim omnia*), and very special (*singularissima*) providence in His secret, eternal, and immutable counsel.[56] '*Singularissima*' is not a term inherited from Calvin and it will be discussed in the next section concerning special providence. However, Beza follows Calvin's interpretation of general providence by stressing that human beings as creation can participate in God's goodness and are appointed to do so. God also endows humans with spirit so that they can witness God's glory in His power, might, wisdom, and goodness.[57]

When Calvin preaches on 1:6–8, he offers a long explanation of God's providence. Calvin ensures the congregation knows that nothing is governed by fortune and that God has full authority over all creatures, including the angel and Satan. When Calvin objects to the misunderstandings of God's providence, he mainly refutes the 'irreligious people', – the Epicureans and the Stoics. Yet, Calvin's interpretation of God's general providence in His goodness, power, justice, and wisdom, is not in this sermon, but in Sermon 46 on Job 12:7–16.[58]

Beza follows Calvin's interpretation of God's general providence in the four elements of goodness, power, justice, and wisdom, but he argues that God's action is in His power, wisdom, and goodness, excluding God's action in His justice. Furthermore, in the Preface, Beza stresses that while God's justice and human righteousness are the major issues in certain areas in the Book of Job, the issue of God's providence is not. Beza also emphasises that the doctrine of God's providence, is already understood by believers and discussed by irreligious people,[59] so he

---

cum electis ad salutem: ita quoque cum reprobis agit per ordinatas causas." *Acta colloquij Montis Belligartensis: quod habitum est,* 1586, 529.

55 "Quis Stoicos nescit ab vno extremo ad alterum prolapsos, causarum mediarum & secundarum vinculis Deum ipsum astrinxisse?" Bèze, *Jobus Theodori Bezae Partim Commentariis,* Job 1:4, 21–22.

56 "Sed & istud statuendum est, nihil Deum in tempore statuere, sed ab eterno constituta immutabili & inscrutabili consilio, tum in genere, tum sigillatim omnia & singularissima quaeque fuisse." Ibid., Job 1:5, 24.

57 "Est enim solus tsadai & ἐπαρκής. Sicut autem mundum & res omnes in eo comprehensas condidit, non necessitate vlla, neque ut emolumentum inde aliquod perciperet, sed prout summe bonus est, ut aliquid extaret quod bonitatis illius suo faceret particeps, & in quo agnosceretur, non alicuius sane commodi causa quod in ipsum conditorem accessione quadam redundaret, sed contra quod ipsius a quo agnoscitur commodo cederet: sic etiam beatos illos Spiritus creauit in quibus homines multo etiam magnificentius quam in hoc mundo aspectabili, potentiam, sapientiam, bonitatem Conditoris contemplentur." Ibid., Job 1:6, 29. Cf. Calvin's interpretation of *providentia Dei* in God's actions in His goodness, power, wisdom and justice, and human participation in *providentia Dei* in chapter 3.

58 See chapter 3 for details.

59 "Et si enim (exceptis paucissimis penitus infanis & suae ipsorum conscientiae repugnantibus) nullus vnquam negauit Dei providentia res omnes conditas administrari: videmus tamen hic quoque illud quod verissime testatur Apost.Rom.I.vers.21 hominibus sola sapientia humana fretis, euenisse,

focuses on other important topics such as God's justice and man's righteousness. Hence, is Beza attempting to separate God's justice from God's providence?

It is pertinent to note that Beza argues that Job's friends understand the meaning of God's justice and providence well but when they apply it to Job's case, they make wrong conclusions about God and human beings. Therefore, Beza intends to highlight God's justice in the doctrine of God's providence[60] instead of separating God's justice from God's general providence: this can be clarified after one has considered Beza's treatment of special providence. To summarise, it is noted that Beza's doctrine of God's general providence shows some features of his decree-execution framework of predestination, especially in respect to God's decree.

Special providence Job 1:12

When commenting on Job 1:12, Beza argues that Satan is not gratified by God at all although He says that everything of Job's is in Satan's hands. God puts Job in Satan's hands in order to make Satan the instrument of his own shame. This shame is revealed when Job refuses to curse God.[61] Satan, as secondary cause, is decreed by God's secret providence and he obeys His will to incur afflictions upon Job.[62] However, Job is protected by God's very special providence, '*singularissma providentia*', which is particularly given to some chosen people. Hence, Job is being

---

nempe ut in suis ratiocinationibus euanescerent. Quis enim Epicureorum impios furores ignorat, suorum atomorum concursui omnia subiicientes? Quis Stoicos nescit ab vno extremo ad alterum prolapsos, causarum mediarum & secundarum vinculis Deum ipsum astrinxisse? Peripateticos autem omnium acutissimos, singularum rerum euenta Providentiae diuinae exemisse? Neque haec duntaxat in profanorum hominum scholis agitata sunt, verum etiam in ipsa Dei schola, minime quidem, An Dei providentia Mundus regatur..." Bèze, *Jobus Theodori Bezae Partim Commentariis*, Job 1:4, 21. Cf. "Deinceps autem ad finem usque huius capitis, & decimi tertis capitis vers.13 a quo potius caput illud exordiri oportuit, docet Iobus pendere res omnes, & earum statum a Deo: neque Deum a rebus a se conditis prout ipsae affectae sunt, consilia sua mutuari, sed e contrario, cunsta inscrutabili nobis vicissitudine diuinitus gubernari." Ibid., Summa et Dispositio Capitis XII, 126.

60 See also: "In hypothesi vero quod hoc vtrumque Iobi personae immerito applicarent, quanuis interea praeclare & vere multa, sed male conclusa & perperam applicata de Dei Providentia & Iustitia different." Ibid., 4.

61 "Hoc igitur concedens Satanae Deus, nihil est ei proprie largitus, sed eum potius effecit suae ipsius infamiae instrumentum, quum illum potius Iobo traderet superandum: seruo autem suo insigne trophaeum iam tum praeparauit." Ibid., Job 1:12, 37.

62 "...Satanae quidlibet de Iobi bonis statuendi, nihil tamen aliud neque aliter statuere & exequi Satanam potuisse quam quod Deus decreuisset: arcano motu, causis omnibus secundis, & earum effectibus, citra exceptionem vllam..." Ibid.

cared for in '*singularissma providentia*', the very special providence.[63] It is found that from the beginning of his interpretation of the Book of Job, Beza considers Job to be one of the Elect.

Similarly, as Calvin, Beza considers Satan as the instrument of God's wrath and he acts according to God's pleasure, but not according to Satan's own will. However, when preaching Job 1:9–12, Calvin's view differs from Beza's as Calvin believes that God's judgement is aimed at both His children and the wicked.[64] Sometimes, Calvin argues that God's judgement including that which falls upon the godly, is contained in His secrets and therefore people, in the present day, cannot comprehend it.[65] Calvin suggests that people should show humility and reverence towards God's hiddenness,[66] and while they cannot understand some aspects of various incidents, the faithful may have an insight to the condition by praying for His revelation,[67] but Beza thinks differently.

Beza's exegesis of Job 1:12 mentions God's special providence, stressing that God endows this '*singularissima*' care to His chosen people. Calvin's exegesis of this verse is different, and he argues that secret providence is God's judgement upon both the godly and the wicked.[68] Hence, Job's affliction is also God's judgement

---

63 "...Dei decreto obsecundantibus: quod negari non potest, quin particularis & singularum rerum providentia impie negetur. Particularem autem, atque adeo singularissimam providentiam esse consitituendam..." Ibid.

64 "...ils sont aussi comme verges, par lesquelles Dieu chastie ses enfans. Brief, il faut que le diable soit instrument de l'ire de Dieu, et qu'il execute sa volonté, non pas qu'il le face (comme nous avons dit) de son bon gré, mais d'autant que Dieu a l'empire souverain sur toutes ses creatures, et qu'il faut qu'il les plie, et les tourne là où bon luy semble." Calvin, Sermon 5 Job 1:9–12, CO33:75. Cf. "Voila ce que nous avons à noter: et cependant nous avons à observer aussi que c'est des iugemens de Dieu, tels qu'il les exerce et sur les bons, et sur les mauvais." Ibid., CO33:77.

65 "... et attendre le iour que nous concevions mieux les secrets de Dieu, lesquels nous sont auiourd'huy incomprehensibles, et que pourtant il faut que nous apprenions à les magnifier, que nous adorions les iugemens de Dieu, qu'ils nous soyent admirables..." Ibid.

66 "...il nous faut humilier, voyant que l'Escriture en parle ainsi..." Ibid.

67 Ibid., CO33:79–80.

68 "Nous voyons donc que quand Dieu veut punir les meschans, et executer son ire à l'encontre, selon qu'ils en sont dignes, il n'attend pas d'estre sollicité par Satan, mais il anticipe. En ce passage quand il est question d'affliger Iob, c'est à dire, que Dieu traite rudement l'un de ses enfans, il faut que cela vienne à la poursuite de l'ennemi...ils sont aussi comme verges, par lesquelles Dieu chastie ses enfans. Brief, il faut que le diable soit instrument de l'ire de Dieu, et qu'il execute sa volonté...Voila (di-ie) comme Dieu besongne envers tous incredules et reprouvez, c'est qu'il donne efficace d'erreur à Satan, tellement qu'il les peut tromper sans qu'ils s'en apperçoyvent. Or il n'en fait pas ainsi envers les siens quand il les afflige...Voila ce que nous avons à noter: et cependant nous avons à observer aussi que c'est des iugemens de Dieu, tels qu'il les exerce et sur les bons, et sur les mauvais." Ibid., CO33:75–77. Calvin's view about special providence is related to general providence in God's actions in His goodness, power, justice and wisdom. Refer to chapter 3 for detailed discussion. Secret providence is the explanation of predestination. Refer to chapter 5 for detailed discussion.

through His secret providence. However, Beza considers that God's use of Satan as an instrument for the revelation of Satan's own shame is in God's beneficial and benevolent secret providence. Beza only emphasises that the judgement of the wicked is God's secret, while the chosen are being cared for in '*singularissma providentia*', the very special/singular providence. Beza is eager to suggest that Job is protected in God's very special providence, but his affliction is not a judgement from God, as Father God offers special care to His children. According to Beza, God's justice is shown in His secret providence (judgement of the wicked) and '*singularissma providentia*' (blessing of the Elect).

Beza is more sympathetic to Job than Calvin is. God can put His children in some evil instruments' hands but only for the purpose of chastisement.[69] Hence, Beza refuses to apply God's judgement to Job's case because Job's suffering is neither a judgement from God nor does it show God's justice. Although Beza reinforces his view that God is just, he also shows that Job's case does not aim to teach that God's will or His act are just but to show human righteousness and God's chastisement as a sanctifying process for human beings. So, if God is not unjust, why does Job suffer? Beza's explanation is that humans also have an active part, in some of the incidents that happened. God moves people to work but the people also move themselves by '*intrinsecus motus*', intrinsic moving.[70] Beza's interpretation of God's special providence shows an outline of the decree-execution framework, especially the part concerning the causality in the very special care for the Elect.

Secret providence Job 28:1

When he comments on Job 28, Beza emphasises that a part of *providentia Dei* is hidden[71] and that this hidden segment relates specifically to the order of nature. To comfort the godly, he uses the examples of the revealed general providence from Job 28 to bring into relief and help the faithful to settle the incomprehensibility of secret providence. He states that God's general providence can be discerned through nature, where people can gaze in awe at both the sky and nature. Although the reasons for the existence of these natural phenomena may be difficult to discern,

---

69 "...vel ut benignus pater suos vel per mala quoque instrumenta castigans: vel ad nominis sui gloriam & suorum commodum quibuscunque libuit modis exercens." Bèze, *Jobus Theodori Bezae Partim Commentariis*, Job 1:21, 54.

70 *Intrinsecus motus* is explained after the section of secret providence.

71 Beze, *Iob Expounded by Theodore Beza: Partly in Manner of a Commentary, Partly in Manner of a Paraphrase* Job 28:1. Also see "Et de rebus quidem apertis ac manifestis, & Dei tum in puniendis sceleratis, tum in protegendis piis providentia hactenus dictum esto. Nunc ad illa occulta & penitus ab hominum captu remota veniamus." Bèze, *Jobus Theodori Bezae Partim Commentariis*, Job 28:1, 183.

answers are still found by those who investigate and explore,[72] however, the hidden part of God's providence is incomprehensible to humankind. This demonstrates God's wisdom and it is not comparable to anything, even the most admirable and precious stones.[73] God's wisdom sets the world in order and this wisdom is too high and wonderful for humankind to attain.[74] According to Beza, secret providence is God's wisdom which is unsearchable by mortal humans.

Beza focuses on the discussion of secret providence in the order of nature when commenting on Job 28:1. Yet, what does he say about secret providence in human history? He delivers this discussion when he comments on Job 1:21, where he agrees that Job's tremendous affliction is a God given trial and that the cause of Job's suffering is in His secret providence demonstrating God's justice and wisdom.[75] However, Beza considers that Job knows both the spiritual and supernatural knowledge of God,[76] implying that God reveals His secret providence to Job and that he is treated in a special way. Since Job is endowed with some special knowledge of God, he can wait for God patiently.[77] Therefore, Beza considers Job as an excellent example to follow in dealing with calamities.[78]

Calvin's exegesis of Job 28 also focuses on God's wisdom and the incomprehensibility of His hiddenness. However, Calvin offers a solution to people when they are confused in God's hiddenness. Firstly, they should fear God as this act shows that they honour and affirm God's goodness. This fear leads people to hope for salvation, which God has prepared for His children in Jesus Christ, showing Himself as a father and a saviour.[79] Secondly, although people have an insight to God's wisdom

---

72 Ibid., Job 28:12, 185.

73 Ibid.

74 "Quandam enim etiam esse occultissimam Dei sapientiam, qua res omnes sic administret, ut eius ratio nulla possit humana opera sagaecitate, industria iniri, & quam adorare non scrutari oporteat: nempe quum vere pios, quorum unum se esse serio testatur & probat, durissime affligit, & e contrario sceleratos patientissime toleret." Ibid., Summa et Dispositio Capitis Job 27–31, 180. Cf. Job 28:12, 185; Job 28:13, 185; Job 28:28, 187.

75 "Sed quid si ut hic nostro Iobo vsuuenit, in istiusmodi calamitatibus…Tum sane omnibus omissis dialogismis haec laus est Deo tribuenda, quod licet nobis occultis de causis Deus sic de nobis statuat, nihil tamen quibuscunque instrumentis aduersum nos vtatur, nisi sapientissime & rectissime agat…" Ibid., Job 1:21, 60.

76 "Iobus autem noster quum naturali tum spirituali & ὑπερφυσικῇ Dei notitia instructus…ad Deum vnum sese totum conuertens, singulare nobis accersendae & obtinendae in omnibus istiusmodi calamitatibus patientiae exemplum praebet." Ibid., Job 1:21, 58. Cf. "Contra vero qui recta ad Dei providentiam assurgunt, &, exemplo Iobi, Deum agnoscunt rerum omnium, etiam singularium iustissimum & sapientissimum gubernatorem…" Ibid., Job 1:21, 59.

77 Ibid., Job 1:21, 58.

78 Ibid.

79 "…que voila tout ce qu'il nous faut savoir, c'est que nous concevions comme Dieu se declare nostre Pere et Saveur, comme il nous a adoptez en la personne de son Fils, et qu'ils nous a voulu faire

in nature and find it incomprehensible, they recognise from the Holy Scriptures that this wisdom is desirable.[80] In Calvin's account, God's incomprehensibility has a positive effect on the godly – to hope for God's salvation and to admire His wisdom.[81] Calvin states that if God's children, who are cared for through Fatherly special providence, read the Scriptures humbly, they will submit to their Father's secrets. Calvin links secret providence to general and special providence, and he provides a solution for the godly, for the confusion in God's hiddenness.[82]

In his commentary on Job, Beza emphasises that God endowed Job with some special knowledge of Himself. However, Calvin encourages the godly to read the Scripture so that they can submit to God's secret providence, and thus there is no actual attainment of God's secret by humans. Beza also highlights that human beings, as God's instruments, are to glorify Him in secret providence,[83] and he elaborates this issue when he discusses the decree-execution framework.

Decree-execution framework

Background – Beza's Job in 1:21

Job says that he is willing to submit to God because "naked he came from his mother's womb, and naked he will depart". (Job 1:21) Beza argues that there are two kinds of human nakedness in Scripture: outward nakedness which concerns the body and material life, and inward nakedness which concerns the spiritual life.[84] Beza believes that Job has a spiritual life, which is enriched by God's gifts,

---

participans de sa bonté et misericorde, en laquelle nostre salut consiste. Nous voyons donc maintenant comme il faut que pour craindre Dieu nous soyons certifiez de sa bonté…" Calvin, Sermon 103 Job 28:10–28, CO34:527–528.

80 "…car nostre Seigneur nous a donné ceste impression-la en nature que nous savons que c'est une chose desirable que la vraye sagesse. Or nostre Seigneur intitule sa parole de ce nom tant honorable, et nous monstre que si nous y profitons, voila où toute nostre sagesse consiste. Cecy donc nous doit bien enflammer à cercher ce qui est contenu en l'Escriture saincte." Ibid., CO34:528. Cf. "Voila donc où nostre Seigneur nous convie, quand il nous veut amener à lui, quand il declare que toute nostre sagesse et intelligence vraye est de l'escouter…" Calvin, Sermon 102 Job 28:10–28, CO34:518.

81 "Or maintenant pous mieux faire profit de ceste doctrine, notons en premier lieu quelle est la bonté de nostre Dieu, en ce qu'il nous communique la sagesse qu'il cognoit nous estre bonne et propre: voire combien que nous en soyons privez et exclus de nature." Ibid., CO34:516.

82 Refer to chapter 3 regarding Calvin's opinion on Job's attitude towards God's hiddenness.

83 "…nihil tamen quibuscunque instrumentis aduersum nos vtatur, nisi sapientissime & rectissime agat…" Bèze, Jobus Theodori Bezae Partim Commentariis, Job 1:21, 60.

84 "Primum hic nobis est de nuditate agendum, quae nobis duplex in scripturis proponitur: vna exterior, quae partim hoc corpus, partim externa omnia huius vitae commoda respicit: altera interior, quae verorum animi bonorum priuationem declarat." Ibid., Job 1:21, 48.

including eternal life,[85] therefore according to Beza, Job's statement means that God has brought him back to his naked state by withdrawing all His great blessings. Yet Job is not grieved at his loss, as he hopes for a better condition in eternal life. The purpose of God's action is therefore, to prevent people from forgetting the better life in eternity.[86]

Beza's Job is not impious but holy and religious.[87] The reason why Job does not aim to regain his wealth, according to Beza, is because Job does not 'love' his possessions.[88] Although Job's focus is not on the material life, Job does have many questions about his sufferings and God's justice. For example, Job is brought to '*aliquam inopiam*', which means that he only suffers a little poverty, and he is not poor like a beggar. However, Job struggles with the question of why is this affliction from God? Job can accept his loss of the 'little possessions' as he was born naked. However, the fact that God showers tremendous blessings upon him and then brings him back to his original state of nakedness, seems to be '*novum*' to Job.[89]

Beza shows that pious Job faces his life challenges well, but he is also eager to know the reason behind all these afflictions from God. Nevertheless, Beza is convinced that Job is a good example of trusting God's providence in His justice and wise governing of everything,[90] and he presents Job as the best example of patience for everybody to follow when facing afflictions.[91] Job's great patience is

---

85 "De hac autem specie posteriore Iobum hic non agere declarat tota ipsius oratio, ex qua intelligitur nunquam illum fuisse veris illis animi bonis, fide videlicet & aeternae vitae spe, & asserendae gloriae Dei zelo locupletiorem…" Ibid.

86 Ibid., Job 1:21, 51.

87 "…illud non modo impie dictum non fuisse, verum etiam pie prorsus ac religiose cogitatum & pronuntiatum fuisse." Ibid.

88 "Itaque recte quidam testatus est, Iobum amittentem opes sine dolore, ostendisse satis super que se illas non possedisse cum eo amore…" Ibid., Job 1:21, 50.

89 "Nudus, inquit, exiui ex vtero matris, ac si diceret, video me quidem non simpliciter ex locupletissimo repente ad aliquam inopiam, sed ad egestatem redactum. Immo quae tam repente mihi diuinitus potius quam humanitus accidisse video, paucolorum etiam eorum quae mihi supersunt spoliationem interminantur. Esto id vero. Mihi tamen noui proprie nihil hic accidit, sed tum potius quum Deus ille meus conditor nascentem operiret, & tandem tot tantisque huius vitae commodis bearet, tum ipse mihi nouum aliquid tribuit: quo nunc ipse me spolians, quaecunque tandem causa huc illum impulerit, ad primam illam & veterem conditionem me reuocar, quod cur aequo animo non ferrem?" Ibid.

90 "Contra vero qui recta ad Dei providentiam assurgunt, &, exemplo Iobi, Deum agnoscunt rerum omnium, etiam singularium justissimum & sapientissimum gubernatorem, illi demum tutissimum & pacatissimum portum inueniunt, in quo quantumuis asperis tempestatibus iactati conquiescant." Ibid., Job 1:21, 59. Cf. "Ut autem ad Iobum nostrum regrediamur, quum, ut ex proxime sequenti membro apparet, haec loquutus sit Iobus fidei & spei plenus, ut qui totus ad Deum laudandum feratur…" Ibid., Job 1:21, 58. Cf. "Contra vero ne hoc quidem illi videtur in mentem venisse, assueto nimirum in Dei providentia spem omnem suam reponere." Ibid., Job 1:21, 60.

91 "…omnibus istiusmodi calamitatibus patientiae exemplum praebet." Ibid., Job 1:21, 58.

especially shown when he does not mention the loss of his children. Viewed in this way, Job's patience is wonderful and therefore Beza believes that God has given the example of Job to the godly to imitate.[92]

Calvin's Job is different. Calvin argues that patience and faith are like two sides of a coin. A person must be patient in order to be faithful, yet patience is not without grief.[93] Calvin encourages the congregation to alleviate sorrow by thinking of God's goodness and in this way, they are showing patience and faithfulness to God.[94] Job tears his clothes, casts himself down, and accepts his loss (Job 1:20), and Calvin considers these gestures show humility, reverence, and patience. However, when Job tears his garments, he makes himself more sorrowful outwardly, intending to get people's attention and empathy, yet according to Calvin, this behaviour should not be condemned because Job's sorrow is truly remarkable.[95] However, what annoys Calvin is that Job is not inwardly patient, and Calvin further asserts that Job's behaviour does not reflect his faith. However, when Job says that he comes out of his mother's womb naked, and therefore he is content with how God acts towards him. Calvin believes that this is proof of Job's patience and willingness to submit to God's will.[96]

Both Beza and Calvin think that Job is patient, but they make their judgements according to different occasions when Job faces his loss and submits to God, therefore, their understanding of Job in chapter 1 of the Book of Job is not totally the same. There is also another crucial difference: Beza's emphasis on the working of secondary causes in God's providence is stronger than Calvin's.

'Intrinsecus motus'

In Job 1:21, when Job says, "The Lord has given and the Lord has taken away", Beza stresses that the speech does not imply that God is the author of sin because God

---

92 "Vere igitur magna, ingens, sublimis fuit haec Iobi patientia, quam nobis donet Deus, ut aliquatenus saltem imitemur." Ibid., Job 1:21, 61.

93 Calvin, Sermon 7 Job 1:20–22, CO33:93. Cf. "…que la patience n'est point sans affliction, qu'ils faut bien que les enfans de Dieu soyent tristes…" Ibid., CO33:96.

94 Refer to chapter 3.

95 "Or ici il est dit, que Iob a desciré sa robe: il semble qu'il se vueille plus picquer pour estre plus triste qu'il n'estoit (car un homme qui se voit ainsi deffiguré, il s'estonne de soy-mesme) et puis quand il vient iusques aux cheveux, on pouvoit dire qu'il a cerché comme des aides pour s'aguillonner et augmenter son dueil, et que c'estoit comme se donner des coups d'esperon. Et cela (comme i'ay dit) seroit bien à condamner : mais en premier lieu notons que l'Escriture nous a ici voulu exprimer, que la tristesse de ce sainct personnage estoit si grande…" Calvin, Sermon 7 Job 1:20–22, CO33:94.

96 "…car Iob n'eust peu mieux approuver sa patience, qu'en se deliberant d'estre tout nud, d'autant que le bon plaisir de Dieu estoit tel." Ibid., CO33:97.

works by eternal and just decree, and He wills and works through instruments in His general and special providence.[97] Beza distinguishes three kinds of instruments: 1. Passive instruments such as non-living things, which cannot move by themselves, but rather are moved by God, or by a living secondary cause; 2. Instruments which are moved by no understanding or reason and which can also move by themselves, such as beasts; 3. Instruments which are endowed with understanding and reason, and therefore these instruments produce some part of the work which can truly be called their own.[98] Beza believes that the nature of human beings was not destroyed after the fall, but was only corrupted. Hence, the '*intrinsecus motus*' of humans still functions, yet the work that the '*motus*' can do is merely sinful.[99]

The merciful God chooses some people out of a group of sinful people and He predestines them to salvation in Christ.[100] The Holy Spirit sanctifies their '*voluntas*' and therefore when God moves them, the Elect 'also' move themselves.[101] This process is ongoing and so human beings can be 'more and more' corrected and changed through the illumination of the Holy Spirit.[102] Beza stresses that God's action and permission should be separated before one can understand that God

---

97 "Non tantum igitur euenta rerum, sed etiam causas omnes secundas a Deo, non certe nesciente siue otioso, multo minus coacte & ab inuito, sed a decernente ac volente moueri, regi, & ad fines suos perduci…(quaedam enim ex illis bene, quaedam male, quaedam nec bene nec male, quaedam denique nullo modo se mouent) aestimandam, sed contra iuste semper Deum velle, mouere & agere quaecunque vult, mouet & agit, idest omnia ac singula…Esti Deus nullis mediis causis ad res omnes quas condidit vniuersaliter & sigillatim regendas…" Bèze, *Jobus Theodori Bezae Partim Commentariis*, Job 1:21, 51–52.

98 "Sunt autem haec instrumenta in triplici differentia. Quaedam enim sunt mere παθητικά ut inani-marae res omnes…ut sesenullo intrinseco motu impellent. Quaedam sic extrinsecus mouentur, ut simul sese etiam ipsa moueant naturali quodam appetitu…Quaedam denique sic mouentur, extra se ut quum, intelligentia & ratione praedita sint, sint etiam ipsorum aliquae agendi partes vnde proprium ipsorum opus nascitur." Ibid., Job 1:21, 52.

99 "Lapsus iste nec Angelos illos nec homines aboleuit, sed naturam duntaxat eorum deprauauit: usque adeo tamen ut intrinsecus omnis illorum motus, manens qualis nunc est, nunquam nisi male sese moueat, ac proinde nunquam vere bonum, sed vitiosum semper opus edat." Ibid.

100 For discussions regarding the continuity of the views of predestination between Beza and Calvin, refer to: Sinnema, "Beza's view of Predestination in Historical Perspective", 219–239; Raymond A. Blacketer, "The man in the black hat: Theodore Beza and the reorientation of early Reformed historiography", in *Church and School in Early Modern Protestantism*, edited by Joardan J. Ballor, David S. Sytsma and Jason Zuidema (Boston: Leiden Brill, 2013), 227–241.

101 "…pro immensa sua misericordia, ex vniuerso hominum genere, in Christo & per Christum saluti destinauit, qui sic a Spiritu Sancto illustrati in intellectu & in voluntate, efficaciter sanctificati, sicut bene a Deo mouentur, sic etiam bene & ipsi sese mouent, ut bonum & rectum sit tum Dei ipsos mouentis, tum ipsorum ses non secundum carnem, sed secundum spiritum mouentium opus." Bèze, *Jobus Theodori Bezae Partim Commentariis*, Job 1:21, 53.

102 "…emendauit autem semper, emendat & emendabit in iis quos…" Ibid.

works justly using instruments, but the instruments, too, move themselves.[103] They contribute to motion but without changing the fact that God ordains everything in His general and special providence, however, when the instruments create good or evil actions, they move themselves according to their own '*motus*'.[104]

In Aristotelian metaphysics, the primary sense of '*motus*' is the process or development from potency to actuality.[105]

> Finite movers both move and are moved – indeed, are moved from potency to act prior to their own self-movements – the chain of causality demands a first mover who moves without himself being moved.[106]

God acts as the first mover, but the instruments also move, which Beza clarifies by extensive use of Aristotelian causality to explain '*motus*' of instruments. Beza's doctrine of predestination suggests that humankind wills to move,[107] and relating the above to Job's case, in His eternal decree, God appoints what is going to happen in Job's life, for Job is an instrument in God's hand to display His glorification and Job's sanctification. In this training process, Job gradually understands as stated in Job 42,[108] that there are several parts involved in God's secret providence.

Beza's doctrine of providence shown in his work on the Book of Job mirrors the image of his decree-execution framework of predestination that he first illustrated in 1555, but in the commentary on Job, he offers a more detailed explanation of

---

103 "Ut autem Dei per illa sese quoque mouentia instrumenta semper iustum opus, ab altero seu vitioso seu recto instrumentorum sese quoque mouentium motu & opere distinguatur, tradita est a veteribus patribus inter Dei Actionem& eiusdem Permissionem distinctio, tam vera & necessaria, si recte & ex illorum sensu intelligatur..." Ibid.

104 "Itaque, quo ad Deum ipsum & proprium eius opus attinet, bene semper vult, decernit, gerit, quicquid ipse per quemcunque, quandocunque & quomodocunque in mundo gerit, id est quicquid in mundo sit & euenit, & generaliter & sigilatim. Instrumentorum autem mediorum sese quoque mouentium respectu, quamuis bene semper quoque illa moueat...Ad mala vero instrumenta & male sese mouentia quod attinet, nempe ad daemones & omnes non regeneratos, vel regeneratos, secundum carnem tamen peccantes: nequaquam in illis agere dicitur, ut qui prauitatem nullam ipsis indat vel inspirer, sed quam in illis reperit non compescendo, illis permittat & potestatem faciat secundum illam male sese mouendi & illius in malum actum exerendae..." Ibid., Job 1:21, 53–54.

105 Richard A. Muller, *Dictionary of Latin and Greek Theological Terms: Drawn Principally from Protestant Scholastic Theology*, Second edition (Grand Rapids, MI: Baker Academic, 2017), 224.

106 Ibid.

107 John S. Bray, *Theodore Beza's Doctrine of Predestination* (De Graaf, 1975), 115–16.

108 "Contra vero quantum est istud tuum in me beneficium quod quum te antea auribus duntaxat cognouerim, ex iis videlicet que patres illos nostros audiuimus de te nobis recitantes, nunc etiam teipsum in isto nimbo mihi praesentem, & inde mecum loquentem sistere sustinuisti?" Bèze, *Jobus Theodori Bezae Partim Commentariis*, Job 42:5, 248.

Job's case by using another Aristotelian term, *'intrinsecus motus'*, to highlight the human role involved in salvation and condemnation. Admittedly, showing most of the features of his decree-execution framework and Calvin's doctrine of heavenly providence, Beza's doctrines of providence and predestination are fundamentally the same.[109] God's providence assures the restoration of the corrupted wills of the chosen with help from the Holy Spirit, through God's training. Although Beza's Job is pious, Beza objects to Job's request for death.

Beza's Job in 3:11

Beza has a positive opinion of Job when Job still commits to God even after the great affliction in chapter 1 of the Book of Job. However, what does he think about Job's request for death in chapter 3? Beza affirms that God's children, who are saved in Christ will receive chastisement in the present life, so although they may suffer from infirmities, the chosen can hope for eternal happiness,[110] as life's afflictions are God's chastisements, but not judgements as sometimes defined by Calvin. So, with this definition, Beza truly thinks that Job's affliction is God's training and that Job would be crowned with victory when he is strengthened on earth through his training for eternity.

Job expresses that he wishes he had never been born or had died when he came out of his mother's womb, to which Beza asserts that this proceeds from an unsettled judgement.[111] Although Beza has sympathy for Job's grief, he believes that Job has forgotten the goodness he received from God and the commitments he made to God in Job 1.[112] Beza even suggests that Job is like an Epicurean who believes there is no eternal life after death.[113] However, Beza recognises that Job's behaviour is only human weakness and he reminds readers that at the end, Job acknowledges God's blessings.[114] He still praises Job as a perfect man and reinforces that if a perfect

---

109 "...providence and predestination go hand in hand." Elliott, *Providence Perceived*, 148.

110 "Et hac quidem est omnium hominum sors communis, iis demum exceptis quorum misereri Deus pro immensa bonitate sua in Christo Seruatore nostro decreuit. In istis igitur manet quidem praesentis vitae miseria, sed ipsorum commodo, siue sic illos Deus paterna ferula castiget: siue sic eos exerceat, partim ne ipsos fallat istius mundi σχῆμα partim ut in ipsorum infirmitate virtus ipsius sese demonstret, aeterna tandem beatitate victores suos athletas coronaturi." Bèze, *Jobus Theodori Bezae Partim Commentariis*, In Caput Tertium πρόλεγόμενα, 85.

111 "Sunt enim haec non a constante & sedato animi iudicio profecta, sed a magnitudine doloris mentis & fides luminibus ad tempus officiente, expressa." Ibid., 87.

112 "...hominis inconsyderati & tot acceptorum beneficiorum, atque adeo suiipsius, & insignisillius apophtegmatis obliti, si bona suscepimus a Domino cur aduersa non sustineamus?" Ibid., 87.

113 "...qui sese viuum respiceret atque adeo qui nihil hominis a morte superesse cum Epicureis sentiret." Ibid., 87.

114 Ibid., 87.

man like Job can behave like this, normal people should pray that God would not allow them to be led into temptation.[115]

Calvin on the other hand, shows that he is displeased with Job when he preaches Job 3:11–19, because while Job is honoured by God in such a gracious way, he nevertheless acts as if he had never tasted God's goodness[116] and he despises all God's blessings that he has received.[117] Both Beza and Calvin reject Job's request for death, but Beza's comments are milder.

Differences between Beza's Job and Calvin's Job

Beza supposes that believers' afflictions are God's training but not His judgement. Based on this understanding, Beza has sympathy for the tragedy Job faces. When Job says, 'The Lord gave and the Lord has taken away…(Job1:21)', Beza thinks that Job does not blaspheme but that he is confessing that God's will and His actions show His justice.[118] However, Beza points out that Job, as one of the chosen, sometimes forgets his status as God's child, and does not hope for eternal life.

Beza explains the participation of secondary causes and the way of moving/willing in election and reprobation, and shows that Job has a good understanding of the reprobation aspect of predestination. However, as one of the Elect, Job thinks rashly when facing adversity and forgets that he is part of the Elect, not one of the Reprobate. Beza also stresses that humankind as secondary cause, is genuinely moved by its own '*motus*' or *movement* to commit evil deeds. Aiming to defend Calvin's doctrine of predestination, Beza's explanation features Calvin's, but when applying this to Job's situation, there are differences. Beza puts more emphasises on the aspect of human righteousness in the election component of the doctrine of predestination. Yet, what do Beza and Calvin think of Elihu's criticism of Job?

---

115 Ibid.

116 "Voila des biens qui sont inestimables: neantmoins tant s'en faut que Iob les prise, qu'il voudroit iamais ne les avoir gousté." Calvin, Sermon 12 Job 3:11–19, CO33:153.

117 "Or nous voyons que Iob les met ici en un faisseau, et despite tout. Par cela donc que nous soyons admonestez si tost que Dieu nous propose quelque benefice que nous aurons receu de luy, d'estre esmeus de sentir sa bonté paternelle, afin de le remercier…" Ibid., CO33:155. See chapter 3 for detailed discussion.

118 "Idcirco primum omnium de hoc Iobi dicto probandum nobis est, illud non modo impie dictum non fuisse, verum etiam pie prorsus ac religiose cogitatum & pronuntiatum fuisse. Deinde istius pronuntiati quis & quantus sit vsus ostendam. Status autem huius quaestionis est, non An Deus auctor sit vllius mali…sed, An vere dici prossit, ac etiam debeat, aliquam atque adeo summam ac praecipuam Dei tum voluntatem tum actionem semper iustam…" Bèze, *Jobus Theodori Bezae Partim Commentariis*, Job 1:21, 51.

Elihu, Job and Calvin

Beza believes that Job's speech in chapter 32 is not blasphemous. He argues that Job knows he is godly, because in his life he has done his best to be upright before both God and man. Job confesses that he was born with sin, but cannot believe that he is a sinner and so he finds it difficult to endure and face the enormous torment attached to this concept.[119] When Calvin preaches on chapter 32, he asserts that Job murmurs about God's heavy hand upon his situation, and in doing so, says that Job justifies himself above God, for Job speaks with great passion and tries to prove that he is more righteous than God. Calvin says that this is blaspheming, and he exhorts his congregation to bridle their grudges and murmuring and to reverence God and submit to His power.[120]

In Beza's eyes, it is Job's friends who cause the problem of his faulty thinking. For while they reason many things excellently and accurately, they only understand part of God's providence and justice, hence they apply their knowledge wrongly to Job's situation, adding one more affliction and inflaming the situation.[121] They make two mistakes. Firstly, they think that it is impossible for God to lay His hands upon the godly and endow riches upon the wicked, for they reason that if God is just in how He judges a person, this person must have sinned. Secondly, since God is just, Job's current miserable state is the result of God's judgement of his sins.[122]

Beza consistently reminds his readers that the overall theme of the Book of Job is concerned about God's providence and justice but in a particular respect, it focuses on human righteousness. This consideration seems to refer specifically to Job's

---

119 "Contra vero Iobus sibi optime conscius, ad prius quidem caput haeret, Quinam videlicet fieri possit, ut tot tantisque calamitatibus tam subito prosternatur qui peccator quidem sit (nec enim hoc ipse negat, imo talem se natum esse confitetur) sed tamen ex animo sancte & honeste pro viribus sese erga Deum & homines gesserit." Ibid., 4.

120 "Quand donc Iob a des passions si vehementes, il n'y a nulle doute qu'en ce faisant il ne se face iuste par dessus Dieu. Et c'est ce que i'ay desia dit, que nous blasphemerons souvent en nos passions sans y penser: et cela nous doit rendre tant plus avisez de ne point lascher la bride à nos passions à fin de n'estre point si miserables que de blasphemer Dieu sans que nous y pensions. Ceste doctrine donc nous est bien utile. Quand le sainct Esprit prononce que tous ceux qui se despitent et murmurent en leurs afflictions, tous ceux qui ne se peuvent assuiettir à la main forte de Dieu pour confesser que tout ce qu'il fait est iuste et raisonnable, que tous ceux-la se font iustes par dessus Dieu..." Calvin, Sermon 119 Job 32:1–3, CO35:8.

121 "In hypothesi vero quod hoc vtrumque Iobi personae immerito applicarent, quanuis interea praeclare & vere multa, sed male conclusa & perperam applicata de Dei Providentia & Iustitia differant." Bèze, *Jobus Theodori Bezae Partim Commentariis*, 4.

122 "In thesi quidem quod ferre posse Dei iustitiam negarent, ut vere boni diuinitus, praesertim tam acerbe de repente affligantur, siue, Non nisi propter peccata hominibus eiusmodi calamitates immitti, ac proinde non posse quenquam simul vere probum fuisse, & tam calamitosum subito fieri." Ibid.

righteousness for Beza regards Job as a victim; however, now Job not only faces his own sufferings, he also needs to vindicate his innocence before God and his friends.[123] While most people consider Job's young friend, Elihu, as a comforter to Job and that Elihu has done the right thing in God's eyes, Beza has some reservations about part of Elihu's speech. Furthermore, although God says nothing against Elihu, Beza stresses that Elihu is not entirely right. Unlike Calvin, Beza defends Job's suffering against his friends' judgement and accusations, while Calvin's opinion of Job's friends, especially Elihu are more positive.

Beza's Elihu helps Job to defend Job's innocence in suffering against the other three friends' accusation, because these three friends surmise that Job's affliction is a result of God's condemnation of his past sin, and that Job therefore is regarded as being a great sinner.[124] However, Elihu still misinterprets Job's situation in that Elihu accuses Job of a different charge by asserting that God is offended by Job's blasphemous speeches (Job 36:16–19).[125] Beza, however, believes that God is not offended by Job's speech and that his speech is not blasphemous. Yet, according to both Calvin and Beza's Elihu, Job's speech is blasphemous, and in this regard, Calvin and Beza's Elihu have the same negative opinion of Job.

In addition, Beza's Elihu seems to agree with the other three friends that Job is punished because God is angry with him.[126] Although Elihu misconstrues Job's speeches, Beza does think that Elihu is divinely sent to let Job witness the majesty and glory of God's providence.[127] So why is Job afflicted? Beza asserts that God has

---

123 "Iobus autem, et si de re tota rectius sentit & iudicat, tamen & doloris magnitudine, & amicorum amarulentia pene oppressus, modum interdum non tenet in asserenda sua, tum apud Deum, tum apud amicos innocentia…" Ibid.

124 Ibid., Capitis 33 Summa et Dispositio, 205 and Capitis 36 Summa et Dispositio, 220.

125 "Sed in eo discrepat ab illis Iobis accusatoribus, quod illi quidem Deum sic falso existimabant Iobo infensum ob anteactam vitam: Elius autem ob ipsius responsa quasi manifeste blasphema v.16, 17, 18 & 19…" Ibid., Capitis 36 Summa et Dispositio, 220. Cf. "At enim, inquies, Elium dicta Iobi non pauca sinistre & aliter quam mens ipsius ferret interpretatum praeteriit, ipsius etiam quasi vestigiis insistens, ut penitus videatur eius accusationi subscripsisse." Ibid., Quinque Reliquorum huius libri capitum Summa et Dispositio, 230.

126 "Quum enim Elius Iobum non tantum ut audacius in disputationem de Dei administratione ingressum, sed etiam quasi impietatis ac blasphemiae reum accusasset amicos autem eius parce admodum & ieiune arguisset, immo etiam illis aliquatenus visus esset in eo assentiri, quod ab irato Deo Iobus castigaretur…." Ibid.

127 "Elium audiuimus rigidiorem quidem, sed necessarium censorem diuinitus praemissum qui calumniis amicorum irritatiorem factum Iobum, grauissimis & sapientissimis sermonibus, ab illo integritatis suae patrocinio, ad moderationem reuocaret." Ibid., Summa et Dispositio Quinque Reliquorum huius libri capitum, 229. Cf. "Respondeo fuisse quidem Elium diuinitus praemissum, qui Iobi non nisi acri re medio cessuri intemperiem, proposita illa summa ac terribili diuinae Maiestatis gloria, compesceret…" Ibid., 230.

'special love' for the Elect which includes Job, his friends, and the wisest men,[128] and because of His mercy, if they repent, He will not forsake them. Furthermore, a just God reasonably provides special care for justified people. Again, Beza claims that Job is one of the Elect, so apparently, he is justified and is being protected in God's special love. Therefore, Job is confirmed to be justified, and hence his suffering is surely not God's punishment but instead, is a training, as Beza explained in his comments on Job 3:11. This training is a process, so human repentance to God should continue as long as human beings continues to be rebellious. Thus, Job can remember to hope for a better life in eternity, as Beza suggested in his comments on Job 1:21. However, while Beza's Job is assured to be one of the Elect, Calvin's Job seems unsure of his prestigious status until Job 42, when Job repents, and thus when facing afflictions, he sways between being saved and condemned. However, through Job's example, Beza conveys a message which shows that salvation is assured for the Elect.

Beza assures that the Elect will not be punished, and that salvation is assured, and he is not the first to address the assurance of salvation, with Susan Schreiner asserting that the certitude of salvation was the concern of most sixteenth–century reformers. In Luther's exegesis of Galatians 4:6, he suggests that when believers, through the working of the Holy Spirit, cry "Abba! Father", they gain a new understanding of God as a Father who wills to save his children through His Spirit. This is an expression of certainty and it produces the noetic healing caused by the human nature of humanity's doubtful mind.[129]

Calvin expounded this verse in a similar way when he preached to his congregation in 1557. He said,

> When we cry through the Spirit, we do so with full certainty that we know and acknowledge that we are members of God's son and by means of Christ we are accepted by God into his heavenly kingdom; the gate is open to us and access is given to us personally.[130]

When Calvin commented on Galatians 4:6 and 4:30 in 1548, he had already stressed that the ungodly cannot taste this kind of certainty,[131] yet, the Elect will inherit

---

128 "...in Deo quidem singularis illa φιλανθρωπία, & erga resipiscentes: omnes ineffabilis clementia: in Iobo vero & ipsius amicis sapientissimorum etiam hominum infirmitas..." Ibid.

129 Susan Elizabeth Schreiner, *Are You Alone Wise? The Search for Certainty in the Early Modern Era*, Oxford Studies in Historical Theology (New York: Oxford University Press, 2012), 58.

130 John Calvin, *Sermons sur l'epitre aux Galates*, CR 78, 588. Also in Schreiner, *Are You Alone Wise?*, 67.

131 "Ideoque hoc argumentum non potest valere nisi inter fideles: quia reprobi nullum huius certitudinis gustum habent." Ioannis Calvini, *Commentarius in epistolam ad Galatas* 1548, Gal 4:6, CO50:228.

the heavenly kingdom in eternity as they are chosen in God's eternal decree as His children in heavenly providence.[132]

While Calvin's comments on Galatians 4:30 were discussed in the previous chapter, it should be noted that his doctrine of heavenly providence also addresses certitude. However, Calvin's method of asserting assurance of salvation using Job's case, is not continued by Beza. Therefore, although Beza's doctrine of providence mirrors Calvin's and Beza also uses this doctrine to assure salvation, his explanation of the roles of Job, and Job's friends, especially Elihu, is entirely different from that of his master.

Beza's use of the scholastic method

Some Reformation scholars regard Beza as the reformer who changed Protestant theology to scholasticism, however, Raitt[133] and John Bray both agree that Beza is 'a transitional figure who bridged the gulf between the biblical-Christocentric position of Calvin and the scholasticism of those who followed him'.[134] Bray reinforces that Beza's work contains no features of scholasticism,[135] but he stresses that Beza in his later years employed a more analytical method to explain predestination.[136] The increase in the use of the meaning of Aristotelian fourfold causality to explain the reprobation aspect of the doctrine of predestination does echo Bray's claim. However, Bray considers that Beza's increased use of the scholastic content is analytical, but not scholastic.

---

132 "…sed haec aliquanto efficacior, dum addit, hypocritas cum sua iactantia nihil aliud profecturos, quam ut eiiciantur ex spirituali Abrahae familia: nobis vero nihil ominus salvam fore haereditatem, utcunque insolenter nos ad tempus lacessant…Locus pulcherrimus, ne turbemur hypocritarum fastu: aut illorum sorti invideamus, quum temporariam cum dignitate mansionem habent in ecclesia: sed patienter exitum, qui eos manet, exspectemus. Multi enim vel spurii, vel alieni locum usurpant in ecclesia: sed fidem perpetuo fixam non habent. Quemadmodum instar alienigenae, eiectus fuit cum posteris suis Ismael, qui tamen primogenitura inflatus initio regnabat. Rident hic nasuti quidam homines Pauli simplicitatem, quod bilem foeminae ex futili rixa natam comparet Dei iudicio: sed non animadvertunt, interpositum fuisse Dei decretum, quo palam fieret totum id coelesti providentia gubernari." Ibid., Gal 4:30, CO50:242.

133 To explain the reality and effectiveness of the Supper, Raitt asserts, "The effectiveness of the Super is wholly from the Holy Spirit who, while using created instruments according to their natural operations, nevertheless causes effects completely beyond any natural power. Here again Beza developed Calvin's doctrine of instrumentality along scholastic lines." Raitt, *The Eucharistic Theology of Theodore Beza*, 70.

134 Bray, *Theodore Beza's Doctrine of Predestination*, 21.

135 Ibid., 21.

136 Ibid., 76.

Raymond A. Blacketer argues that the scholastic way is a modern academic method rather than a method with specific and predictable doctrinal content.[137] Reformed theologians pursued the academic method of making careful distinctions and definition from exegesis. Furthermore, Blacketer adds that when Reformed theologians adopted Aristotelian fourfold causality, they did not abandon the tradition of Protestantism but rather they engaged in Renaissance humanist dialectic.[138] He reinforces that Beza's use of fourfold causality is to provide a 'coherent understanding of Pauline teaching.'[139] This statement is helpful but it should be noted that Beza does not involve a verse-by verse rhetorical analysis, a typical renaissance humanist dialectic,[140] in explaining the doctrine of predestination in *Tabula praedestinationis* or in the commentary on Job. Beza uses Scriptures widely, but his analysis is not humanistic in style.

Jeffery Mallinson observes that all Reformed religious epistemologies are uniquely concerned with the role of the knowing subject.[141] The analysis of Beza's application of the doctrine of divine providence on Job's situation echoes this argument. However, Mallinson's suggestion of the objective and subjective relation in Beza's epistemology remains negotiable. Mallinson recognises the importance of Aristole to the approach Beza adopted to teach dialectic, and he argues that it is imprecise to assume Beza's adherence to Aristotle's philosophy.[142] In Mallinson's arguments, he distinguishes the terms 'subjective' and 'objective' regarding faith although these terms were not used by Beza.[143] Mallinson argues that to Beza, Scripture is objectively historical and authentic, and therefore, it is demonstrable even to the ungodly.[144]

In *Tabula pradestinationis*, when Beza explains the execution of reprobation, he stresses that although the ungodly also hear the Gospel, they understand it with

---

137 "Beza's analysis is in fact a verse-by verse rhetorical analysis of the text, typical of renaissance humanism's preoccupation with examining arguments." Blacketer, "The man in the black hat: Theodore Beza and the reorientation of early Reformed historiography", 230, 237, 240.

138 Ibid., 230.

139 Ibid., 238.

140 Ibid., 237.

141 Jeffrey Mallinson, *Faith, Reason, and Revelation in Theodore Beza, 1519–1605*, Oxford Theological Monographs (Oxford/ New York: Oxford University Press, 2003), 59.

142 Mallinson, Faith, Reason, and Revelation in Theodore Beza, 1519–1605, 236.

143 Mallinson also agrees that the terminology of subjectivity and objectivity is foreign to Beza's time. Mallinson, *Faith, Reason, and Revelation in Theodore Beza, 1519–1605*, 20. Jill Raitt, Review of *Faith, Reason, and Revelation in Theodore Beza (1519–1605)*, by Jeffery Mallinson, *American Society of Church History*, vol. 73, no. 4 (Dec 2004), 857–858.

144 Mallinson, *Faith, Reason, and Revelation in Theodore Beza, 1519–1605*, 235.

general faith.[145] This general faith is objectively ascribed to everyone but not all are willing to assent to this truth because of their human sinful nature. Therefore, the only way people can attain true faith is by responding to the Gospel subjectively, and thus Christ subjectively endows them with grace.[146] The faith Jesus granted to the faithful and the faith by which the faithful respond to the preaching, are both described as subjective by Mallinson. The matching of the objective and subjective relation to the operation of divine predestination seems explainable. However, one has to note that Beza's interpretation of the doctrines of providences and predestination in his *Tabula praedestinationis* and his exegesis on the Book of Job do not use 'subjective' and 'objective'. Instead, Beza employs a combination of methodologies available in the sixteenth century to help him to clarify his theology, or perhaps for apologetic argumentation.

While these methodologies and the scholastic terms Beza adopted help him to explain his doctrines, they have no effect on leading Beza on a different path away from Calvin. Beza is a bridge to later Reformed scholastics after 1600. He certainly adopts many fundamentals of Calvin's doctrines of predestination and providence to formulate his decree-execution framework, therefore, both Beza and Calvin are essentially similar. Their differences lie in how they apply the doctrines differently in Job's situation, whereas Beza wants to highlight Job's righteousness.

Conclusion

After examining Beza's work, *Tabula praedestionationis* 1555, it is found that Beza's decree-execution framework used to explain the doctrine of double predestination, consists of significant features of Calvin's doctrine of '*providentia coelestis*', which Beza follows in formulating *Tabula paredestinationis*. While Calvin's doctrine of heavenly providence is soteriological, Beza's doctrine of predestination is providential. After examining *Jobus Theodori Bezae partim commentariis partim paraphrasi illustratus* 1589, it is discovered Beza and Calvin's difference of opinion concerning Job, originates from Beza's consideration for human righteousness and his assertion of the certainty of salvation for the Elect. From *Tabula praedestionationis* to

---

145 'Sunt alis praeterea quorum intelligentiam excitat ad ea percipienda & credenda quae audiunt: sed hoc sit generalis illa fide, quae praediti Diaboli contremiscunt.' Bèze, *Summa totius Christianismi sive descriptio et distributio causarum salutis electorum, & exitii reproborum, ex sacris literis collecta*, Chapter 5, 192.

146 'Primum autem hic Spiritus facit in electis ut calamitatis illius suae sensu vere afficiantur: deinde fidem in ipsis create, ut possint conditionem praedicationis Euangelis adnexam praestare.' Ibid., Chapter 4, 186.

Jobus Theodori Bezae partim commentariis partim paraphrasi illustratus, Beza increases his usage of scholastic terms to explain his doctrine of predestination and to expound his apologetics, but this increase does not mean that his theology has diverged from Calvin's doctrine of divine providence. Furthermore, Beza's doctrine of predestination introduces a discussion of causality, as a defence against God as the author of sin and gradually moves to the discussion of human righteousness, to assure salvation for the Elect.

Heavenly Providence

The doctrine of providence is known to be central in Calvin's theology and has been the focus of considerable Reformation scholarship. This study builds upon this body of work, while clarifying that Calvin's doctrine of divine providence is truly heavenly providence, allowing human beings, as the second cause, to participate in God's action on earth. Furthermore, this study underlines that while God's providence in Calvin's theology is gradually less associated with soteriological matters for the ungodly, Calvin in his early years asserted that everyone could attain God-given life through Jesus Christ.

> *A fountain from which all drink, and from which streams flow and are derived, is said to have water in itself, yet it has it not of itself but of the source, which constantly supplies what may suffice both for the running streams and the men who drink of it. Accordingly, Christ has life in himself, i. e. fullness of life, by which he both himself lives and quickens others; yet he has it not of himself, as he elsewhere declares that he lives by the Father.* (John Calvin, 1534).

Psychopannychia 1534

The main theme of *Psychopannychia* 1534 is not to exemplify the doctrine of *providentia Dei*, but to refute the false Anabaptist teaching concerning the afterlife. However, Calvin does discuss this situation based on *providentia Dei*, and he uses the image of the fountain to explain the function of God's providence in relation to eternal life. Drawing from the Book of Baruch 3:14, Calvin illustrates that *providentia Dei* is God's power, and the source of life, which operates like a fountain, gushing out goodness of both material and eternal benefits for humankind. Calvin uses this concept to refute his opponents who believe that storehouses are God's providence.

According to a verse from 4 Esdras 7:32, which specifies that "the earth will render up those things which sleep in it, and dwell in silence; and the storehouses will render up the souls which were committed to them", the Anabaptists argue that the soul sleeps or dies in the afterlife. They believe that the storehouse is God's providence, and so when a person dies, his soul dies as well but the souls of the faithful are kept in the storehouse, which is known as God's providence. Furthermore, they allege that souls are thoughts and that the Book of Life displays these thoughts in storehouses. Calvin does not agree with these interpretations of the soul and reminds his readers to take note of 4 Esdras 4:35 as it says, "did not the souls of these petition in their abodes, saying, how long do we hope this, O Lord? When will the harvest of our reward come?" Therefore, the soul does not die but instead it hopes for the reward of resurrection. Calvin argues that God's providence is not storehouses but God's power, and that souls are not thoughts but life. The soul never loses its life. So, what does God's power do to the souls when people die? Calvin uses the Book of Baruch 3:12–14 to deliver an explanation.

Calvin adopts the image of the fountain as a heuristic key to unlock the meaning of God's power and argues that God's providence is His power, which functions as a fountain. God's power benefits all people in the world, including the godly and ungodly. Calvin continued to use this image of the fountain to illustrate God's power and *providentia Dei* in his first two editions of the *Institutes*. God gives life that endures for all, and life of a spiritual quality to the Elect.

The 1536 *Institutes*

Calvin stresses that rulers are vicars of God, and as such they should model themselves on the image of divine providence, protection, goodness, benevolence, and justice. This description is an echo of Calvin's description of God in the first paragraph of the first section of his 1536 *Institutes*. In the first section of the 1536 *Institutes*, Calvin quotes from Baruch 3:12–14 and he argues that God is infinite wisdom, righteousness, goodness, mercy, truth, power, and life. In *Psychopannychia*, Calvin had already used Baruch 3:14 to describe God as being like a fountain which gives the fullness of life, and the same passage of the Apocrypha or the Deuterocanonical books is adopted to support his interpretation in the 1536 *Institutes*. Although the term *fons* is not found in this first section of the 1536 *Institutes* when Calvin describes God, this term appears twice in this edition of the *Institutes*. These two instances show that one can find the fountain of living water in Christ and this living water is from the fountain source of God, who provides immortal life to those who believe in Him.

In the 1536 *Institutes*, Calvin also introduces 'aeterna Dei providentia' in which God chooses people to be adopted as member of the Church. Yet, what is the relationship between God's wisdom, righteousness, goodness, mercy, truth, power and life, and eternal providence? It seems that there is a strong connection but Calvin's explanation in the 1536 *Institutes* has not yet been fully developed. However, this teaching of God's providence for the Church constitutes a sense of salvation. Furthermore, Calvin continues to relate God's providence to God's wisdom, righteousness, and life, which spring from the source of God's fountain.

Calvin's use of the term *fons* in the 1539 *Institutes* displays an inconspicuous but significant difference. He adds the term, fountain, to both the Latin and French editions without reference to the Book of Baruch.

The 1539 & 1541 *Institutes*

In the first chapter (Knowledge of God) of the second edition of the *Institutes*, published in Latin in 1539 and in French in 1541, Calvin argues that God is the *fons* and *fonteine* respectively: that is, God is the source of all truth, wisdom, goodness, righteousness, judgement, mercy, power, and holiness, and he does so without reference to the Book of Baruch in this edition. In this expanded volume of a dogmatic handbook, Calvin wants to highlight that God is the fountain of life, and something more. Calvin argues that God not only has power over earthly blessings and immortal life, but He also endows humanity with holiness, which is salvation for the Church. This list is reinforced at the end of this chapter of 'Knowledge of God' and Calvin reminds readers to gain the knowledge of God in His truth, wisdom, goodness, righteousness, judgement, mercy, and power together, then His holiness will shine in them. The reinforcement of the list, displaying God's 'things' (God's *res*) by Calvin at the end of chapter one in the 1539 and 1541 *Institutes* shows the importance of the list to Calvin. God's operation in His providence shows His truth, wisdom, goodness, righteousness, judgement, mercy, power, and holiness.

It is only with the second edition of Calvin's *Institutes*, that he directly relates God's 'things' to salvation, which signify sanctification and immortality. However, in doing so, he omits reference to the Book of Baruch, indicating his avoidance of the Apocrypha and the Deuterocanonical books. This does not imply that Calvin has come to a stage to have a clear interpretation of *providentia Dei*, as the texts of both the Latin and French editions show that he is indecisive in defining the meaning of special providence. That might be the reason why in the 1539 and 1541 *Institutes*, Calvin distinguishes two kinds of providence: general and special, which guide both the matters of this world and of the faithful respectively. However, Calvin does not provide a distinction between special providence (for all humankind) and very special providence (only for the Elect), and he is hesitant about the definitions of special providence and very special providence.

Calvin discusses the doctrines of predestination and providence in the same chapter, while he uses his interpretation of *providentia Dei* to explain his doctrine of double predestination, by assuring the Elect that they are endowed with salvation, life, and immortality from the fountain of life in Christ. In contrast, the Reprobate, by God's providence, are set apart for destruction. To echo Calvin's concern about salvation and the holiness of the Church at the beginning of the second edition of the *Institutes*, Calvin uses the doctrine of predestination to exemplify the situation that false Christians are not heirs of God's kingdom, but the Elect are God's children and can inherit a place in His kingdom. In the 1539 and 1541 *Institutes*, Calvin's doctrine of *providentia Dei* is now related directly to soteriological matters. Furthermore, Calvin follows most of his predecessors and suggests that providential activities are in some sense salvific.

Commentarius in epistolam Pauli ad Romanos 1540

In 1540 when Calvin wrote the *Commentarius in epistolam Pauli ad Romanos*, he showed that reprobation is included in *providentia Dei*, and he uses the image of the fountain to defend the argument against God as the author of sin. In his exegesis of Romans 9:17, he argues that Pharaoh is predestined to ruin in the hidden fountain of God's providence, as God's judgement for the Reprobate originates from God's hidden providence for the purpose of glorifying His name.

In his works prior Calvin's *Commentarius in epistolam Pauli ad Romanos*, Calvin portrays God as a fountain to show that He is the source of eternal life and all benefits. In *Commentarius in epistolam Pauli ad Romanos*, Calvin uses the word, fountain, to describe that in God's hidden fountain of providence, He condemns some people. The usage of the image of the fountain displays one of the actions of God: judging the sinners, and this usage is not a reference to the Book of Baruch anymore.

De aeterna Dei praedestinatione 1552

Calvin's definitions of general providence and special providence started to assume a distinct form in the 1539 &1541 *Institutes,* but this is only shown explicitly in his *De aeterna Dei praedestinatione*, where Calvin offered three distinctive definitions for three kinds of *providentia Dei*. In *De aeterna Dei praedestinatione* 1552, Calvin distinguishes three kinds of '*providentia Dei*': firstly, there is a general government of the world so that everything is kept in its proper and natural state. Secondly, there is a special government of particular parts of the world, but this care is especially for humans. Thirdly, there is *providentia* '*praesentissima Dei*' in which God protects and guides the Church by His fatherly care. Yet, is '*praesentissima Dei*' the same as '*aeterna Dei providentia*' which Calvin discussed in the 1536 *Institutes*? He offers an answer in his *Sermon sur le livre de Iob, De occulta providentia Dei* and in the 1559 *Institutes*.

The image of the fountain is used to describe double predestination. In this work, Calvin argues that it is God's will that the '*fons gratiae*' should flow through all the godly, and in the '*omnis iustitiae fons*', God judges the ungodly. God is the sole source, and the fountains of grace and justices both are sprung from Him. However, this fountain of justice originates from a deep secret, which echoes Calvin's interpretation of the hidden providence of God's fountain in his *Commentarius in epistolam Pauli ad Romanos*. The fountain of justice is hidden, which means that it is incomprehensible to human reason. In other words, in God's fountain of grace, which is His providence, He saves the members who are also the Elect in Christ. While in God's fountain of justice, which is His hidden providence, He condemns the Reprobate. The fountains of grace and justice are different, and they serve separate purposes. However, in another place in *De aeterna Dei praedestinatione*, it is described that the fountain of all evil deeds is the corruption of human nature. Therefore, Calvin's use of this image of the fountain is not pointing to the source of life as he first adopted it, but instead functions as Calvin's writing style, and now becomes loosely related to his doctrine of *providentia Dei*. Calvin gradually moves away from portraying God's providence as a fountain because God's providence is more than what can be illustrated by the image of a fountain as one can see in his three definitions of *providentia Dei* in *De aeterna Dei praedestinatione*. God's action is not passive as a fountain implies. In addition, God's providence does not imply passivity in the role of believers.

Sermons sur le livre de Job 1554 to 1555

From 1554–1555, Calvin delivered 159 sermons on the Book of Job, and he also gave an elaboration of the doctrine of *providentia Dei* to assure salvation for the congregations to whom he preached. Calvin demonstrates that there are two kinds of providence: general providence and special providence. General providence is God's action in His order of creation which can be seen in His power, goodness, justice, and wisdom, but this kind of providence also has an effect on human lives. Special providence is God's action acted upon human beings. Human participation in God's providence is possible, especially in God's goodness, but only the godly can realise and appreciate this participation. Job participates in God's general and special providence, but Calvin endeavours to inform the Genevan churches that Job does not recognize his participation because he acts like an ungodly person. However, when Job repents, as shown in chapter 42, he truly knows that he participates in *providentia Dei*.

Calvin believes that God will both bless and punish His children and that Job's suffering is God's chastisement and judgement. In some of his sermons on the Book of Job, Calvin even considers Job as a non-believer. Therefore, Calvin thinks that only from that moment when Job truly repents and is justified (in chapter 42), can Job notice his participation in God's providence. Thus, Calvin intends to show that only believers can acknowledge God's providence, which raises the question, are believers being cared for by a distinctive kind of God's providence? Certainly, some people are protected in God's '*providentia coelestis*', which is the very special providence for the Elect only, also known as '*specialissima*' by theologians after Calvin. Although Calvin suggests that only the godly can understand God's providence, the ungodly can live a life on earth in God's protection in His general and special providence. Election and reprobation are decreed in '*providentia coelestis*', and God uses some instruments to execute these two processes. It is found that one has to read *Sermons sur le livre de Job, De occulta providentia Dei* 1558 and the definitive 1559 *Institutes* to grasp a complete meaning of '*providentia coelestis*'.

In *Sermons de le livre de Job*, Calvin directly regards God's actions in His 'things': power, goodness, justice, and wisdom as *providentia Dei*, however, this is not the first work where he offers this discussion. In the first paragraph of the first chapter in both of the 1536 and the 1539 *Institutes*, Calvin shows a list of God's 'things', but Calvin does not relate God's actions in His 'things' directly to *providentia Dei*. However, *Sermons de le livre de Job* constitute the definition of God's providence in relation to God's 'things', His action and '*providentia Dei*'.

Three kinds of providence: general providence, special providence, and heavenly providence appear together in *Sermons de le livre de Job*, but it does not mean that Calvin only develops these three terms when he preached these sermons in 1554. Most scholars of Calvin studies agree that Calvin spends his whole life teaching general and special providence, but while Calvin teaches these two kinds of providence, he demonstrates in 1536 a germination of the third kind of providence concerning salvation. Moreover, in the 1539 *Institutes*, the addition of 'holiness' to the list of God's 'things' formally shows Calvin's consideration of human salvation in relation to *providentia Dei*. The detailed explanation of Calvin's doctrine of *providentia Dei* in *Sermons sur le livre de Job* confirms that Calvin's doctrine of *providentia Dei* takes shape in 1539, as all the elements in the doctrine of *providentia Dei* are firstly discussed in the 1539 *Institutes*. The picture is clearer when one examines his later works from 1558–1559.

Commentarius in librum Psalmorum 1557

When Calvin preached his sermons on the Book of Job, he commented that Job does not deal with life's suffering in a godly way, and thus he recommends the example of David to the congregation as a better model to follow. The reasons Calvin shows special fondness for David are both personal and pastoral. From a personal perspective, Calvin sees himself in David admitting there are resemblances in their young lives, their life sufferings, and the attacks of their enemies although Calvin considers he falls far short of equalling David. From a practical perspective,

Calvin regards the Book of Psalms as a handbook teaching the godly how to practice piety.

In *Commentarius in librum Psalmorum* 1557, Calvin explains that David is a faithful servant because he sees suffering as reparation for his sins, thus, every time when he is afflicted, David does not complain but begs for God's pardon. Calvin appreciates David tremendously because of David's awareness of God's wrath and his endeavours to be humble. Calvin's David has no difficulty in understanding God's general providence, special providence, and providence especially for the Church because he prays faithfully. When David witnesses and enjoys God's wonderful blessings in general providence, he praises God with his whole body. When David prays to God amid his opponents' attacks, God delivers him. When David prays for God's pardon of his sin, God forgives him, and God extends His deliverance to the whole Church. David prays earnestly and he is the one who enjoys God's benevolence and eternal happiness on earth in *providentia Dei*.

Calvin depicts David as submitting to God's providence and shows how David, through prayer, continuously praises God's wonderful works in general providence, awaits God's deliverance in special providence and beseeches God to grant salvation especially for the godly in the Church, in His providence. Calvin recommends all children of God to read the Book of Psalms as he considers it is a guide for Christian sanctification, as many of the situations experienced by David as described in this book applied to the experiences of the Church during Calvin's time. Calvin especially honours David's prayer and he emphasises that humankind is able to see some revelation of God's providence through prayer, where prayer makes both God and His providence known. David is an exemplar who truly tastes *providentia Dei*, and therefore Calvin uses David as an illustration of a genuine existence of secondary causes in God's providence.

The doctrine of *'providentia coelestis'* in *Sermons sur le live de Job* **1554** to **1555,** *De occulta providentia Dei* **1558** and the **1559** *Institutes*

Reading *Sermons sur le live de Job* 1554–1555, *De occulta providentia Dei* 1558 and Book 1 of the 1559 *Institutes* together is important for an understanding of Calvin's meaning of *'providentia coelestis'*.

Early in 1548, Calvin wrote *Commentarius in epistolam ad Galatas*, and dedicated it to Christoph of Württemberg, aiming to encourage him in the intense and difficult situations oppressing in the Church. Calvin's major discussion in this commentary is not about *providentia Dei* but the proper organization of the Church, and so he stresses that believers inherit a place in the Church, while false Christians, will be cast out like strangers. This is governed by *'providentiae coelestis'*, and this term is repeated and explained more precisely in his later works.

When Calvin preaches the sermons on the Book of Job, in 1554–1555, he suggests that general and special providence are God's actions in His goodness, power, justice, and wisdom. However, Calvin argues that only the people who are saved, can understand general and special providence, while he further asserts that in God's '*providentia coelestis*', He endows His children with fatherly goodness, and governs the world with justice. In *De occulta providentia Dei*, Calvin argues that God in His secret decree, as the '*coelestis pater*' and the '*coelestis iudex*', ordains some people to be the Elect and the rest to be the Reprobate. God's secret providence, which is hidden, is the explanation of predestination, especially the controversial part of the reprobation in this doctrine.

In Book 1 of the 1559 *Institutes*, Calvin considers '*providentia coelestis*' as a doctrine related to the knowledge of God, and its purpose is to encourage the godly to worship God, and hope for eternal life as God's clemency and His judgement are not yet fulfilled in the present life. God has very special care for the Elect, as they inherit a place in the Church, and Calvin elaborates this matter in Book 2 and 3 of the 1559 *Institutes*. God wills to predestine some to be His children, and to exclude the rest from the inheritance of salvation and those who have not become part of Christ will not inherit God's kingdom. These people are condemned to eternal death by '*aeterna Dei providentia*'. Calvin again discusses the doctrine of eternal providence in Book 4 when he confirms that the salvation of church members rests upon the unshakable nature of the Church, and that the Church stands firm because God's election is in His eternal providence.

Calvin has already used the doctrine of eternal providence starting with the 1536 *Institutes*, to describe how God's election gathers the faithful as members of the Church. He discussed this doctrine briefly in 1536, but he elaborated on it further in his definitive edition of the 1559 *Institutes*. '*Providentia coelestis*' is God's special care given only to the Elect, and Calvin refers to it with different terms at various stages of his life: '*aeterna Dei providentia*' (1536), '*providentia coelestis*' (1548), '*praesentissima Dei*' (1552), '*providence celeste*' (1554), '*coelestis pater* and *coelestis iudex*' (1558), and finally back to '*providentia coelestis*' and '*aeterna Dei providentia*' in 1559. The term '*providentia specialissima*' is used in the seventeenth century after Calvin. The definitions of the doctrine of *providentia Dei* in the first edition (1536) and the definitive edition (1559) of the *Institutes* echo each other, showing that although there is a gradual development and clarification of Calvin's interpretation, the meaning of the doctrine Calvin refers to is consistent, and his position on the doctrine of *providentia Dei* has not changed.

When Calvin wrote *Commentarius in epistolam Pauli ad Romanos* 1540 and *De aeterna Dei praedestinatione* 1552, he used the image of the fountain to describe hidden providence and evil deeds respectively. The instance of people's sin as the fountain of the sinners' adversities and mishaps is a prime example that the use of the image of fountain is not a reference to the Book of Baruch.

Later in works such as *Sermons sur le live de Job* 1554–1555, *De occulta providentia Dei* 1558 and the 1559 *Institutes*, Calvin seems to drop the image of the *fons* and starts to consolidate his doctrine of *providentia Dei*, by assuring the faithful that they are cared for by God's '*providentia coelestis*'. He asserts that the faithful are members of God's unshakable church and therefore in His eternal providence, they are entitled to inherit God's kingdom. Although Calvin's interpretation of the doctrine of *providentia Dei* does not consist of the image of the fountain, the argument concerning guaranteed eternal salvation as the 'care' God provides is consistently present.

To Calvin, God's providence was like a fountain but the description of God's providence using an image of a fountain is limited, for God's action is active, but the fountain is stagnant and passive. In addition, the image of the fountain displays that God as creator and judge and thus secondary causes are restricted. Therefore, the image of the fountain is used in a more descriptive way, instead of as theology, in Calvin's later works. The idea of God's providence in relation to predestination simply cannot be explained thoroughly using the image of the fountain but can be explained through '*providentia coelestis*'. As Calvin advocates in the definitive edition of the *Institutes*, *providentia Dei* is truly '*providentia coelestis*', which is '*providentia Dei*' for the Church. It seems that Calvin defines the meanings of general providence, special providence, and the very special providence progressively, however, there is only one kind of *providentia Dei*: '*providentia coelestis*', from the Elect's point of view.

Theodore Beza's *Tabula praedestinationis* 1555, *Jobus Theodori Bezae partim commentariis partim paraphrasi illustratus* 1589

After Calvin's death, his academic colleague, Theodore Beza succeeded him as leader of the Genevan churches. He follows Calvin in many interpretations of doctrine such as providence and predestination, however, their applications of doctrine are different. For instance, Beza's decree-execution framework suggested in his work, *Tabula raedestinationis*, which is a work to defend the argument against God as the author of sin, shows a line of continuity with Calvin's doctrine of '*providentia coelestis*', but there is a clear divergence when he uses the doctrine to analyse Job's case.

When Beza comments on chapter one of the Book of Job, he suggests that Satan's action, as the secondary cause, is decreed by God's secret providence and that Satan obeys God's will to incur afflictions upon Job. However, Beza depicts Job as being protected by God's '*singularissma providentia*', the same as Calvin depicts in '*providentia coelestis*'. This providence, according to Beza, is particularly given to the chosen, so Job is being cared for in God's very special providence, and Job's affliction is neither a judgement nor a punishment from God, as Father God offers very special care to His children. Beza is more sympathetic to Job than Calvin, and he reinforces his assertion that Job's case is to show God's chastisement of humans and human righteousness. While Calvin encourages his congregation by stressing that God is the father of His chosen, Beza reinforces his argument that there is salvation for the godly, by emphasising human righteousness through faith in Christ. Beza explains that people suffer because they move themselves by '*intrinsectus motus*', which is truly a moving of their own accord. While the term '*intrinsectus motus*' is derived from Aristotelian metaphysics, Beza, in adopting some scholastic terms, suggests that there is a genuine existence of human beings as the secondary cause in the course of salvation and condemnation.

In Calvin's early work, the explanation of the image of the fountain is not related to scholasticism, but to a medieval theology which connects itself to Christian spirituality. When Calvin explains the doctrine of *providentia Dei* in his later works, although he incorporates some scholastic ideas and methods such as causality and a distinction between decree and execution, he never accepts scholastic ideas the same way Beza does. Calvin tends to stay away from using scholastic teaching, while Beza increases the use of some scholastic terms in his explanation of the doctrine of predestination. Beza introduces a discussion of causality, as a defence against the idea that God is the author of sin and gradually moves to a discussion of human righteousness, to assure salvation for the Elect.

Further research possibilities – '*providentia coelestis*'

Modern studies on Calvin's doctrine of *providentia Dei* tend to be limited to the discussion of two kinds of providence: general providence and special providence, as these studies usually only focus on one or two of Calvin's works, namely the 1539 *Institutes*, *De occulta providentia Dei* or the 1559 *Institutes*. Therefore, these studies arrive at an incomplete conclusion of Calvin's interpretation of *providentia Dei*. I have argued here that a more comprehensive picture of the development of Calvin's doctrine of God's providence is formed by collecting many pieces of the puzzle, through an historical analysis of the doctrine of *providentia Dei* in Calvin's work, including treatises, commentaries, sermons, and polemic writings from 1534 to 1559. If this method is followed, a more accurate understanding of Calvin's doctrine of *providentia Dei* can be obtained as this doctrine was developed in different stages. Calvin's formulation of the doctrine of *providentia Dei* started from a reception of an image of a fountain adopted from the Book of Baruch, portraying God as a source of everything, and ended at '*providentia coelestis*' to assure salvation for the godly, portraying God as a heavenly Father and a heavenly Judge.

From 1534–1559, the relationship between *providentia Dei* and salvation shows a gradual separation from the point of view of the ungodly, but it shows the opposite for the godly. Calvin advocates that *providentia Dei* is '*providentia coelestis*' for the godly:

> *Thus, he clearly shows himself the protector and vindicator of innocence, while he prospers the life of good men with blessings, relieves their need, soothes and mitigates their pain, and alleviates their calamities, and in all these things he provides for their salvation…By setting forth examples of this sort, the prophet shows that what are thought to be chance occurrences are just so many proofs of heavenly providence, especially of fatherly kindness. And hence ground for rejoicing is given to the godly, while as for the wicked and the reprobate, their mouths are stopped.* (John Calvin, 1559).

The four different books in the 1559 *Institutes* summarise Calvin's journey in his understanding of divine providence. In Book 1, Calvin argues that God, as Creator, governs human beings and all of His creation universally to direct and preserve the world, and because human beings are in God's special care, they are distinguished from other creatures. In Book 2, Calvin discusses the corrupt nature of humankind and God's salvation plan. Book 3 asserts that some people are predestined to enjoy God's very special care in eternity, for when they are justified by faith through Jesus Christ, they are endowed with eternal life as they are protected by God's heavenly care. In Book 4, Calvin argues that the people who are in God's very special care, are part of the true Church, and therefore they are assured of salvation.

Calvin's doctrine of *providentia Dei* is like a biblical story walking us from Creation in the Old Testament to Redemption and the assurance of salvation in the New Testament. However, the practice of placing the doctrines of providence and predestination together in his earlier works does not resonate with the biblical theme above, as it suggests that redemption is unnecessary, and thus to rectify this situation, Calvin separates these two doctrines in the 1559 *Institutes*. It is only in the definitive 1559 *Institutes* that Calvin finally puts the doctrines of *providentia Dei* and predestination in their right 'biblical place'. This is confirmed by the analysis of the development of Calvin's doctrine of *providentia Dei* in his works before 1559 in this research, and Calvin's discussion of redemption and the doctrine of predestination being placed separately in Book 3 of the 1559 *Institutes*. Therefore, the argument about the insignificance of the doctrines of providence and predestination being placed separately is not tenable. The historical approach taken in this research casts new light on this issue.

The Elect, as God's children, participate in God's providence by having a taste of His goodness, power, justice, and wisdom while they are on earth. Part of God's providence can be revealed in His will because of the prayer of the Elect. Evidently, an historical analysis of Calvin's works on the interpretation of divine providence shows that there is a genuine existence of secondary cause in heavenly providence. Some scholars argue that Calvin rejects human agency but the historical analysis of Calvin's doctrine of *providentia Dei* shown in this work does not resonate their voice.

Calvin uses the doctrine of '*providentiae coelestis*' to help explain the governance of false Christians and hypocrites in the Church when he wrote *Commentarius in epistolam ad Galatas*, in which providence is not primarily the central theme. Does Calvin use the doctrine of heavenly providence in other commentaries, or even other genre of his works which are not directly related to divine providence? The doctrine of '*providentia coelestis*' has not received any scholarly attention in the past hence this work is a beginning of highlighting the doctrine of heavenly providence in Calvin's works and there is much more to be explored this doctrine. The exploration of the position of this doctrine in Calvin's other works is worthy of further investigation.

Bibliography

Primary Sources

Augustine. *De Praedest. Sanct.*

Bèze, Théodore De. "Life of John Calvin". In *John Calvin, Tracts and Treatises on the Reformation of the Church*. Translated by Henry Beveridge, lvii–cxxxviii. Grand Rapids, MI: WM.B. Eerdmans Publishing Company, 1958.

Beza, Theodoro. *Quaestionum et responsionum christianarum libellus: In quo praecipua Christianae religionis capita*. Genève: Musée historique de la Rèformation, 1570.

_____. *Jobus Theodori Bezae Partim Commentariis Partim Paraphrasi Illustratus*. Genève: Bibliothèque de Genève, 1589.

_____. *Iob Expounded by Theodore Beza: Partly in Manner of a Commentary, Partly in Manner of a Paraphrase*. London: Printed by Iohn Legatt, Printer to the Vniversitie of Cambridge. And Are to Be Sold at the Signe of the Sunne in Paules Churchyard in London, 1589.

_____. *Summa totius Christianismi sive descriptio et distributio causarum salutis electorum, & exitii reproborum, ex sacris literis collecta*. Geneva: Ioannis Crispini, 1570.

_____. *Tractationum Theologicarum, in quibus peleraque Christianae Religionis dogmata adversus haereses nostris temporibus renovates solide ex verbo Dei defenduntur*. Genevae, 1582.

_____. "Summa Doctrinae de re Sacramentaria". In *Theodori Bezae Vezelii volumen primum tractationum*, 206–210. Genevae, 1582.

Calvin, John. *Ioannis Calvini Opera Quae Supersunt Omnia: Ad Fidem Editionum Principum et Authenticarum Ex Parte Etiam Codicum Manu Scriptorum, Additis Prolegomenis Literariis, Annotationibus Criticis, Annalibus Calvinianis, Indicibusque Novis et Copiosissmis*. 59 vol. Ioannis Calvini Opera Quae Supersunt Omnia 1–59. Brunsvigae: apud C. A. Schwetschke et filium (M. Bruhn), 1863. (*CO*)

_____. *Supplementa Calviniana Sermons inédits*. Volumen I, iussu Corporis Presbyterianorum Universalis. Neukirchen: Neukirchener Verlag der Buchhandlung des Erziehungsvereins, 1961.

_____. *Calvin's Commentary on Seneca's De Clementia*. Edited and translated by Ford Lewis. Battles, and André Malan Hugo. Published for the Renaissance Society of America. Leiden, Netherlands: E.J. Brill, 1969.

_____. *Sermons of Maister Iohn Caluin, vpon the booke of Iob*. Translated by Arthur Golding. Londini: Impensis Georgij Bishop, 1574.

_____. *Sermons on 2 Samuel Chapters 1–13*. Translated by Douglas Kelly. Edinburgh: The Banner of Truth Trust, 1992.

_____. *Soul Sleep: Psychopannychia*. Translated by Henry Beveridge. Legacy Publications, 2011.

_____. *Institutes of the Christian Religion* 1536. Translated and annotated by Ford Lewis Battles. London: Collins, 1975.

_____. *Institutes of the Christian Religion* 1541. Translated by Elsie Anne McKee. Grand Rapids, MI: William B. Eerdmans Publishing Company, 2009.

_____. *Institution de la religion chrétienne* 1541. Critical edition by Olivier Millet. Genéve: DROZ S.A., 2008.

_____. *Institutes of the Christian Religion* 1559. Translated by Ford Lewis Battles. Edited by John T. McNeill. The Library of Christian Classics. Vol. 20–21. London: SCM, 1961.

_____. *Concerning the eternal predestination of God*. Translated by J.K.S. Reid. London: J. Clarke, 1961.

_____. *The Bondage and the Liberation of the Will: a defense of the Orthodox Doctrine of human Choice Against Pighius*. Edited by A.N.S. Lane and translated by G. I. Davies. Grand Rapids, MI: Baker, 1996.

_____. *Treatises Against the Anabaptists and Against the Libertines*. Grand Rapids, MI: Baker Book House,1982.

_____. *The Secret Providence of God*. Edited by. Paul Helm. First edition. Wheaton, IL: Crossway Books, 2010.

_____. *Commentary on Romans*. Translated and edited by John Owen. Grand Rapids, MI: Christian Classic Ethereal Library, 1849.

_____. *Commentary on Psalms*, Volume 1–5. Translated by James Anderson. Grand Rapids, MI: Christian Classics Ethereal Library, 1571.

_____. *Commentary on Jonah, Micah, Nahum*. Translated by John Owen. Grand Rapids, MI: Christian Classics Ethereal Library, 1847.

_____. *Commentary on Daniel*. Translated by Tomas Meyers. Grand Rapids, MI: Christians Ethereal Library, 1852.

_____. *Commentary on Galatians and Ephesians*. Translated by William Pringle. Grand Rapids, MI: Christian Classics Ethereal Library, 1854.

Castellion, Sebastien. *De haereticis an sint persequendi*. Introduction by Sape van der Woude. Genève: Droz, 1954.

Saint Gregory. *Homily*.

Marsiglio da Padova. *Defensor Pacis*, Monumenta Germaniae Historica. Turnhout: Brepols Publishers, 2010.

_____. *The Defender of the Peace*. Edited and translated by Annabel Brett. Cambridge: Cambridge University Press, 2005.

Melanchthon, Philipp. *Loci communes rerum theologicarum seu hypotyposes theologicae*. Vvittembergae: Zentralbibliothek Zürich,1521.

_____. *Melanchthon on Christian doctrine Loci communes 1555*. Translated by Clyde Leonard Manschreck. NY: Oxford University Press, 1965.

_____. *The chief theological topics: Loci praecipui theologici 1559.* Translated by Jacob A. O. Preus. St Louis, MO: Concordia Publishing House, 2010.

_____. *Opera quae supersunt omnia.* Edited by C.G. Bretschneider and H.E. Bindseil. Corpus Reformatorum, vol. 1–28. Halle, 1834–52; Brunswick, 1853–60, CR7:930

Zwingli, Huldrych. *Ad illustrissimum Cattorum principem Philippum, sermonis de providentia Dei anamnema.* Tiguri: Zentralbibliothek Zürich, 1530.

_____. *Huldreich Zwinglis Sämtliche Werke.* Berlin, Leipzig, Zurich, 1905–.

_____. "Reproduction from memory of a sermon on the providence of God, dedicated to his highness, Philip Hesse August 20, 1530". In *On providence and other essays,* chapter V, 128–234. Eugene, OR: Wipf and Stock Publishers, 1999.

Ad acta colloquii Montisbelgardensis Tubingae edita,. Theodori Bezae responsionis, pars prior. Editio secunda. Genève: Bibliothèque de Genève, 1588.

Acta colloquij Montis Belligartensis: quod habitum est, anno Christi.1586. fauente Deo opt.max. Praeside, ... Friderico, comite VVirtembergico et Mompelgartensi, &c. inter clarissimos viros, D.Iacobum Andreae, praepositum & concellarium Academiae Tubingensis: & D.Theodorum Bezam, professorem... Georgium Gruppenbachium, 1587.

Jakob Andreae, Beze Theodore de, and Clinton J. Armstrong, *Lutheranism vs. Calvinism: the Classic Debate at the Colloquy of Montbeliard 1586.* Concordia Publishing House, 2017.

Biblia Sacra Vulgata. Editio quinta. Deutsche Bibelgesellschaft, 2007.

Secondary Sources

Abraham, William J. "Divine Action in Predestination in John Calvin". In *Divine Agency and Divine Action, Volume II,* 176–197. Oxford: Oxford University Press, 2017.

_____, *Divine Agency and Divine Action, Volume I: Exploring and Evaluation the Debate.* Oxford: Oxford University Press, 2017.

_____, *Divine Agency and Divine Action, Volume II: Soundings in the Christian Tradition.* Oxford: Oxford University Press, 2017.

_____. *Divine Agency and Divine Action, Volume III: Systematic Theology.* Oxford: Oxford University Press, 2018.

Balserak, Jon. *John Calvin as Sixteenth-Century Prophet.* Oxford: Oxford University Press, 2014.

Bavaud, Georges. "La position du Réformateur Pierre Viret à face aux Deutérocanoniques". In *Le canon de l'Ancien Testament: sa formation et son histoire.* Edited by Jean-Daniel Kaestli and Otto Wermelinger, 245–252. Geneva: Labor et Fides, 1984.

Beeke, Joel R. "Calvin on Sovereignty, Providence, and Predestination". In *Puritan Reformed Journal* 2, no. 2 (2010): 79–107.

Billings, Todd J. *Calvin, participation, and the gift: the activity of believers in union with Christ.* Oxford: Oxford University Press, 2009.

Blacketer, Raymond A. "The man in the black hat: Theodore Beza and the reorientation of early Reformed historiography". In *Church and School in Early Modern Protestantism.* Edited by. Joardan J. Ballor, David S. Sytsma and Jason Zuidema, 227–241. Boston: Leiden Brill, 2013.

Bohatec, Josef. "Calvin's Vorsehungslehre". In *Calvinstudien: Festschrift Zum 400. Geburtstage Johann Calvins,* 339–441. Leipzig: Rudolph Haupt, 1909.

_____. "Gott Und Die Geschichte Nach Calvin". In *Philosophia Reformata,* vol. 1, no. 3, (1936):129–161.

Bolliger, Daniel. *Infiniti Contemplatio. Grundzüge der Scotus–und Scotismusrezeption im Werk Huldrych Zwinglis. Mit ausfiihrliclier Edition bisher unpublizierter Annotatione Zwinglis* [Studies in the History of Christian Thought 107]. Leiden/Boston: Brill, 2003.

Bouwsma, William J. *John Calvin: A Sixteen-Century Portrait.* Oxford: Oxford University Press, 1988.

Bray, John S. *Theodore Beza's Doctrine of Predestination.* De Graaf, 1975.

Breen, Quirinus. *John Calvin: a Study in French Humanism.* Hamden, CT: Archon Books, 1968.

_____. *Christianity and Humanism: Studies in the History of Ideas.* Edited by Nelson Peter Ross, 107–129. Grand Rapids, MI: W. B. Eerdmans Publishing Company, 1968.

Brunner, Emil. *The Christian Doctrine of God Dogmatics* vol. I, 324–326. Lutterworth Press, 1949.

Bucanus, Gulielmus. *Institio theologica.* Lausanne, 1605.

Buckner, Forrest. "Calvin's Non-Speculative Methodology: A Corrective to Billings and Muller on Calvin's Divine Attributes". In *Calvinus Pastor Ecclesia,* ed. Herman J. Selderhuis, 233–243 Gottingen: Vandenhoeck & Ruprecht, 2016.

Buisson, Ferdinand. *Sébastien Castellion, sa vie et son œuvre (1515–1563). Étude sur les origines du protestantisme libéral français.* Paris: Hachette, 1892.

Canlis, Julie. *Calvin's Ladder: a Spiritual Theology of ascent and ascension.* Grand Rapids, MI: W.B. Eerdmans Publishing Company, 2010.

Chan, Suk Yu. "Is Job a participant in God's providence? Calvin's Interpretation of Human Participation in *providence de Dieu* in his *Sermons sur le livre de Iob* (1554–1555)". In *Calvinus Frater in Domino Papers of the Twelfth International Congress on Calvin Research.* Edited by Arnold Huijgen and Karin Maag, 189–202. Gottingen: Vandenhoeck & Ruprecht, 2020.

Crisp, Oliver D. "Calvin on Creation and Providence". In *John Calvin and Evangelical Theology: Legacy and Prospect.* Edited by Sung Wook Chung, 43–65. Louisville: Westminster John Knox Press, 2009.

De Greef, Wulfert. *The writings of John Calvin, an introductory guide.* Translated by Lyle D. Bierma. Grand Rapids MI: Baker Books, 1993.

_____. "Calvin as commentator on the Psalms". Translated by Raymond A. Blacketer, and edited by Donald K. McKim in *Calvin and the Bible,* 85–106. Cambridge: Cambridge University Press, 2006.

DeLapp, Neveda Levi. *The reformed David(s) and the question of resistance to tyranny: reading the Bible in the 16th and 17th centuries*. London: T&T Clark, 2016.

Dowey, Edward A. *The Knowledge of God in Calvin's Theology*, 239–240. Grand Rapids, MI: W.B. Eerdmans Publishing Company, 1994.

Dreyer, Wim A. "John Calvin as 'public theologian' in view of his 'Commentary on Seneca's De Clementia'". *HTS Teologies Studies/Theological Studies*, 74, no. 4, (June, 2018), a4928. https://doi.org/ 10.4102/hts.v74i4.4928

Elliott, Mark W. *Providence Perceived: Divine Action from a Human Point of View*, 141–148. Berlin/Boston: De Gruyter, 2015.

Engel, Mary Potter. *Perspectival Structure of Calvin's Anthropology*. Eugene, OR: Wipf and Stock Publishers, 2002.

Fergusson, David. "Reformed Tradition and Tolerance". In *Public Theology for the 21st Century*. Edited by William F. Storrar and Andrew R. Morton, 107–121. London: T&T Clark, 2004.

_____. *Church, State and Civil Society*. Cambridge/New York: Cambridge University Press, 2004.

_____. *The Providence of God: A Polyphonic Approach*, 84–109. Cambridge: Cambridge University Press, 2018.

Ferrario, Fulvio. "Calvin et la providence: actualité provocatrice d'un thème embarrassant". In *Études théologiques et religieuses* 84, no. 3 (2009): 359–372.

Freudenberg, Matthias. "Vorsehung und Freiheit: Calvins Freiheitsverständnis am Beispiel seiner Auseinandersetzung mit den Libertinern". In *Calvinus clarissimus theologus: Papers of the Tenth International Congress on Calvin Research*. Edited by Herman J. Selderhuis, 311–325. Göttingen: Vandenhoeck & Ruprecht, 2012.

Gamble, Richard C. "Exposition and Method in Calvin". In *Westminster Theological Journal* 49 (1987): 153–165.

_____. "Calvin as Theologian and Exegete: Is There Anything New?" In *Calvin Theological Journal* 23 (1988): 178–194.

Ganoczy, Alexandre and Lortz, Joseph. *Le Jeune Calvin: Genese Et Evolution De Sa Vocation Reformatrice*. Wiesbaden: Franz Steiner Verlag GMBH, 1966.

_____. *La Bibliothèque de l'Académie de Calvin. Le Catalogue de 1572 et ses Enseignments*. Genèva: Librairie Droz, 1969.

Gordon, Bruce *Calvin*. New Haven: Yale University Press, 2009.

_____. "Huldrych Zwingli". In *Expository Times* (December, 2014): 1–12.

_____. *John Calvin's Institutes of the Christian Religion: a Biography*. Princeton: Princeton University Press, 2016.

Gordon, Bruce; Baschera, Luca; Moser, Christian. "Emulating the Past and Creating the Present: Reformation and the Use of Historical and Theological Models in Zurich in the Sixteenth Century". In *Following Zwingli: Applying the Past in Reformation Zurich*, 1–39. Surrey: Ashgate Publishing Limited, 2014.

Garcia, Aurelio A. "'Summum Bonum' in the Zurich Reformation: Zwingli and Bullinger". In *Zwingliana* 144 (2017): 179–197.

Harkins, Franklin T. "Christ and the Eternal Extent of Divine Providence in the *Expositio super Iob ad litteram* of Thomas Aquinas". In *A Companion to Job in the Middle Ages*. Edited by Franklin T. Harkins and Aaron Canty, 161–200. Leiden: Brill, 2017.

Helm, Paul. *Calvin and the Calvinists*, 16–17. Edinburgh: The Banner of Truth Trust, 1982.

_____. "Calvin (and Zwingli) on Divine Providence". In *Calvin Theological Journal* 29, no. 2 (1994): 388–405.

_____. *John Calvin's Ideas*, 93–128. Oxford: Oxford University Press, 2004.

_____. "Calvin, the 'Two Issues', and the Structure of the Institutes". In *Calvin Theological Journal* 42, no. 2 (2007): 341–348.

_____. "Providence and Predestination". In *Calvin at the Centre*, 132–162. Oxford: Oxford University Press, 2009.

_____. *Calvin at the Centre*. Oxford University Press, 2011.

_____. "Calvin and Stoicism". In *Philosophie der Reformierten*, edited by Günter Frank and Herman J. Selderhuis, 169–181. Stuttgart: Frommann-Holzboog, 2012.

Heppe, Heinrich. *Reformed Dogmatics Set Out and Illustrated from the Sources*. Edited by Ernst Bizer and translated by. G.T. Thompson. London: Allen, 1950.

Holmes, Christopher R.J. *Revisiting the Doctrine of the Divine Attributes in dialogue with Karl Barth, Eberhard Jüngel and Wolf Krötke*. New York: Peter Lang, 2007.

Holmes, Stephen R. "Calvin on Scripture". In *Calvin, Barth and Reformed theology*. Edited by Neil B. MacDonald and Carl Trueman, 149–162. Milton Keynes: Paternoster Press, 2008.

Hopkins, Samuel. *The System of Doctrines: Contained in Divine Revelation, Explained and Defended. Showing Their Consistence and Connection with Each Other. To which is Added, a Treatise on the Millennium*, Volume I. Boston: Isaiah Thomas and Ebenezer T. Andrews, 1793.

Hunt, Stephen Leigh. "Predestination in the Institutes of the Christian Religion, 1536–1559". In *An Elaboration of the Theology of Calvin*. Edited by Richard C. Gamble, 185–192. New York: Garland, 1992.

Jaeger, Lydia. "Le rapport entre la nature de Dieu et sa volonté dans l'Institution chrétienne". In *European Journal of Theology* 11, no. 2 (2002): 109–118.

Kim, Sung-Sup. *Deus Providebit-Calvin, Schleiermacher, and Barth on the Providence of God*. Minneapolis: Fortress Press, 2014.

Kingdon, Robert M. "Reviewed Work: *Calvin's Commentary on Seneca's De Clementia*, by John Calvin". *Renaissance Quarterly*, 25, no. 4 (Winter, 1972): 467–469.

Kirby, W. J. Torrance. "Stoic and Epicurean? Calvin's Dialectical Account of Providence in the Institutes". In *International Journal of Systematic Theology* 5, no. 3 (2003): 309–322.

König, J. F. *Theologia Positiva Acroamatica* (Rostock 1664). Edited and translated by Andreas Stegmann, §260, 277. Tübingen: Mohr Siebeck, 2016,

Krusche, Werner. *Das Wirken des heiligen Geistes nach Calvin*. Göttingen: Vandenhoeck & Ruprecht, 1957.

Lane, A.N.S. "Introduction". In John Calvin, *The Bondage and Liberation of the Will*, xiii–xxxiv. Grand Rapids, MI: Baker Books: 1996.

Lestringant, Frank. "Stefan Zweig contre Calvin (1936)". In *Revue de l'histoire des religions*, 1 (2006): 71–94.

Link, Christian. "Wie handelt Gott in der Welt?-Calvins Vorsehungslehre". In *Calvin entdecken: Wirkungsgeschichte—Theologie-Sozialethik*. Edited by Traugott Jähnichen, Thomas K. Kuhn, and Arno Lohmann, 65–79. Berlin: Lit, 2010.

Mallinson, Jeffrey. *Faith, Reason, and Revelation in Theodore Beza, 1519-1605*. Oxford Theological Monographs. Oxford/New York: Oxford University Press, 2003.

Manetsch, Scott, M. "The Journey towards Geneva: Theodore Beza's Conversion, 1535-1548". In *Calvin, Beza, and Later Calvinism: Calvin Society Papers 2005*. Edited by David Foxgrover. Grand Rapids, MI: CRC Produce Services, 2006.

Martinich, A.P. "Scotus and Anslem on Existence of God". In *Franciscan Studies*, vol. 37 (1977): 139–152.

Mays, James Luther. "Calvin's Commentary on the Psalms". In *John Calvin and the Church*. Edited by Timothy George, 195–204. Kentucky, Westerminster/John Knox Press:1990.

McGrath, Alister. *A Life of John Calvin: A Study in the Shaping of Western Culture*. Cambridge, MA: Basil Blackwell, 1990.

McCray, Alden C. "'God, We Know, Is Subject to No Passions.' The Impassibility of God in Calvin's Commentaries as a Test-Case for the Divine Attributes". In *Calvinus Frater in Domino*, Papers of the Twelfth International Congress on Calvin Research, edited by Arnold Huijgen and Karin Maag, 295– 308. Gottingen: Vandenhoeck & Ruprecht, 2020.

Meyer, Ruth. "A Passionate Dispute Over Divine Providence: Albert the Great's Commentary on the Book of Job". In *A Companion to Job in the Middle Ages*. Edited by Franklin T. Harkins and Aaron Canty, 201–224. Leiden: Brill, 2017.

Miln, Peter. "Hommes D'une Bonne Cause: Calvin's Sermons on the Book of Job". PhD diss., University of Nottingham, 1989.

Moreau, Pierre-François. "Calvin: fascination et critique du stoïcisme". In *Le Stoïcisme au XVI et au XVII siècle – Le retour des philosophies antiques à l'Âge classique*, edited by Pierre-François Moreau, 51–64. Paris: Albin Michel S.A., 1999.

Muller, Richard A. *Christ and the Decree: Christology and Predestination in Reformed Theology from Calvin to Perkins*. Durham, NC: Labyrinth Press, 1986.

————. "Ordo docendi: Melanchthon and the Organization of Calvin's Institutes, 1536–1543". In *Melanchthon in Europe-his work and influence beyond Wittenberg*. Edited by Karin Maag, 123–140. Grand Rapids, MI: Baker Books, 1999.

————. *The Unaccommodated Calvin: Studies in the Foundation of a Theological Tradition*. Oxford: Oxford University Press, 2000.

————. "The Placement of Predestination in Reformed Theology: Issue or Non-Issue?" In *Calvin Theological Journal*, 40, (2005), 184–210.

————. "The Use and Abuse of a Document: Beza's *Tabula praedestinationis*, the Bolsec Controversy, and the Origins of Reformed Orthodoxy". In *Protestant Scholasticism: Essays in Reassessment*. Edited by Carl R. Trueman and R. Scott Clark, 33–61. Eugene, OR: Wipf & Stock, 2006.

_____. "Reception and Response Referencing and Understanding Calvin in Seventeenth-Century Calvinism". In *Calvin and His Influence, 1509-2009*, 182–196. Oxford Scholarship Online: 2011.

_____. "The Reception of Calvin' in Later Reformed Theology: Concluding Thoughts". In *Church History and Religious Culture* 91, no. 1–2 (2011), 255–274.

_____. *Dictionary of Latin and Greek Theological Terms: Drawn Principally from Protestant Scholastic Theology*. Second edition. Grand Rapids, MI: Baker Academic, 2017.

_____. *Divine Will and Human Choice*. Grand Rapids, MI: Baker Academic, 2017.

_____. "Calvin on Divine Attributes: A Question of Terminology and Method". In *Westminister Theological Journal* 80, no. 2 (2018), 199–218.

Murphy, Joseph P. *The Fountain of Life in John Calvin and the Devotio Moderna: Metaphorical Theology of the Trinity in Word and Sacrament*. Palo Alto, CA: Academica Press, 2011.

Naphy, William. *Calvin and the consolidation of the Genevan Reformation with a new preface*. Louisville, KY: Westminster John Knox Press, 2003.

Niesel, Wilhelm. *The Theology of Calvin*. Translated by Harold Knight, 61–79. London: Lutterworth Press, 1956.

Oakley, Francis. "The Absolute and Ordained Power of God in Sixteenth- and Seventeenth-Century". In *Journal of the History of Ideas*, vol. 59, no. 3 (July 1998): 437–461.

Oberman, Heiko A. "Subita Conversio: The Conversion of John Calvin". In *Reformiertes Erbe*, vol. 2. Edited by Heiko A. Oberman et al, 279–295. Zürich: Theologischer, Verlag, 1993.

Ong, Meng Chai. "John Calvin on Providence: The *Locus Classicus* in Context". PhD diss., King's College, London, 2003.

Opitz, Peter. "Scripture". In *The Calvin Handbook*, edited by Herman J. Selderhuis, 235–244. Grand Rapids, MI: Eerdmans, 2009.

Pak, Sujin. *The Judaizing Calvin: Sixteenth-Century Debates over the Messianic Psalms*. New York: Oxford University Press, 2010.

Parker, T.H.L. *John Calvin: A Biography*. London: J.M. Dent & Sons Limited, 1975.

_____. *Calvin's Old Testament Commentaries*. Edinburgh: T&T Clark, 1986.

_____. *Calvin's New Testament Commentaries*. 2nd ed. Edinburgh: T&T Clark, 1993.

Partee, Charles. *Calvin and Classical Philosophy*. Studies in History of Christian Thought 15. Leiden: E.J. Brill, 1977.

_____. *The Theology of John Calvin*. Louisville, Kentucky: Westminster John Knox Press, 2008.

Petris, Paolo De. "Calvin's 'Theodicy' in His Sermons on Job and the Hiddenness of God". PhD diss., McGill University, 2008.

Pitkin, Barbara. *What pure eyes could see: Calvin's doctrine of faith in its exegetical context*. New York: Oxford University Press, 1999.

_____. "The Protestant Zeno: Calvin and the Development of Melanchthon's Anthropology". In *The Journal of Religion*, vol. 84, no. 3 (July 2004): 345–378.

_____. "Calvin's Commentary on Psalm 1 and Providentia Faith: Reformed Influences on the Psalms in English". In *Crossing traditions: essays on the Reformation and intellectual history in honour of Irena Backus*. Edited by Maria-Cristina Pitassi and Daniela Solfaroli Camillocci with collaboration of Arthur Huiban, 164–181. Leiden, Boston: Brill, 2018.

————. *Calvin, the Bible, and History-Exegesis and Historical Reflection in the Era of Reform*. New York: Oxford University Press, 2020.

Pipa, Joseph A., Jr. "Creation and Providence: Institutes 1.14, 16–18". In *A Theological Guide to Calvin's Institutes: Essays and Analysis*. Edited by David W. Hall and Peter A. Lillback, 123–150. Phillipsburg: P & R Publishing, 2008.

Plath, Von Uwe. "'Die Mücke gegen den Elefanten'-Castellio gegen Calvin? Einige Anmerkungen zu dem Basler Exemplar von Castellios 'De haereticis an sint persequendi', zu Ferdinand Buisson und zu Stefan Zweig". *Archiv für Reformationsgeschichte* 109 (2018): 428–441.

Potgieter, Pieter C. "Perspectives on the Doctrine of Providence in Some of Calvin's Sermons on Job". In *Hervormde Teologiese Studies* 54, no. 1–2 (1998): 36–49.

Potgieter, Pieter C. "Providence in Calvin: Calvin's View of God's Use of Means (Media) in His Acts of Providence". In *Calvinus Evangelii Propugnator: Calvin, Champion of the Gospel. Papers from the International Congress on Calvin Research, Seoul, 1998*. Edited by Anthony N. S. Lane, Jon Balserak, and David F. Wright, 175–190. Grand Rapids, MI: CRC Product Services for the Calvin Studies Society, 2006.

Raitt, Jill. *The Eucharistic Theology of Theodore Beza: Development of the Reformed Doctrine*, AAR Studies in Religion, no. 4. Chambersburg: American Academy of Religion, 1972.

————. *The Colloquy of Montbéliard: Religion and Politics in the Sixteenth Century*. New York, Oxford: Oxford University Press, 1993.

————. "Lessons in Troubled Times: Beza's Lessons on Job". In *Calvin and the State: papers and responses presented at the Seventh and Eighth Colloquia on Calvin & Calvin Studies*. Sponsored by the Calvin Studies Society, edited by Peter De Klerk, 21–45. Grand Rapids, MI: Calvin Studies Society, 1993.

————. Review of *Faith, Reason, and Revelation in Theodore Beza (1519–1605)*, by Jeffery Mallinson. In *American Society of Church History*, vol. 73, no. 4 (December 2004): 857–858.

Rziha, John. *Perfecting Human Actions: St Thomas Aquinas on Human Participation In Eternal Law*. Washington, DC: Catholic University of America, 2009.

Sanchez, Michelle Chaplin. "Providence: from pronoia to immanent affirmation in John Calvin's Institutes of 1559". PhD diss., Massachusetts: Harvard University, 2014.

Schreiner, Susan. "Exegesis and Double Justice in Calvin's Sermons on Job". In *Church History*, vol 58, 03 (September 1989): 322–338.

————. "Why do the wicked live? Job and David in Calvin's sermons on Job". In *The Voice from the Whirlwind*. Edited by Leo G. Perdue and W. Clark Gilpin, 129–143. Nashville, TN: Abingdon Press, 1992.

————. *Where Shall Wisdom Be Found? Calvin's Exegesis of Job from Medieval and Modern Perspectives*. Chicago: The University of Chicago Press, 1994.

————. *The Theater of His Glory: Nature and the Natural Order in the Thought of John Calvin*. Grand Rapids, MI: Baker, 1995.

_____. "Calvin as an Interpreter of Job". In *Calvin and the Bible*. Edited by Donald K. McKim, 53–84. Cambridge: Cambridge University Press, 2006).

_____. "Creation and Providence". In *The Calvin Handbook*. Edited by Herman J. Selderhuis, 267–275. Grand Rapids MI: William B. Eerdmans Publishing Company, 2009.

_____. *Are You Alone Wise? The Search for Certainty in the Early Modern Era*. Oxford Studies in Historical Theology. New York: Oxford University Press, 2012.

Selderhuis, Herman J. *Calvin's theology of the Psalms*. Grand Rapids, MI: Baker Academic, 2007.

_____. "God, the Caring One: The Providence of God According to Calvin's Psalms Commentary". In *La Revue Farel* 1 (2006): 17–32.

Sinnema, Donald. "Calvin and Beza: The Role of the Decree-Execution Distinction in Their Theologies". In *Calvinus Evangelii Propugnator; Calvin, Champion of the Gospel*. Edited by Anthony Lane, Jon Balserak, 191–207. Grand Rapids, MI: Calvin Studies Society, 2006.

_____. "Beza's view of predestination in historical perspective". In *Théodore de Bèze, 1519-1605: actes du colloque de Genève, septembre 2005*, Travaux d'humanisme et Renaissance. Edited by Irena Backus and Institut d'histoire de la Réformation, no. 424, 219–239. Genève: Droz, 2007.

Snavely, Iren. "'The evidence of things unseen': Zwingli's Sermons on Providence and the Colloquy of Marburg". In *Westminster Theological Journal* 56 (1994): 399–407.

Stauffer, Richard. *Dieu, La Création Et La Providence Dans La Prédication De Calvin*. Bern: P. Lang, 1978.

Steinmetz, David C. *Calvin in Context*. New York; Oxford: Oxford University Press, 1995.

Stephens, W.P. *The Theology of Huldrych Zwingli*. Oxford: Oxford University Press, 1986.

_____. "Election in Zwingli and Bullinger: a comparison of Zwingli's *Sermonis de providentia Dei anamnema* (1530) and Bullinger's *Oratio de moderatione servanda in negotio providentiae, praedestinationis, gratiae et liberi arbitrii 1536*". *Reformation and Renaissance Review* 7.1 (2005): 42–56.

Stroup, George. *Calvin*. Nashville: Abingdon Press, 2009.

Tavard, George H. *The Starting Point of Calvin's Theology*. Cambridge: William B. Eerdmans Publishing Company, 2000.

_____. "The Mystery of Divine Providence." In *Theological Studies* 64, no. 4 (2003): 707–718.

Thomas, Derek. *Proclaiming the Incomprehensible God: Calvin's Teaching on Job*. Fearn: Mentor, 2004.

Torrance, Thomas F. *The Hermeneutics of John Calvin*. Edinburgh: Scottish Academic Press, 1988.

Trueman, Carl R. "The Reception of Calvin: Historical Considerations". In *Church History and Religious Culture* 91, no. 1–2 (2011): 19–27.

Turretin, Francis. *Institutes of Elenctic Theology*. Translated by George Musgrave Giger. Edited by James T. Dennison Jr. vol. Phillipsburg, NJ: P&R Publishing, 1992.

Van Stam, Frans P. *The Servetus Case An appeal for a new assessment.* Genève: Librairie Droz, 2017.

Venema, Cornelis P. "The 'Twofold Knowledge of God' and the Structure of Calvin's Theology". *Mid-America Journal of Theology* 4, no. 2 (1988): 156–182.

Warfield, Benjamin Breckinridge. "Calvin's Doctrine the Knowledge of God". In *Calvin and Augustine*, edited by Samuel G. Craig, 29–130. Philadelphia: Presbyterian and Reformed Publishing Company, 1956.

Webster, John. "On the Theology of Providence". In *The Providence of God Deus Habet Consilium*. Edited by Francesca Aran Murphy & Philip G. Ziegler, 161, 164, 166–169. London: T&T Clark, 2009.

Wendel, François. *Calvin: Origins and Development of His Religious Thought.* New York: Harper & Row, 1963.

Wisse, Maarten. "Scripture between Identity and Creativity A Hermeneutical Theory Building upon Four Interpretations of Job-John Calvin Perspective of Job". In *Ars Disputandi Supplement Series*, Volume 1. Edited by Marcel Sarot, Michael Scott and Maarten Wisse, 51–76. Netherlands: Utrecht University Library, 2003.

Wittmer, Michael E. "Providence and Human Agency in the Thought of John Calvin". PhD diss., Calvin Theological Seminary. Grand Rapids, MI, 1996.

Wright, Shawn D. *Our Sovereign Refuge: the Pastoral Theology of Theodore Beza.* Milton Keynes: Paternoster, 2004.

————. *Theodore Beza: The Man and the Myth.* Fearn, Ross-shire: Christian Focus, 2015.

Zachman, Randall C. Review of *The Theater of His Glory: Nature and the Natural Order in the Thought of John Calvin*, by Susan Schreiner. In *Journal of Religion*, vol. 73, Issue 3 (July 1993), 413–414.

————. *Reconsidering John Calvin.* Cambridge: Cambridge University Press, 2012.

————. "Contemplating the Living Image of God in Creation". In *Calvin Today*. Edited by Michael Welker, Michael Weinrich & Ulrich Möller, 33–47. London; New York: Bloomsbury T&T Clark, 2013.

Zuber, Valentine. "Les conflits de la tolérance (XIXe–XXe siècles). Michel Servet entre mémoire et histoire". PhD diss., 1997.

Zweig, Stefan. *Erasmus and the Right to Heresy.* Translated by Eden and Cedar Paul. London: Condor Book Souvenir Press E&A Limited, 1979.

Appendix

The development of Calvin's interpretation of the doctrine of divine providence

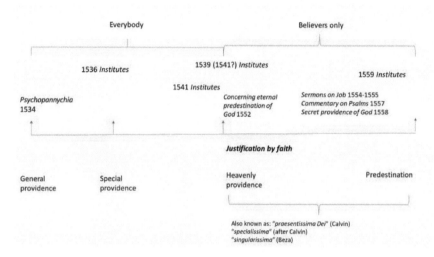

Fig. 1   Distance between the years on the scale is not in proportion

Index of Scriptures

Index of Names

Index of Subjects